Luminos is the Open Access monograph publishing program from UC Press. Luminos provides a framework for preserving and reinvigorating monograph publishing for the future and increases the reach and visibility of important scholarly work. Titles published in the UC Press Luminos model are published with the same high standards for selection, peer review, production, and marketing as those in our traditional program. www.luminosoa.org

Nairobi Hip Hop Flow

Nairobi Hip Hop Flow

Diasporic Blackness and Embodied Performance in the Underground

RaShelle R. Peck

UNIVERSITY OF CALIFORNIA PRESS

University of California Press
Oakland, California

Suggested citation: RaShelle R. Peck. *Nairobi Hip Hop Flow: Diasporic Blackness and Embodied Performance in the Underground*. Oakland: University of California Press, 2025. DOI: https://doi.org/10.1525/luminos.229

Cataloging-in-Publication data is on file at the Library of Congress.

ISBN 978-0-520-38979-3 (cloth)
ISBN 978-0-520-38648-8 (pbk.)
ISBN 978-0-520-38649-5 (ebook)

GPSR Authorized Representative: Easy Access System Europe, Mustamäe tee 50, 10621 Tallinn, Estonia, gpsr.requests@easproject.com

34   33   32   31   30   29   28   27   26   25
10   9   8   7   6   5   4   3   2   1

To Nakami and to Ajani, thank you

CONTENTS

ACKNOWLEDGMENTS

As I care for my ancestral altar, I am reminded that the person I am today is because of their continued work in the spirit world, and for that, I am grateful.

My children, Nakami and Ajani, have hung strong with me through academic nomadism and relocations. I feel grateful to be a parent to them—I thank them for their patience, guidance, and wisdom through the process. To my entire family for love, including my brother, late mother, father, aunts, and cousins. To my sister Arika: thank you for the coffee mugs and the encouragement. To my Nana, who always believed in me. And to my Aunt Nancy, who continued to ask when this book will be published—thank you for the nudge! Thank you to all the spiritual advisors I have had on this journey, especially Jude, Lana, and Maureen. And I cannot forget Wande and Keli!

I thank my current department, the Department of Ethnic and Race Studies at the Borough of Manhattan Community College (BMCC), and the chair, Patricia Mathews, for encouragement and support. While in the final stages, I earned a BMCC Faculty Development Grant, which enabled me to complete the project. The several writing groups I have been involved in remind me that writing, while solitary, can be and should be a collective endeavor. I have shared space with Lissette Acosta Corniel, Judith Anderson, Kersha Smith, Anika Thrower, Linta Varghese, Prathibha Kanakamedala, and Monica Foust. While at the Center for Historical Analysis and the Black Bodies Seminar at Rutgers, I wrote, among other things, my book proposal in community with Michael Casiano, Anna Hinton, Miya Carey, Rachel Miller, Jasmine Samara, and Johnny Bailey; may he rest in peace. We exchanged work and gave each other feedback, and I grew as a scholar because of these groups. I also became a better writer because of feedback from Msia Clark, Lisa Regan, and Therí A. Pickens.

There are many comrades I need to lift up: Yveline Alexis for her revolutionary praxis, Danielle Terrazas Williams for our shared wanderlust. I especially honor Yveline and Danielle, who stepped in during family crises gently and with love, and for that, I will never forget. I am especially grateful for Jennifer Black, a friend, worker of roots, and activist, for reading versions of chapters and for continually encouraging me through the arduous journey of academia. I remember, at this moment, scholar Jacquie Scott, whose ancestral force has marked a spot in my life. I imagine that somewhere in this cruel world, your writing lies dormant and awaits our unearthing.

While at Oberlin, I sharpened my desire for Black Studies through teaching and programming in the Department of Africana Studies, which reframed this book in critical ways. I am grateful for those significant experiences, particularly working with Dio Aldridge, Afia Ofori-Mensa, and Candice Raynor. I learned how to better work with and alongside students, which in turn transformed me into a more committed professor.

My participation in the Black Bodies Seminar at Rutgers allowed me to continue sharpening my theoretical interventions. Thank you, Quiyana Butler, for your wisdom, fun, and support. There, I expanded my appreciation for the archives, the places where, during my fieldwork, I impatiently struggled to spend time. For this expansion of my knowledge and feedback on my work, I thank Marisa Fuentes and Kali Gross. They also enabled the funding for our writing group, which provided us with much-needed resources as we endeavored our next moves. I completed another postdoctoral fellowship with AMESALL, and I thank Ousseina Alidou and Alamin Mazrui for their mentorship, feedback, and guidance.

As a disillusioned and disheartened graduate student, I reached out to Aisha Durham after reading her work to thank her for her presence and incomparable brilliance. From there, every so often, she would email me to see how I was. Although we eventually lost touch, I will never forget her gestures of kindness and solidarity, which were, in fact, a type of labor she did not have to perform. While at Ohio State, I helped organize a hip hop literacies conference with Elaine Richardson along with others. Her vision and dedication encouraged me in ways that I did not realize at the time, and I thank her for that now.

I thank Daniel Banks, whose brief mentorship in the Association for Theater in Higher Education's (ATHE) Performance Studies Emerging Scholars initiative encouraged the development of my research. I also remember and appreciate Jason McGill, who provided much-needed advice and encouragement.

I thank wholeheartedly Philip Wekunda for his feedback and assistance with Swahili and Sheng and Jaja Yogo for his translation assistance. While at Ohio University, my Swahili teacher, Peter Otiato, was foundational in how I learned and understood the language, and I am indebted to him. Thank you also to Diane Ciekawy for assistance with my research. I also thank musician and scholar Izzy Mizell for helping me identify the sonic qualities in many of the songs analyzed in this book. Their invaluable assistance helped me frame my analysis more clearly.

Thank you, Rita Trimble, my forever writing partner, for reading writing drafts, random poetry, and so many other things that left my head and landed on paper. You will forever be a significant person in my life. While at Ohio State and well after I completed my doctorate, Barry Shank, my advisor and mentor, and Nina Berman, my mentor, have helped me in innumerable ways as I polished my scholarship and navigated the next steps in the job market. I will always have gratitude, which I continue to carry into my work with students. Maurice Stevens, Dan Reff, and Kwaku Korang all assisted in shaping me into the scholar that I am, and I am forever grateful. I additionally thank Pablo Mitchell for his advice, guidance, and support as I moved from Oberlin to Rutgers.

My trips to Kenya would not have been possible without Janette Watila, who came with me to the most unique places as we learned about the Nairobi underground. I also thank Lavenda Watila, Ruth Wekunda, and Anne Wekunda for accompanying me to events. Manasseh Wekunda and Diana Wekunda, your willingness to host me was selfless and invaluable. Manasseh, Diana, and Lavenda's connections to artists and other industry players were critical in this project. I could not have completed this work without your assistance. Thank you so much.

I appreciate all the artists, producers, and deejays who took time out to speak with me.

Lastly, I thank all the Black feminists who have carved paths and forged academic and activist spaces.

Introduction

2-5-Flow!

An artist excitedly moves onto a stage with the mic in their hand, taking a deep, steadying breath. As the sound emerges, they look to the crowd and bob their head, first slightly and rhythmically up and down, then back and forth, using their shoulders to frame the gesture. The beat drops. They look toward the horizon of the crowd, clutch the mic, and deliver their rap bars, stretching words into rhymes. Their body is a knowledgeable vessel of the culture, enlivened and energetic but always composed. Sonic arrangements of the song structure the syllabic emphases of the lyrics. Every time the artist reaches a verbal climactic point, their momentum surges. They move back and forth, toward and away from the crowd, and movements mix intentionally cadenced motions and dances. Audience members participate by bobbing, swaying, shouting, pointing toward the stage, and rapping to the lyrics, all responding to how the rapper's performance engages with the encompassing sonic energies. The rapper receives the arena's abundant verve and experiences the euphoria of embodied sonic pleasure.

This is just one description of hip hop flow: the various performance practices of rappers and other practitioners of the music. The flow of an artist includes how they gesture as they spit rhymes and how their rapping and movements work with and give energy to song beats. These embodiments not only interact with the immediate surroundings of the stage, the music video, and the cypher; they also contribute to societal and global conversations about power and social difference. I use several key terms in this book to consider the cultural and sociopolitical significance of hip hop corporeality: *ludicity, political seriousness, orature, diasporic blackness, cultural anxieties*, and *sound*. I focus on the specific performative embodiments of flow in Nairobi, Kenya, and contend that rappers' use of these themes indicates the complex processes by which the music becomes Kenyan.

"2-5-Flow!" Whenever we hear rappers, announcers, DJs, and party planners shout "2-5-Flow!" we are listening to Kenyan rap music. The partly hackneyed, partly celebrated term plays off +254, Kenya's country code. Artists reference it in lyrics or create songs with that title, using the term to form a musical community while asserting themselves as primary contributors to how Kenyan hip hop has materialized. "2-5-Flow" inspires the book title and harkens to the major explorations within these pages—how the embodied, the performative, and the sonic converge, while also underscoring the relationship that the music has with conceptions of the global and local. If Kenya's country code marks its geopolitical boundaries, it also locates the country within a global sphere because those who have left and call into Kenya must use the code. Therefore, flow in Nairobi speaks to local specificities as much as it gestures toward how Kenyan hip hop participates in an imagined global rap culture. Although many Nairobi artists lack ongoing radio and television airplay, they find methods to disseminate their product and take part in the music's global rhythms. They contribute to rap culture not only sonically and lyrically but also through the embodiments of performative flow, and together, these practices develop a critical interrogation about race, diaspora, gender, nationality, postcoloniality, and the city space of Nairobi.

I emphasize the critical significance of examining the misunderstood and passed-over beauty of underground embodiments, which, for me, is described in Tavia Nyong'o's offer, "afro-philo-sophy, the love of black wisdom on the lower frequencies."[1] Instead of focusing on the purely linguistic or sonic, this book considers those elements by placing the artistic, disaffected, cool, styled, embodied performance practices at the conceptual center and as a method of enriching our understanding of sound and lyrics. As opposed to concluding that the gestures and stances are external imitations of Black Americanness, something always already foreign, and the linguistic as the home of the innovative and local, I gather the embodied, the lyrical, the visual, and the aural together as one comprehensive collection of practices and consider the complicated and innovative projects of Nairobi artists. In so doing, we can understand performances as interfacing with the modalities of resistance within traditions of Kenyan music, as well as within an imagined global hip hop diaspora.

WHAT IS NAIROBI UNDERGROUND HIP HOP?

While "2-5-Flow!" references any form of Kenyan hip hop, I focus on the non-commercial underground hip hop found in Nairobi scenes. Like most forms of underground sounds worldwide, this Nairobi music is attentive to the poor and marginalized and focused on raising the consciousness of disenfranchised people. It is mainly resistant to mainstream music standards and broader social norms. Artists tell stories from some of Nairobi's most well-known neighborhoods, such

FIGURE 1. Graffiti art in Nairobi, 2012. Photo by author.

FIGURE 2. Graffiti art in Nairobi, 2012. Photo by author.

as Dandora, Kibera, Githurai, Ngara, Jericho, and Ziwani. The music has certain core themes. It holds a defiant position against both the media entities that exclude them and the continuously corrupt state. Underground music also has a complicated perspective of other modalities of power in Kenya, such as capitalism and the churches and NGOs that periodically host their events. These compromises are not always foreclosures but rather the music's contradictions. Listening to the archives of this underground and noncommercial rapscape, one can hear the tensions, the hustle, the cacophonous, the symphonic.

In the Nairobi underground, many rappers construct diasporic meeting points by using a Mau Mau cultural aesthetic, a class-based consciousness and artistic method of marginality that has roots in how they remember the anticolonial Mau Mau war. Mbũgua wa Mũngai confirms, "Mau Mau history supplies critical tropes by which popular musicians seek to apprehend and explain the tensions in their everyday lives, especially those to do with identity and power."[2] The legacy of artists drawing on Kenya's well-known freedom struggle has allowed them to imagine themselves participating in the global traditions of the music that take up the political struggle for African and Black liberation. Hip hop in Kenya rose to fame with Kalamashaka's 1998 hit single, "Tafsiri Hii." Kalamashaka and the groundbreaking Ukoo Flani Mau Mau made a compilation of music that set the stage for underground culture. Dandora, the poor Nairobi area of Eastlands, has been the most mentioned place and is a continual reference point in these songs.[3] It is arguably the birthplace of Kenyan rap culture. Ukoo Flani Mau Mau is best known for their 2004 album *Kilio cha Haki* (A Cry for Justice), which was inspired by the Ali Mazrui play of the same name about political corruption and social change. Their constant evocation of the Mau Mau is less about the actual events of the armed conflict and more about how rappers remember and draw on the army and its revolutionary themes.

Many of the artists I follow were once a part of UFMM, having friends or mentors from the group. In the last fifteen years, direct references to the Mau Mau have faded, transitioning into generalized themes of war, warriors, fighting, struggle, underclass marginality, poverty, political repression, and state corruption. Keeping with the traditions of global hip hop sentiment and Kenyan rap, these artists have continued to imagine their work as socially and individually transformative. Each rapper defines this characteristic differently; some artists believe that gospel rap is suitable to make interventions about social change, while others make hardcore music rooted in ghetto life. There is a deep component of cultural nationalism, meaning that rappers feel that culture is the joining fixture in Kenyans' lives that can unite people, erase divisions, and (re)constitute the nation. Artists use cultural nationalism to show allegiance to Kenya as they consider how their work challenges mainstream nationalism, resists the state, and holds committed ties to transnational rap culture.

Rapper L-Ness comes out of UFMM and is from a family of musicians, namely the acoustic guitarist Peter Akwabi, who is her father. She has made music for over fifteen years, and on *Kilio cha Haki* she had the song "Msanii" (Artist). She took the name L-Ness after the mighty animal, "lioness," and she builds on that name with quick and fierce lyrical deliveries. L-Ness released *Gal Power* in 2012, a collaborative album with other African and Kenyan women artists like Nazizi and Xtatic. L-Ness remains involved with various projects, including the Babishai Poetry Festival in Uganda, Nairobi's StoryMoja Festival, and the Nairobi-Berlin initiative SPOKEN WOR:L:DS Project.

Many artists come from working-class areas in Nairobi. Evaredi hails from Embakasi, Sue Timon is from Ngara, and Judge is from Dandora and grew up in Ziwani, all of which are lower- and working-class areas of Nairobi. When I first met Sue, she was making gospel music, and about a year after meeting her, she joined the queer group I Am, recorded music, and continued to perform at Sarakasi with the group for a short time. Judge made his start with his brother, Mo Phat, in their group, Black Duo. He has also worked on solo projects, and ones with Washamba Wenza, hosting and performing at numerous events, like Hip Hop Fest at Sarakasi Dome. Rapper Nafsi Huru, meaning "free soul," moved to Nairobi as a young adult and hailed initially from Magongo, a poor neighborhood in Mombasa. His name has become central to his brand, and he often wears T-shirts bearing Nafsi Huru or the English translation. As a teen, he formed the rap group Skali Flani before moving to Nairobi. He has hosted the Hip Hop Hookup at the Sarakasi Dome and has performed with Juma Tutu and the Swahili Jazz Band for many years. Nafsi fuses hip hop with jazz music and reggae influences because, as he regularly states, he is influenced by the genres of global Black music.

Most underground rappers often imagine their work as fundamentally dissimilar to mainstream music through sound and content. They believe that their music is exceptional because of its commitment to socially meaningful messaging without regard to whether it appeals to a mainstream sound. Practitioners often attempt to be unconcerned with fulfilling the commercial appetites of listeners, and they regard themselves as cultural stewards of society who are unfazed by obstacles and determined to make music that benefits Kenyan society. As Anthony Kwame Harrison describes, underground music "[works] to secure and sustain distinctions between their music/culture and its commercial counterpart."[4] The majority of radio airplay goes to American and British hip hop and pop, Nigerian Afrobeats, Afropop from East Africa, and mainstream Kenyan rap that draws influences from many of the above-mentioned genres. Underground and noncommercial artists often feel sidelined by the privileging of genres with smooth sounds, danceable beats, and palatable lyrics. Many consider music that is too watered down and too much about carefree celebration and leisurely fun as lacking substance, relevance, and value. Noncommercial rap often "sounds" underground, with hard bass-infused beats that fit with usually fast-paced lyrics. Sonically, the kick drum accompanies instruments like the horn, piano, guitar, or saxophone, which are typically produced technologically. These sounds evoke solemn, uplifting, persevering, and gritty tones and are critical to the underground ethic. For rappers true to this game, these lyrics cannot be empty of meaning, and they must affirm the author's presence as an MC and articulate some investment in social change.

To compare, Afropop is a synthesized electronic dance music that can incorporate rap, Congolese dance and music, South African house, and Jamaican dancehall. Afropop is similar to West African Afrobeats. Within Kenya, Afropop music is sometimes called *kapuka* or *boomba* music. *Kapuka* "is specifically known for its repeated beats and lyrics meant to enhance the song's draw for dancing [and] many sounds in *kapuka* are generated from existing computer tunes."[5] Often contrasted with *kapuka, genge* and *gengetone* rely on rap more heavily and borrow from dancehall and synthesized East African Afropop.[6] *Genge* artists tend to rap more in their songs, while *kapuka* artists tend to sing. While many may distinguish between *kapuka/boomba* and *genge* music, underground artists do not. Mostly, they view mainstream music as valueless and empty, fleecing the best elements of hip hop to make it marketable to a broad audience of people who would not generally like hardcore rap music. Conversely, many commercial artists believe underground sounds are not danceable or upbeat and are too controversial to be sold in stores and played on the radio.[7] Despite these divisions, some artists straddle the underground and mainstream. I profile Baby T, who did a remix collaboration with mainstream artist Octopizzo (also featuring Rabbit, Collo, Frasha, and J'Mani) on his song "Bila Mic" (Without the Mic). Her notable songs have since included "Utanitii"(You Will Obey Me), "Dandiwa" (Jumped On) and "Bado" (Not Yet), many of which have appeared on television and radio. Additionally, she teamed up with L-Ness and other women artists on the noncommercial song "Looking Up," which I analyze in chapter 2.

HIP HOP AS ORATURE

Hip hop is best analyzed using the African term orature. Capturing political potency and ludic energies, orature describes how the music is a collection of sonic elements, corporealities, and verbal dexterity that work together to formulate a holistic performance practice. I use orature to advocate for a turn away from an overly heavy focus on lyrical analysis to illuminate how artists indigenize the music. In much of global hip hop studies (usually defined as non-U.S. hip hop studies), there has been an emphasis on highlighting the contributions of non-U.S. artists and the various methods employed to make the music local through lyrical content and language practices, from which the field of global hip hop literacies has made significant interventions.[8] I proffer an examination of the performative elements of orature to consider the profound insight that might be missed in a linguistic-heavy evaluation. Relying on performance as a frame of reference, I insist that we use embodied performance practices as a contextual center to understand artists' interventions. The now well-cited term orature was first put forth by Ugandan literary theorist Pio Zirimu, followed by Kenyan playwright, author, and theorist Ngũgĩ wa Thiong'o.[9] Ngũgĩ argues that in African contexts, written European forms of literature were imported, but that does not mean literature itself is foreign. There have been other types of literature in Africa, especially those focusing on orality and performance. Orature describes how Africana performances often have elements of song, literature, music, and dance. Thus, in African cultures throughout the globe, the boundaries between literature (which can be oral) and dance and movement (which can tell stories) are often fluid.

Therefore, studying the music through the lens of orature means that we must consider how embodied performances interact with the speech-act of rapping. Rather than study lyrics on their own, using orature we need to consider how lyrics are best analyzed in relation to elements of the cultural, the political, the sonic, the technological, and the embodied. The Kenyan feminist writer Mĩcere Mũgo writes, "African orature is an art form that uses languages to create artistic verbal compositions. The verbal art culminates in dramatized utterance, oration, recitation and performance."[10] Hip hop draws from and continues the long traditions of how people used orature to confront and subvert domination, particularly among the landless poor and working class. Both Ngũgĩ and Mũgo note how the oppressed have found orature fundamental to self-determination and political struggle during and after colonial rule. Ngũgĩ writes:

> [African] languages were kept alive in the daily speech, in the ceremonies, in political struggles, above all in the rich store of orature—proverbs, stories, poems, and riddles. The peasantry and the urban working class threw up singers. These sang old songs or composed new experiences in industries and urban life and in working-class struggle and organizations.[11]

Mũgo builds on this idea. She asserts that *mapinduzi* orature (revolutionary orature) occurs in everyday African spaces like farms, factories, and *matatus* (public transportation), as well as in slave narratives, political movements, and protests.[12] Like the forms that Mũgo and Ngũgĩ mention, the orature of rap music draws on the lived experiences of lower-class folks to produce meaning-making about practitioners' lives.

Rapping is an example of orature. Embodied performance, storytelling, interactions with sonic characteristics, social theories, and world-making ideas are all present. While the lyrics matter, it is how one articulates their words, what they put emphasis on, how their verbalities meld and interact with sound, and how those embodied emphases resonate with fans and other artists. Just as lyrics articulate culture, so too do embodiments, and at the center of orature is the performing body conveying knowledge and producing notions of agency. Thomas DeFrantz's elaboration of Black social dance as "corporeal orature" draws from Ngũgĩ and others. He argues that simply spectating Black dance is insufficient; one must participate in understanding the philosophies produced within bodily movement.[13] Rappers, producers, and musicians can help set the parameters for flow. The types of flows may differ depending on skill, experience, and embeddedness in the culture, yet flow itself is an embodied performance in which all devotees can participate. If rappers can create flow, so too can the crew in a music video, the audience members at a concert, and the fans listening with headphones in public transportation. These shared cultural practices do not mean that everyone who is a hip hop head can rap, but there is a democratizing force to the culture where all are invited in, even in its most competitive moments.

This embodied knowledge is in the form of performances of slickness, coolness, defiance, and subversion. Rappers enact what Robert Farris Thompson defines as African cool, the embodiment of "control, stability, and composure," and what Katrina Hazzard-Donald calls a "hip hop persona," which "emphasizes . . . postures of self-assurance in the face of unbeatable odds."[14] For her, "hip hop dance possesses an air of defiance of authority and mainstream society."[15] Including diasporic frameworks like Thompson's and U.S. Black performance theorists like Hazzard-Donald and DeFrantz points toward one of the central themes that runs throughout this book—that the orature in Nairobi is also always a diasporic project drawing on the embodiedness of U.S. blackness. Sometimes, the presence of U.S. Black performance citations is explicit and upfront; other times, it is simply a trace or specter. In whatever way it appears, Nairobi rappers pull on and draw from U.S. styles as part of their music-making processes of orature. These subtle performative and lyrical tributes are found throughout the music. Hence, the orature of Kenyan rap uses a collection of signifiers of diaspora and blackness to reference and discuss the contexts of their local sociopolitical conditions.

Hip hop orature combines embodiment and vocalities, like rapping and ad-libbing, in conversation with sounds from synthesizers, computers, sound systems, and musical instruments. Among the bass and snare, piano and violin motifs, and horn sounds often created with computer production, it is not uncommon to see a freestyler spitting rhymes to the sounds of an acoustic guitar. Encountering a musician strumming next to a rapper's lyrical rhymes and in the absence of the expected bass of the kick drum might sound clumsy to an outsider's ear, but what we should hear is the union of Afrodiasporic poetic forms given the guitar's long presence in Kenya, which I discuss in following chapters. Moreover, as Julian Henriques offers, it is through practitioners' performative interventions, like DJing and production, that technologies put forward musical sounds.[16] The subjectivity of artists as rappers is understood through their relationships with the sonic, precisely how the sonic undergoes racialized, gendered, classed, and nationalized significations.[17] Even those who spit in a cypher or freestyle without recording devices rely on their familiarity with sonic technologies to structure lyrics.

Nairobi hip hop additionally has transnational characteristics because of how sound technologies have been racialized globally. African and Black people's perceived relationships to instruments and other technologies have long been used to define desire and taste. European interest in twentieth-century African bands was steeped in the notion of what supposedly primitive subjects do with musical technologies coded as white and modern, similar to what Jeremy Lane names in the context of jazz as the "seductive affective force" of the "techno-primitive hybrid."[18] Nairobi rappers are just one more group that participates in forming what Alexander Weheliye calls "technosonic blackness." In the oft-cited *Phonographies: Grooves in Sonic Afro-Modernity*, Weheliye argues that the Black subject has been constructed from notions of modernity and sound through their conflicted relations with technologies, specifically the phonograph as a sonic machine.[19] Hip hop is another contemporary example of how racial codes are imbued within ideas of music and sound. Nairobi rappers' use of music-making machines structured by globalized blackness, in turn, informs how the embodied performance practices of rap culture materialize.

THE POLITICAL AND THE LUDIC

Nairobi underground orature comprises two dominating themes, the political and the ludic. The political or political seriousness describes how the music takes on earnest themes and embeds itself into the social fabric of society, critiquing social inequalities and the ineptitudes of the state. I use the term political seriousness to describe the recurring theme of earnestness that I encountered in my fieldwork, such as this statement from DJ Mos:

> Hip hop basically is like a culture. . . . It's something serious, like . . . any other profession. And at the end of the day, it's not a joke. I can say in society it's not that common, but amongst the youth, it's something that is serious.[20]

After a few conversations like this, it became difficult to ignore how artists demanded recognition in contexts where nondevotees write off the music. DJ Mos's comments align with Maina wa Mutonya's concerns about how the political tonalities within Kenyan genres are stitched into the banality of life. Mutonya writes: "Music does not reside in music texts themselves but in their articulation with society. The articulation then encapsulates the politics of everyday life."[21] In the sonic characteristics of the music, political seriousness is solemnity and melancholy, and even when perseverance is present, it can sound like lost hope. Just like these sounds pierce and intrude, so too do the lyrics.

Artists use political seriousness to demand recognition. Their sacrifices to make music often yield little profit, a fact they believe elevates them to cultural ambassadors who have and should have more legitimacy than mainstream musicians and corrupt political elites. Also, the earnestness is a rejoinder to the quandaries of postcoloniality, the harsh conditions that helped birth hip hop, the commonalities found among Black, African, and other oppressed peoples, and the anxieties that surround the music in the calls for cultural independence and Kenyan pride. Practitioners combat the long-standing and widespread claim that rap is antithetical to Kenya or Africa by creating a counterdiscourse that only authentic artists who love hip hop and Kenya can craft music with devotion and seriousness. Artists spend much time proving to themselves, fans, and others that their music is a serious diasporic and Pan-African style that locally takes on Kenyan social issues, which works to stave off the reduction of Kenyan rap to mimicry. They respond to cultural anxieties in several ways: by representing their neighborhoods through music videos and lyrics, by rapping about Kenyan social issues, and by policing sounds determined to be excessively commercialized and thus judged as inauthentic to Kenyan culture. Artists also rap in Sheng, which is a regularly shifting language tied to urban areas and considered a youth-originated vernacular, with a linguistic base in Swahili that also incorporates English, Arabic, and other Kenyan languages.[22]

Political seriousness in Nairobi underground rap has at least four characteristics: its compromises with neoliberalism, a resistance to the state, a notion of a politicized hip hop love, and a commitment to masculinized rap spaces. Rappers also sometimes use Christian themes and gospel to frame their music as socially useful and significant. Like many other iterations, Nairobi's version holds a deep contradiction: it is dedicated to social change while simultaneously espousing problematic alliances. Underground rap resists some elements of capitalism, like music standardization and commercialization, by arguing that their music eschews mainstream success and only seeks to benefit disenfranchised communities. However, rap's commitment to neoliberal principles promotes personal self-discipline, especially as it rejects the state as a corrupt body. Underground artists' tendency to rap about economic achievement as a measure of human worth is a component of political seriousness. This notion of personal encouragement to become a thriving economic actor is how artists express agency. Political love, which is the notion that the love of and dedication to hip hop is innate, powerful, and the source of rappers' creativity, also serves to argue that they are authentic artists who do not imitate. Similarly, the masculinization of underground music is seen as beneficial and purposeful because it is so intensely entwined with a broader practice of romanticizing Mau Mau histories. Artists create and further notions of cismen as warriors and fighters, directly drawing on the anticolonial conflict. Rappers have departed from the more explicit references to the war but find meaning in a generalized "Mau Mau consciousness."[23] The impacts of the war's shaping of national imaginaries and popular cultures, including hip hop, cannot be understated. This conflict was a distinctly Kenyan event. It thus signifies Kenya, and the ways that artists draw from it have long assisted them in claiming that their music is specific to the country. The cultural themes started under UFMM, such as political seriousness, social justice, and even exclusive masculinities, are primary ways for their rap to be seen as uniquely and legitimately Kenyan.

This book not only details political seriousness but also discusses the conditions to which political seriousness responds. Mbũgua wa Mũngai notes that young people have encountered anxieties about poverty, lack of jobs, and social uncertainty and use music to "[encode] their politics in a mode that transgresses mainstream tastes" and "perform the tensions between the mainstream's traditional worldview and their own sense of dissatisfaction with it."[24] Although rappers resist the status quo, as Mūngai writes, they equally concern themselves with hip hop's validity, insisting that the genre should be considered within the catalogs of the country's music. To add to Mūngai, hip hop and its political seriousness respond to long-held anxieties around music regarded as non-Kenyan. The music situates itself within the ongoing apprehensions about influxes of external music, both historic and contemporary, steeped within societal conditions of a rigid industry and a continuously iniquitous state. Kenyan rap is caught between two political truths: first, its participation as a part of the long tradition of music resistance in the country, and second, its residence within an environment that has always hosted non-Kenyan sounds. This complication creates tension about where to locate the music as an often-regarded outside genre that is politically dissident and one that rappers have innovatively made locally relevant. Within this conundrum, artists use the theme of political seriousness as an indigenizing thrust meant to confront, disrupt, and quell cultural anxieties that continue to hover around the music.

Ludicity is the dominant characteristic found especially in bodily expressiveness that, like political seriousness, confers knowledge about the world. A steady focus on embodied performance practices, which can be improvisational, unconscious, or rehearsed, opens a textural component of rap culture often overlooked. I pinpoint the playful as a dominant characteristic in the culture and as a way to think about how artists divest from, buck, dodge, and dance around discourses and structural conditions of power, allowing them space, reprieve, and joy to continue their political engagements. Victor Turner writes that the ludic "arises from excess energy," which is the substance of possibility, and a "part of that surplus fabricates ludic critiques of presentness, of the status quo, undermining it by parody, satire, irony, slapstick."[25] In hip hop, the ludic attempts to erode the grip that power has over people's lives by sculpting something different, even if it is strung or connected to the norms rappers try to elude. Lindon Barrett designates such efforts, particularly through the Black singing voice, as "sly alterity." Barrett writes that amid enslavement, dispossession, and torture, African Americans have drawn on Africanist cultural impulses that center and celebrate that which has been stolen. Moreover, in contexts in which written literacy conveys a false primacy of knowledge, he asserts that Black sonic vocality narrativizes and theorizes about people's lives.[26] Ludicity also holds a creative intangibility, what Édouard Glissant defines as opacity. Glissant theorizes that opacity is an otherness that is potentially undefinable, an alterity that holds the possibilities of multiple meanings and interpretations, and a "density" that occurs over "duration."[27] Through divestment, untranslatability, and a clever dodging, hip hop play becomes a political alternative articulating the expansive possibilities in the music.

Embodied creativities are subversive, often indecipherable, gendered, and diasporic. Artists of all genders seize an armor that is working class, largely ableist, and masculinist, which is fraught with exclusive registers that purport that all are "let in" to a space created and maintained by cisgender men. As part of a movement-centered Black transnationality, performances are one of the primary ways that the music culture is imagined and constituted as diasporic by its practitioners. In Kenyan rap, the ludic performances move back and forth, flirting with power and freedom. A single performance can articulate transgressive anti-establishment sentiments through deployments of a body that rely on the privilege of physical able-bodiedness and masculinity. This duality reveals one way that the relationship between the political and the ludic is complex and neither wholly subversive nor explicitly compliant. In Kenyan rap, lyrics and music are often intensely solemn, while bodily enactments play with social boundaries and resist some of the conformity of lyrics that encourage self-policing and disciplining behavior. Even rappers' performances of armor, masculinity, and toughness rely on a shifty disaffection of cool, and these enactments of the playful assist in resisting those larger subsuming systems, like the state and the music industry.

The political and the ludic are not strict but porous, integrated, and dynamic categories that constitute hip hop orature. Political seriousness sets the stage for the emergence of playful embodied practices. In this way, the ludic in underground rap is never separate from the political commitments that artists express; it is at the heart of the music and culture. Moreover, ludic elements are often present in lyrics, rhymes, and wordplay in the same way that performances can appear as serious and intense. Artists additionally use lyrics, graffiti art, musical beats, and other elements to play with boundaries for aesthetic explorations and their artistic pleasure.

BLACKNESS, DIASPORA, AND PERFORMANCE IN KENYAN HIP HOP

Nairobi Hip Hop Flow addresses how artists create and circulate music about the specifics of the large urban capital city and Kenya by relying on notions of hip hop diasporic blackness. The music's embodiedness articulates an underclass masculinized diasporic sentiment that consistently refers to and negotiates a U.S. Black–derived quality. Therefore, global blackness as a performative aesthetic is a cultural rubric in the long-standing and indigenization practices of Nairobi styles.

A lingering tension exists in non-U.S. hip hop scholarship involving researching blackness in hip hop culture. Global hip hop studies has long used notions of indigenization to describe the processes that non-U.S. artists use to make music relevant and creative in their own contexts to center the agency of rappers.[28] Some scholars have had an uneasy time with how blackness is globalized, pitting global against notions of Black. The most well-referenced example is in *Global Noise*, where Tony Mitchell writes that American hip hop is "atrophied, clichéd, and repetitive" against the vibrancy of non-U.S. styles.[29] The editors of *The Vinyl Ain't Final*, Dipannita Basu and Sidney J. Lemelle, write against Mitchell's notion that non-U.S. global hip hop has distanced itself from American styles to produce good and viable rap music.[30] In *Global Linguistic Flows*, to which Mitchell is a contributor, H. Samy Alim acknowledges that Mitchell's past comments are "reductive" and a "misrepresentation of Black American Hip Hop."[31] In a review of *Global Linguistic Flows*, U.S. Black feminist scholar Elaine Richardson still finds snags with Mitchell, his collaborator Pennycook's work, and other contributors. She writes, "[There] is a tendency to de-emphasize the globalized African American and Afrodiasporic discursive foundations of hip hop."[32] Richardson goes on to state her contentions with Mitchell and Pennycook's dichotomous presentation of "African American hip hop" and "global hip hop."[33] Richardson and Gwendolyn Pough coedited a special issue of *Social Identities* entitled "Hiphop Literacies and the Globalization of Black Popular Culture," continuing the examination of U.S. blackness within the transnational circulation of the music.[34] What remains true, and what their issue highlights, is that *Black* and *global* have never been mutually exclusive, and the historic and continual global circulation of Black popular culture makes any Black/global dichotomy both challenging to conceive and predicated on erasure.

In African hip hop studies, two trends fall short of conceptualizing African rap's relationship to U.S. blackness. Either scholars briefly indicate U.S. artists or blackness as a contributing framework at the beginning of the work, having it fall away as the discussion progresses past the introduction (including in my own previous work), or they do not focus on it at all.[35] Eric Charry, in *Hip Hop Africa: New African Music in a Globalizing World*, writes in the introductory chapter that the music on the continent formed when artists "made it their own" by no longer rapping in English and African American accents.[36] He asserts its popularity came from it being flexible and youth-oriented: "Rap was a youth music, which was its most attractive quality" and "it was a malleable form and could be shaped to fit local circumstances."[37] Although Charry does mention a persistent drawing on Black culture in the conclusion of the book, he does not account for the myriad ways that African youth drew on and cited U.S. Black art and how those citations, often interstitial and slight, were one of the many markers of creativity within the music.[38] In their edited volume *Hip Hop and Social Change in Africa: Ni Wakati*, Msia Clark and Mickie Koster conversely flesh out the prevalence of African youth who find resonance with the struggles of Black people in the U.S. and globally and contend that hip hop is a Pan-African cultural movement.[39] I build on Clark and Koster, as well as on a number of scholars who identify a diasporic conversation in the ways that non-U.S. rappers use U.S. Black rap culture to create local music.[40]

I continue this conversation and state that there is more to say about the deep sensibilities within the sound and style that travel through borders. First, I contend that an evidentiary diaspora exists that contains components, characteristics, and traces of a negotiated U.S. hip hop blackness. This diasporic blackness is sorted through using people's individual experiences, created through knowledge of the music across the African continent and in the U.S., and influenced by U.S. popular culture's pervasive presence. Second, diaspora is embodied and performed, at various times imperfect and flawed, flexible, and profoundly affectively pleasing. Artists of all races and ethnicities negotiate and can perform a signified blackness in their indigenization processes, many times using it as part of a lower-class ethic of subversion deeply tied to what I call political seriousness. Last, Nairobi artists use diasporic blackness to explore themes of Kenyanness, Pan-Africanism, and Africanity. Many use these diasporic connections to contend that rap music is an inherently African music form that has materialized in the U.S. before spreading around the globe. They use these linkages to Africanity to create the music as inherently Kenyan, while many times drawing distinctions between Africanity and U.S. blackness.

Examining hip hop as a holistic performance practice allows us to identify how this blackness can appear in fine details of embodiment and small moments of liminal creativities. I investigate blackness in Nairobi rap culture as one, though of course not the only, element that adds to the deep texture of the culture. Under the modalities of orature, diasporic blackness occurs in the corporeal, the sensorial, and the verbal, and in so doing, says something specific about Nairobi life. These performances often surface not in opposition to ideas of tradition and Kenyanness but as a method to create locality in this global music. In short, blackness is an indigenizing force.

I am motivated by a U.S. Black hip hop feminist lens, which treats hip hop blackness as intersectional, undergoing classed and gendered significations as it moves and travels before arriving on non-U.S. concrete. Hip hop feminism has been long established within the legacies of Black feminism, developing significant and applicable methods to investigate the music and the world at large.[41] The analysis contained in the following chapters is indebted to thinkers like Cheryl Keyes, who identified rap as not only an embodied practice but as one that holds intrinsic diasporic traditions: "Africanisms also appear in abstract levels of performance [in hip hop]."[42] Keyes discusses how Black women develop active identities in the music, such as Queen Mother, Lesbian, Fly Girl, and Sista with Attitude, which are not mutually exclusive or static.[43]

I use hip hop feminist approaches to formulate how women and others of marginalized genders use political seriousness to engage with the Kenyan underground. In addition to Keyes, Joan Morgan reminds us that "hip-hop on the womanist tip" involves "black-on-black love[, which] is essential to the survival of black women and the black community."[44] Tricia Rose contends that women rappers are full participants in "dialogic processes" with men rappers, resisting the idea there exists a gendered binary between women who are automatically feminists and men who are inevitably sexist.[45] Gwendolyn Pough observes that Black women participate in the performative practice of "bringing wreck" to demand their place in hip hop and public space.[46] Keyes, Rose, and Pough's observations are all instructive in how I examine Nairobi spaces, where the music should not be reduced to an automatic misogynist space, but it still holds that women must vie for recognition to do their work. There is much gray to fuck with in Nairobi rap spaces, to reference Joan Morgan's famous line, and doing so allows me to understand the complexities that artists both create and navigate.[47] Brittney C. Cooper, Susana M. Morris, and Robin M. Boylorn, among others, make up the Crunk Feminist Collective and drive this point home, specifically naming their work as "percussive feminism," which deals with the tensions and fissures that surround the music and "finds its way, its mode, its articulation in the spaces of noises, cacophony, and controversy."[48] Moreover, the ways Tanya Saunders have examined gender, feminism, blackness, and transnationality in their study of Cuban activist practitioners have been especially useful in conceptualizing how blackness appears throughout my work.[49] Hip hop is an artistic practice that is constituted through transnational flows and rises out of and feeds off specific societal tensions. For instance, in Kenyan society, anxieties around urban women's independence abound, and women rappers confront this discourse while also appealing to ideals of gendered respectability informed by rejecting global figures like the tomboy and overtly performative femme rapper, often rendered oversexualized. Thus, I use feminism to investigate politics, dynamics, and events in the research, as well as focus on how women and other rappers of all genders make use of the music's frictional qualities.

My methodology involves studying orature as a collection of experiences that uses diasporic blackness as an interwoven characteristic of performance throughout the Nairobi underground. I investigate the smallest details of corporeality and identify how artists create subtle, direct, and innovative throughlines of diaspora. I rely on scholars of U.S. Black performance, who find that amid the constrictions of society, at some point, embodiments yield instances and speculations of Black freedom. In *Black Movements: Performances and Cultural Politics*, Soyica Diggs Colbert explores how performances in folk narrative, film, music, dance, and fiction connect to the past and embark on a reclamation of Black humanity. She notes that Black narratives like Flying Africans "[imagine] futures within the black diaspora that are predicated on understandings of the human that exceed the physical instantiation in the body."[50] Kyra Gaunt's *The Games Black Girls Play* has pioneered hip hop performance studies, where she adeptly identifies how Black girls' double-dutch games and the practices of "musical play" set the foundation for the emergence of hip hop culture.[51] Gaunt situates Black girls' knowledge production as a verbality and embodiedness called kinetic orality, which works to form what she terms "musical blackness," a participatory set of communicative and community practices. Musical play induces "symbolic and performative moment[s] of freedom."[52] I find that both Gaunt and Diggs Colbert offer rich starting points from which to conceptualize the inner workings of blackness as an ur-text that then helps to structure a hip hop diaspora.

The analytical structure of U.S. Black hip hop performance studies can enrich the observations made in Kenyan hip hop studies. For far too long, the assumption has been that the farther the music is from the Black U.S., the more it has nothing to do with Black life and blackness as a conceptual signifier. Furthermore, although unspoken, it seems that when African rappers collaborate with white rappers or NGOs tied to European countries, this means that U.S. blackness, notions of diaspora, and Black citationality are absent from the equations. This book calls for global hip hop studies to end the ways the music is uncomfortably and inaccurately dislocated from U.S. Black references. Focusing on orature in hip hop is one way to avoid the elision of blackness and its move through borders.

This study investigates how Nairobi rap practitioners formed imagined notions of solidarity through fusions of the political and the ludic. During interviews, artists stated matter-of-factly they owed respect to U.S. rap, but more importantly, participated in a significant citational practice in the music, gesturing toward U.S. Black life, rappers, and hoods as they sought to make their unique style specific to Nairobi contexts. These sentiments mirror H. Samy Alim's discussion of rap's navigation of racial politics, what he terms a "transnational blackness," which he briefly describes as "equally concerned with broader racial politics and specific Indigenous histories."[53] I focus on embodiment as a lens and as an object of study, and through this, I identify how U.S. blackness in the music serves as a connective web at times, and a nominal but enduring presence at others, all of which work to tie artists to an imagined global culture. The making of hip hop diaspora has shortcomings, as it can be bound to the politics of antiblackness. While many artists draw important connections to U.S. Black rappers and others in the diaspora, often those same artists disavow the most popular figures within the music, the deviant masculinized thug or gangsta or oversexualized femme rapper, without making room for nuances and imperfect interventions. According to most rappers, the gangsta and sexualized feminine figure fly in the face of Nairobi underground's objectives of political seriousness and their campaign to prove rap's worth in society.

I focus on how artists create commonalities and sameness within conceptions of diaspora and blackness. I avoid hybridity as an approach because it ignores the similarities and commonalities of Afrodiasporic culture, historic political resistance, and the political economies of music. Framing the music's indigenization as the coming together of two seemingly oppositional or disparate characteristics delimits the ever-present African and Black diasporic commonalities that pervade all of hip hop. While hybridity aims to recognize an artist's ingenuity—how well they/she/he can make music out of two opposing cultures—the term fails to capture the totality of creative processes. "Hybridity," Catherine Appert writes, "—as traced in sound and musical form—reinscribes the limitations of western-centric models of cultural globalization that don't necessarily account for how music makers understand themselves in relation to a globally interconnected world."[54] We must thus attempt to study the commonalities within musics, what Kofi Agawu's calls a "hypostatized presumption of sameness," as an endeavor to recognize the similarities among people, contexts, and various cultural expressions.[55] The hip hop sameness of blackness is a set of musical and cultural practices in Kenya that construct a diaspora, which is undoubtedly complex. Nairobi artists are active participants in deciding how to navigate the music's racial politics and create their own visions of Kenyan and African continental hip hop. Rappers make choices about blackness, Africanity, and Kenyanness, which appear in the music and lyrics and embodied practices and thus are part of hip hop orature.

I see the blackness in Nairobi rap culture, which can be the ludic embodiments that express diaspora, as well as the solemn earnestness in sound and lyrics, as interconnected with the city's cultural politics. Kenyan hip hop studies has addressed diverse topics, which have helped inform how I think about the political, the ludic, diaspora, and blackness. Scholars' investigations include an exhaustive list: historic colonial struggle and postcolonial politics,[56] language innovations,[57] the vibrant and troubled music industry,[58] indigenization,[59] ethnicized, urban, and postcolonial notions of identity,[60] religious interrogations,[61] and Nairobi's urbanity,[62] to name a few. Of particular importance to my research are the explorations of masculinities and deployments of gender in rap music spaces that are in continual conversation with the urbanity of Nairobi.[63] Kimani Njogu and the scholars with whom he produces edited volumes elaborately explore the cultural politics of Kenya. In *Culture, Performance and Identity*, he writes how through the media, literature, and music, practitioners explore the historic, ethnicized, and politicized formations of identity, concluding that identity occurs through performances, which are "instruments of practical experiences."[64] Njogu's discussions parallel how I approach studying hip hop from a historical perspective, framed around the conversations that emerged out of colonial contact and continue into the present.

Chris Wasike brings conversations of society and music to the present, writing, "[*genge*] is indeed an expression of local and global urban fears and anxieties within the city space of Nairobi. . . . [It] is the masculine tensions that are more highlighted through rap music because both (the music and city spaces) are dominated by men."[65] Relating to how U.S. blackness surfaces, Mbũgua wa Mũngai argues that Kenyan rappers move through American tropes and Kenyan genres to draw on what is helpful in their process of creating music: "Youth rappers appropriate the surface representations of African American popular culture . . . to explore local social-cultural space," and "young people are continually contesting predominant concepts of identity while simultaneously repackaging some traditional ideas into 'new' performative modalities."[66] Like Wasike and Mũngai, Esther Milu identifies Kenyan and transnational qualities in the music. "Ethnic and linguistic activism" scrutinizes the ongoing politicization of Kenyan ethnicities through wordplay usages of Sheng. Milu writes such activism "[challenges] hegemonic practices of ethnic and racial identification and [forges] cultural and linguistic identities that mark them as true Kenyans, both in local and global contexts."[67] In my study, I focus on the topics that Wasike, Mũngai, and Milu broach—masculinity, urbanity, identity, linguistics, race, ethnicity, globality, "tradition," and Kenyanness—and argue they can and should be thought of as a part of the music's earnestness and embodied performativities.

RESEARCHING HIP HOP IN NAIROBI

Nairobi Hip Hop Flow is an interdisciplinary investigation of embodiment that uses ethnographic methods, political and cultural histories, and performance analysis, all of which help to tell the story of underground orature. I discuss the history of the music industry, which helps to contextualize the apprehensions that have long endured around the genre. With Nairobi serving as a prominent regional hub of music recording and production, especially since the postwar era, the city has attracted musicians and recording companies from outside Kenya. The development of the industry coincided with colonial restrictions and bans on music and performance deemed subversive. In the 1960s, Kenya formed as a newly independent state and witnessed Congolese music's popularity explode, opening huge questions about the role of Kenyan music traditions and culture in the country. The '80s saw how Moi's dictatorship added to the difficulty Kenyan music encountered, especially politically defiant sounds. By the time hip hop entered the scene in the late '80s and early '90s, several long traditions were in place: banning Kenyan music, hosting outside artists, and the rich and enduring creation of subversive tunes. In post-Moi Kenya, restrictive copyright policies have replaced bans, and the influx of music from around Africa, the United States, and Europe has been continuous. This book details how rap music fits into and engages with this complicated and burdened setting by responding to various political urgencies, engendering cultural anxieties, and exemplifying what cultural production looks like in a postcolonial African city.

I examine underground music culture in the capital city of Kenya while also understanding that there are scenes in other places in Kenya, like Nakuru, Naivasha, and Mombasa.[68] Artists travel between these major cities to perform at gigs, record with others, and have followings in these places. At times, they travel to Uganda and Tanzania for collaborations and concerts. Nairobi, in this context, serves as a cultural center amid other centers like Dar es Salaam and Mombasa, as well as an economic crossroads within and outside of Africa. This study is not generalizable to all Kenyan hip hop, as there are artists who do not emerge from the UFMM camp. Additionally, mainstream sounds have a different story to tell. The discussions I have about underground rap in Nairobi are perhaps most similar to other forms of rap in Anglophone African countries, specifically those in East Africa, given the shared British colonial history and the widespread use of Swahili. Categories like political seriousness and ludicity are specific to my research and found in other hip hop spaces. It is not difficult to imagine that practitioners everywhere are known for spirited verbal sparring, the corresponding playful bodily movement about the stage or in a music video, and the political commitments to social change. Seriousness is found throughout global rap cultures as a way to engage with notions like inequality, cultural affirmation, and political resistance. However, how these concepts interact with the given locality of Nairobi is specific to the cityspace and Kenyan cultural histories.

Studying hip hop's multiplicities must be undertaken with robust approaches. I draw on James Spady's hiphopography, which H. Samy Alim builds out, writing that it is a method that "integrates the varied approaches of ethnography, biography, and social, cultural, and oral history to arrive at an emic view of Hip Hop Culture."[69] I spoke with various actors within the music industry, dug through files at the Kenya National Archives, and conducted participant observations at concerts, bars, and music stalls in Nairobi's city center, all of which helped me stitch together the story of the embodied and the political. Economic barriers and family responsibilities often prevented extended stays, and I carried out intense fieldwork trips in 2008, 2011, 2012, 2014, 2016, and 2018, ranging from three weeks to two months. I followed several artists on social media, which provided me with updates on events I missed. I sought to have artists shape my research, as they held critical knowledge about their marginal place in the economic system and as citizens who fought for their creative agency within limiting conditions. I had a range of inquiries, including their views on the political system and the music industry, the place of rap within Kenyan society, what they accomplished in their songs, and the meaning of embodiment in the culture, the latter being the most difficult to discuss. The conclusions I draw are based on field research, probes of the music industry and the state, interviews with various actors, examinations of music videos, and observations at Sarakasi Dome.

Practitioners have various and often faulty investments in power that need to be identified, such as with capitalism, able-bodiedness, normative masculinity, and homophobia. Even though men outnumber women heavily in underground rap, I intentionally prioritize women by considering their voices, experiences, and performances. In my research, I only met one artist who described himself as having a disability: a cisman who had a cleft palate. He volunteered that he was determined not to allow that to limit his possibilities and that others welcomed him and were open to collaboration, though his career struggled. Hip hop privileges able bodies, those that can move, rap, and dance. Similarly, homophobia and transphobia exist in the community, although rappers have hesitated to admit this. A few artists I interviewed discussed at length their navigation with sexuality and the pressures they felt to be heterosexual even though they were not. Although all I interviewed identified as either a cisman or ciswoman, at times I use the pronouns "they/them/theirs," the terms "marginalized genders" and "gender-expansive people," and wording such as "artists of all genders" to hold space for those rappers who continue to explore their gendered self-making.

I conducted structured and recorded interviews with sixteen rappers—some of whom I introduced above, a rapper turned DJ, two graffiti artists, two music producers, one DJ on a mainstream radio station, and a gospel artist who did not make hip hop. I had impromptu, informal, unrecorded conversations with a handful of other music producers and about a dozen other rappers. The briefness of my trips impacted how I interacted with many practitioners. I continued to encounter an ethical dilemma concerning my role as a researcher, obtaining information about their challenging experiences and knowledge of the industry. I sought to mitigate the politics of extraction that had long plagued Kenyan and African music scenes, which led me to provide a small stipend to anyone I formally interviewed. I realized what feminist ethnographer Karla Slocum notes as the ongoing "impossibility of dislodging the imbalance in the researcher-informant relationship."[70] Paying artists helped to acknowledge the power relations between working- and lower-class rap practitioners and me as a privileged American researcher.[71] I aimed to recognize their labor of sharing knowledge and mediate any minor difficulties that meeting me might cause. In most cases, we met in a café in a central area, which required them to pay for public transportation and spend time in the city center.

I was mindful of how I structured fieldwork trips, given the complications of paying a stipend. I purposely visited venues at the beginning of my stay and then, toward the end, conducted interviews. My presence in venues was less disruptive this way because not many knew I would then be providing stipends. However, some understood I was an American researcher, and additionally, while mixed race and Black, I could pass for white or *mzungu* in Kenya, which also meant my presence conferred privilege. I also moved around to different places—I visited most NGOs where events took place, and I spent time at the Kenya National Theatre, random street events, outdoor music festivals, and nightclubs and bars in wealthier areas. With this, I often encountered new groups of people, again meaning that I could observe and interact with others without the complication of my presence as a researcher who offered remuneration for interviews. Toward the end of my research, I conducted follow-up virtual conversations with artists I continued to follow closely and again paid a stipend, motivated not only by recognizing their knowledge sharing but also by how expensive internet service is to maintain a ninety-minute discussion. Doing interviews before and after deciding to pay a stipend meant that I was able to compare conversations. I noticed no vast differences between how the conversations unfolded, aside from those receiving the stipend being less likely to cancel or reschedule. Yet, how our interactions were mediated by economic exchange and the shorter duration of fieldwork trips prevented the formation of in-depth relationships.

I spent time at Sarakasi Dome, Goethe-Institut, Alliance Française, and the British Council, all international nongovernmental organizations (NGOs). Additionally, I attended events at the Godown Arts Centre, which models itself as an organization that promotes community arts and music through training and events. It envisions relying on funding from Kenyan individuals, corporations, and global partners and has received support from entities like the British Council and the Ford Foundation.[72] From the places mentioned, I spent the most time at Sarakasi, which receives sponsorship from several foreign donors, primarily from Scandinavia, including the Royal Netherlands Embassy, the Danish Embassy, Stichting Doen Netherlands (a Dutch foundation), and FK Norway (a Norwegian state entity).[73] Artists have long relied on NGOs and cultural organizations to host events. These places regularly hold various cultural and language classes, workshops, concerts, festivals, and training programs. Regardless of the incredible diversity and quality of many events, these entities often perpetuate and maintain global north/south power relations. NGO programming, interest, and investment do not undo or challenge the privileged position these centers or their countries of origin hold. Consider Maurice Amutabi: "[NGOs] are gatekeepers, situating themselves between [Africa] and donors, exercising so-called benevolent hegemony."[74] The artists I followed recognized that foreign organizations are interested in listening and funding politically conscious rap. However, the role of NGOs in the underground world has not been stable. During the course of the research, I noticed fewer events at these places. When I approached artists with this inquiry, they stated that many NGOs have increasingly requested that events produce monetary profit. Some artists apply for and obtain grants from NGOs, but these funds have decreased over the years. Therefore, artists charge devotees to get in at the door, which invariably limits those who want to attend but lack the expendable cash to do so. The decline of events has meant that many artists have relied more on the digital world to circulate music.

Music videos have been fundamental to my research analysis because they are critical storehouses of hip hop oratured performances. Practitioners contribute to creating an underground archive that exists on platforms like YouTube, Mdundo, and ReverbNation, which rarely translates into direct income. Rappers repeatedly stated that to break into the industry, one must have videos.[75] During one interview, a gospel singer from Ongata Rongai named Snooker stated, "In Kenya, you can be a hip hop artist, you can be well known, you can spit sixteen bars, but as long as you don't have a video, you are not considered to be anywhere."[76] The greater truth is that for many underground artists, videos do not serve as a promising ticket to access mainstream visibility on television and radio. Thus, the music video, in many ways, seems to be not only an industry and genre standard but also, for these rappers, a response to the exclusions and a primary way artists express their cultural agency. Practitioners explained that though trained producers developed the

FIGURE 3. Graffiti artist Esen at Sarakasi Dome, 2011. Photo by author.

FIGURE 4. Graffiti artist Wise at Sarakasi Dome, 2011. Photo by author.

finished product, they gave input into the shape and texture of the video. Wanting to retain creative control, rappers helped frame background scenes, experimented with props, and positioned their bodies in specific ways related to the camera. The critical role of this visual technosonic text has acquired significance over time as the industry has shifted away from CDs and toward digitality as a primary mechanism of circulation.

Underground videos challenge our traditional notions of the media archive. The noncommercial archive is distinct from mainstream music because it lacks commercial visibility. These musicians often work with studios to release the videos. Although they enter an economy of circulation and reproduction, the music exists on a different stratum than mainstream Kenyan sounds. Noncommercial rap videos rarely make it to television and, therefore, do not have the same visibility as the work of commercial artists or U.S. hip hop that often receive regular play on television.

With the decrease of events at NGOs, music distribution has altered. For underground artists, by 2016 or 2017, gone were the days when one could hawk CDs at NGO concerts and earn some income. It is important to note that CDs are still sold in Kenya to a small market. While one can encounter a salesperson making rounds between cars on the city streets, such practices no longer work well for underground artists. The digital marketplace and virtual world have made it easier for rappers to host their own freestyle battles and small concerts. Rappers use Twitter, Instagram, Facebook, and music-sharing platforms like ReverbNation and Mdundo to make their songs and music videos more visible. Of course, the downside to such shifts is a marked difficulty in acquiring profit. Given the limitations of the industry and artists' demand to be heard and seen, the weight and force of the music video becomes vitally apparent.

POLITICAL TIMELINES OF RESEARCH

The time period of this book is from 2011 to 2018, although I reference events both before and after these dates. I trace both the political conditions of the country at large as well as the music industry itself, on which I started research when I lived in Kenya in 2000–2001. I studied public transportation vehicles, *matatus*, and specifically the imagery and the African American and Afro-Caribbean references made on the exterior of brightly colored and graffitied vehicles. This early research occurred at the end of Daniel arap Moi's presidency and coincided with the music of early artists like Kalamashaka and the Ukoo Flani Mau Mau collective. Their music interfaced with harsh political repression and the long-lasting effects of structural adjustment programs (SAPs), especially as urban poverty worsened due to inflation, the gutting of public funds, and the elimination of jobs. Moi had begun opening markets, selling state parastatals, and embracing neoliberal reforms, responding to IMF and World Bank stipulations, insistence from donor countries, and internal political pressure.[77] In 2002, hip hop ushered Mwai Kibaki into power. He rode the wave of political optimism with the help of Gidi Gidi Maji Maji's song "Unbwogable," which rallied young people and energized the atmosphere of Kenya.[78] Murunga and Nasong'o describe an "enthusiastic euphoria" and "heralded expectations that a new political era of democracy had dawned in Kenya."[79] Under Kibaki, Kenya's adoption of neoliberalism as an answer to the dictatorship years, for both better and worse, has set a significant tone for underground rap. In all the change, hip hop culture played its own part in integrating a political outlook of optimism and a renewed commitment to advocating for capitalism's promise that hard work would equivocate success and monetary return.

The Kibaki presidency brought the flourishing system of bootleg music to a grinding halt. By the early 2000s, new copyright policies prevented practitioners from easily selling their burned copies of music. Additionally, the colorful and booming *matatus* under then-new Michuki state regulations were absent, replaced with quiet(er) and slower monochrome vehicles with a tacky yellow horizontal stripe across the exterior.[80] While Moi's dictatorship was gone, the Kibaki governance brought new difficulties for musicians. The state aggressively eliminated bootlegged and copied music. The copyright policies, imposed by WTO regulations, were in place to benefit artists and prevent the bootleg economy from profiting from musicians' music.[81] The Kenya Copyright Board (KECOBO) and the Music Copyright Society of Kenya (MCSK) created a restrictive and constraining music industry to ensure that musicians supposedly received royalties and abided by copyright laws. While the *matatu* and copyright laws were supposed to be beneficial, they resulted in a noticeable muting of hip hop culture. Such changes meant that artists had to be creative and aggressive in their pursuits and continue collaborating with NGOs like the British Council, Sarakasi Dome, and the Goethe-Institut. The Kibaki presidency was plagued by rampant corruption and postelection violence in 2007–8, and in the following years, rappers would use the music like a salve on these open wounds.

Uhuru Kenyatta assumed the presidency in 2013, and rappers and others settled in and collectively recognized that, although the state has the burden and responsibility to help the populace, it will not. Five years later and after the postelection violence, it became clear that the newly elected President Kenyatta and Vice President William Ruto (Ruto was also elected to the presidency in 2022) would dodge their International Criminal Court (ICC) trials for their roles in orchestrating the election mayhem after trial postponements, media campaigns declaring themselves victims of western imperialist meddling, and accounts of witness intimidation and silencing.[82] If Kibaki ushered in a jubilation of postdictatorship shifts and then shattered it under his administration's corruption and postelection violence, Uhuru's presidency meant an acidic acceptance that at the level of the state, real change and accountability seemed unviable. The mantra "everybody is corrupt" sounded in barroom conversations, in *matatus*, and on stages. Under Kenyatta, the enforcement of some music restrictions put in place during Kibaki's time had weakened, although these policies had not benefited artists even when enforcement was stronger. Those who complained about the utter ineptitude of the Music Copyright Society of Kenya (MCSK) and their promises of royalty payments in the early 2010s believed that the organization has slowly become more corrupt and mismanaged. Musically speaking, rappers grew accustomed to the hustle of the industry, the lack of venues and radio play, and an absence of copyright protection.

CHAPTERS

As with any other work on music, the reader must listen to the songs and watch music videos mentioned to appreciate the analysis and the careful work of placing embodiment at the conceptual crux of investigation. Chapter 1, "Cultural Anxieties, Music Commodities, Rapping Bodies," sets the scene for the underground and music more generally, detailing the social urgency of hip hop and the general apprehensions that arise around cultural expressions. I argue that rap's political seriousness has responded to the cultural anxieties over the long-standing presence of non-Kenyan music. To understand this, I discuss the early music industry formed in the 1920s through the practices of music extraction and commodification, just as the Kenyan colony was taking shape. As the industry grew, it hosted non-Kenyan genres like Congolese and South African music. Alongside this, the colonial state repressed all forms of dissent, including several instances of resistance music, dance, and performance. The consistent hosting of non-Kenyan genres and the silencing and censorship of some Kenyan music throughout the colonial epoch and into the first two presidencies created a hostile atmosphere for artists, regardless of whether they aimed for their music to be subversive. New copyright policies have replaced state censorship, continuing the hardship that plagues Kenyan music, resulting in the long-standing cultural anxieties of "foreign" sounds that hip hop has continued to incite. The U.S. Black hip hop performing body is at the center of current apprehensions, which usher in claims of mimicry and the supposed empty value of U.S. music. Rap's political seriousness grows out of this anxiety, rejecting the claim that the music is another example of a foreign genre privileged in an already challenging music scene.

Chapter 2, "Play and Gender," clarifies how embodied creativities operate through performatives of gender and play. Rappers use the ludic within the imperfect political, where songs condemning injustice rely on the playful unpredictability of practitioners' performances to fashion the creative repertoires of rap music. Both the political and the ludic coexist to form notions of global Black rap solidarities. At the same time, the performing body of the Nairobi rapper induces potentialities, movements, and circulatory knowledge in seemingly foreclosed settings. In that sense, artists imagine their bodies as immune from normative structures. This playfully obscure body signals beyond borders and contexts, thus enacting what practitioners enumerate as a global rap culture. Ludicity is part of a larger pattern of movement-centered Black transnationality. Its creative force celebrates the playful narrations of bodily storytelling, actively resisting the antiblackness that follows hip hop around the globe. In this chapter, I introduce the term the *armor of gender*. The now-established idea that gender is indeed a set of performances means that to analyze gender in rap spaces is to investigate embodied performance practices. Here, I explore how cismen and ciswomen seize a gendered armor that is working class, largely ableist, and masculinist. The armor of gender is fraught with exclusive registers that purport that all are "let in" to a space created and maintained by cismen. Nonetheless, women and others of marginalized genders use political seriousness to stage their interventions.

Chapter 3, "Diaspora, Love, and Limits," contends that political love is the foundation of a hip hop diaspora. Underground rap's continual reference to love is not just about fondness toward the music. This political love solidifies the authenticity of practitioners who exercise the innate and undying commitment to the culture, Kenyans, and Africana peoples in general. In Nairobi rap, diaspora is orature. The force of lyrics and the creative embodiments synthesize to espouse a globalized blackness that constantly cites the United States. Elements of diasporic blackness are embraced, sorted through, sometimes rejected, and reworked into a signifier of lower-class solidarity. Not only do diaspora and love facilitate Pan-African sentiments, but these themes are indigenizing mechanisms that rappers use to create uniquely Kenyan music. The film *Ni Wakati* and the South African–based Afrikan Hip Hop Caravan exemplify how diaspora and blackness in rap cohere around motifs of transit, or a "diaspora in motion," a common theme in the music.

Chapter 4, "The Sounds of Imperfect Resistance," argues that the sonic confers with rap corporeality to produce a distinct underground aesthetic. Sound is one dominating characteristic that critics use to discount the music. Likewise, underground practitioners also use sonority to guard their genre, claiming that commercial rappers may use politically conscious lyrics asserting that this music sounds American and "not from the hood." These noncommercial rappers accuse wealthy rappers of imitation and focus on how affluent artists copy the wealth-based braggadocios of swag embodiments. In this manner, these practitioners imagine themselves as having a final say in the debates around imitation and mimicry of U.S. music. I use sound to claim that rappers hold conflicting anticapitalist ideas. They see their participation in capitalism as hard workers and promising entrepreneurs within the industry as a remedy to a corrupt state. However, these same artists also reject commercial standards in part fueled by capitalist practices, seeing the aurally pleasurable sentiments of mainstream music as a significant problematic that waters down the force of hip hop. In turn, these artists use harder sonic qualities to interface with their corporeal interventions, producing sustained conversations about Kenyan society, the state, and music's commercialism.

In the conclusion, "Hip Hop Flow as Kenyan, as Black," I build on P. Khalil Saucier and Tryon P. Woods's assertion that hip hop studies needs to reclaim its radical traditions and become Black studies.[83] Saucier and Woods's contention enhances the interventions within both global hip hop and Kenyan hip hop scholarship by insisting on the music's Black foundational elements. Adding performance theory to this way of studying the music in Nairobi not only deepens the analysis of how artists create and think through a Black-informed diaspora but also intensely focuses on the manners in which rap speaks to and rises out of the specificities of Kenya's realities. I acknowledge, and indeed hope, that the ludicity and opacity of performances prevented complete readings. The descriptions contained herein were as ample as possible, and it is also unfeasible to account for every detail of orature given the dodginess and intentional incomprehensiveness of the music's aesthetic beauty.

1

———

Cultural Anxieties, Music Commodities, Rapping Bodies

Kenyan hip hop has entered a complicated musical landscape. Historically, state restrictions and industry exclusiveness have resulted in the emptying out of Kenyan sounds while outside genres have been pumped in, unsettling a populace that has long heeded nationalist calls to exercise self-determination and celebrate Kenyan culture. Left in the wake of these difficult conditions is an ongoing anxiety about how to articulate what Kenyan music is and what to do with the persistent presence of sounds from other locales. Like other popular genres circulating within the country, hip hop has embedded itself in the country's postcolonial meaning-making processes, helping to tell the story of the country. Rap, including its political seriousness and playful diasporic corporeality, responds in a diversity of creative ways to this cultural landscape that has offered the music a frosty reception.

Many factors, often unaccounted for, have played pivotal roles in the treatment and perspectives of Kenyan music. Past and current bans, inconsistent state policies, and the failures to implement much-desired quotas for radio play have all added to how the public has come to understand the country's music, including hip hop. State actors on both sides of Kenya's 1963 moment approached music with suspicion, wary of its potential to rally people. The industry limitations on the country's genres forced fans and consumers, and those interested in notions of culture writ large, to respond rigidly in defining and defending Kenyan music. Debating what counts as Kenyan and what does not reflects what Mbũgua wa Mũngai terms "post-independence anxieties" about American cultural imperialism, non-Kenyan music, and notions of appropriation and mimicry.[1] For Mũngai, three institutions—the government, the church, and the East African academy—proffered notions in the lead-up to independence and afterward about what it meant to be Kenyan (and East African and African). Mũngai rightly contends that hip hop artists and young people use the music, often what the media provides, to expand notions of Kenyanness and explore their identities in multicultural urban environments like Nairobi. I build on Mũngai's discussion here because it is not solely institutions proffering discourse that shape these worries; the political and economic conditions also contribute to questions about Kenyan culture and what artists do within this arena. Hence, the first two sections of this chapter pan outward beyond Mũngai's three prongs and examine colonial and postcolonial state-instituted bans and a flourishing historic Nairobi industry that long privileged Congolese genres. Not only does this discussion on policy and commerce situate the historical arc of cultural anxieties, but it also helps to contextualize the contemporary state practices hostile to artists explored at the end of the chapter.

The following two sections address how the state and music industry have stymied Kenyan sounds. While there was a marked boom in production during the Kenyatta era (1963–78), much of the focus was on Congolese styles. During the Moi (1978–2002) and Kibaki (2002–13) years, the industry and the state, in different capacities, limited Kenyan music. While Moi was concerned with dissidence, Kibaki's implementation of WTO copyright policies adversely affected the circulation of products that long depended on informal economies. Radio stations and multinational corporations promoted tunes from outside the country during this time. These entities, state power, the music industry, and the World Trade Organization (WTO), in different ways, have held much sway over the appetites of music culture, resulting in challenges defining what it means for a music to be Kenyan, a real quagmire in a context where the country has had its ear to foreign genres for decades. In the section "Radio Play," I discuss that artists must have wealth, connections, and a specific mainstream sound to make it consistently to media airwaves. Here, I delve into the obstacles that underground artists have in obtaining long-standing media airtime, with many blaming the state and its failure to create and implement much-desired quotas, which supposedly would allow for a healthy block of Kenyan music.

The last two sections address the loaded claim that people make of each other: "Kenyans do not appreciate Kenyan music." This common accusation appears in various arenas, such as on television and radio, and often when anything related to music is broached as a topic. Musicians, producers, and fans alike will utter the declaration in casual conversation. I connect this weighty statement to the cultural anxieties around hip hop and all genres that move within the country. In this respect, the idea that "Kenyans do not appreciate Kenyan music" reflects and encapsulates the elements of political, cultural, and intellectual history explored in this chapter. The quip helps to tell the story of a lengthy span of outside sounds and people's responses, given the appeals to center Kenyan culture. It also enables an understanding of how the industry framed the parameters of music and how people have negotiated through these conditions. The notion that Kenyans do not value or treasure Kenyan music is laden with meaning. Media hosts will frame the conversation as a matter of truth: "Of course, we all know that Kenyans have struggled to support and appreciate their artists, but the success of [event X] is testimony to how far we have come." Musicians mention this complaint to lament that they need more opportunities to perform in front of mostly Kenyan audiences and find ways to sustain a fan base and sell their products. Many feel they cannot compete with Congolese, American, Nigerian, and other sounds and find the popularity of genres from these places unnerving. When rappers are accused of making hip hop because they do not appreciate the country's music, they respond with the stern assertion that their music is Kenyan and earnestly located within the contexts of those who live around them. The ways that artists craft political seriousness in hip hop, in other words, is a response to the "Kenyans do not appreciate Kenyan music" accusation. Moreover, the entrenched idea that the citizenry does not enjoy sounds from their country and the retorting political seriousness in rap belong to the same historicized discourse that calls people to prioritize Kenyan cultural expressions within a difficult setting.

Unpacking this loaded claim reveals that focusing on taste conceals structural conditions. Rather than placing the blame on the buying public, I shift the focus to bans, policies, and industry practices. While it is understandable to conclude that Kenyans turn their ear toward all music beyond the borders, there is more to this story than consumer preferences. Entertainment establishments have played Jamaican dancehall and Tanzanian Bongo Flava, and in Nairobi's city center, there has been a plethora of American, Congolese, Nigerian, Tanzanian, and South African music to buy. Television shows air Kenyan artists, yet much airplay has gone to songs from the places just mentioned. Many genres of Kenyan music, from commercial Afropop to Benga, have drawn influences from Congolese music and dance culture. The media's choices in playing these genres or artists' decisions to borrow from styles from around and outside Africa cannot rest solely on the consumer or musician. Absent from many of these conversations is how the long stretches of state censorship and the formation of production industries with a commercial ear to outside music have critically impacted entertainment scenes, and it is from these perspectives that I discuss Kenyan music history.

I establish that music production and state censorship, as well as current policies and politics, have shaped, sometimes indirectly and other times explicitly, the widely circulated beliefs about underground rap and Kenyan styles more generally. These dynamics together fuel racialized conceptions about hip hop and its place in Nairobi. Therefore, I discuss the imported notions of American antiblackness that have ridden in with the music that causes nondevotees to be judgmental and rappers to mount a defense of their craft. From this comprehensive understanding, I contextualize the implications of the imported figure of the U.S. Black rapper who traveled to the country in the 1980s as American hip hop began to make its global rounds. Practitioners recognize that their music all too easily shores up notions of derivativeness that feed into hip hop's status as a genre of racialized otheredness. Therefore, political seriousness has a dire job of filtering out attacks on the culture and affirming hip hop's place within a field that easily writes off rappers.

HIP HOP AND HISTORY

Kenyan hip hop has emerged within and continues to participate in the long traditions of dissent launched against both colonial and postcolonial state power. Within this dynamic, hip hop uses political seriousness to give form to the music's legitimacy within the country's cultural geography. Much of Kenyan rap has served as a vibrant archive for dissecting how the violence of colonialism is presently felt, as illustrated in the famous 2008 Ukoo Flani Mau Mau music video, "Angalia Saa" (Look at the Time). The song induces themes of urgent longing and unfinishedness with its slow pace, solemn beats, and a chorus of high-pitched masculine moaning matched with word-heavy, concentrated verses. Scholars have paid particular attention to how it juxtaposes historical and contemporary notions by displaying various images next to each other.[2] Evan Mwangi writes, "'*Angalia Saa*' [is] a mourning song seeking to memorialize the dead, the raped, and the injured in anticolonial and post-independence Kenya. At the same time, it refuses closure to suggest to the listener that the Mau Mau liberation war is still going on."[3] Scenes of home guards and white authorities checking for *kipande* work passes, pictures from the attempted 1982 overthrow of the Moi government, an image of the tragic capture of Dedan Kimathi, and the 1950s mass detention of Africans during the State of Emergency all work to construct the notion that freedom is a continual struggle.

One moment worth mentioning is the song's brief allusion to activist Mary Muthoni wa Nyanjiru. She organized a protest in the 1920s supporting imprisoned labor organizer Harry Thuku. His advocacy and leadership within the East African Association (EAA) (formerly the Young Kikuyu Association) attracted the ire of the authorities. In 1922, his supporters gathered at the police station across from the Norfolk Hotel, demanding his release. Mary Muthoni wa Nyanjiru was among many other women in the increasingly agitated crowd who threw their loyalty behind Thuku for his concern over how labor conditions exacerbated women and girls' exploitation and sexual assault. After a day of protest, they left, unsuccessful. That night, a frustrated Nyanjiru and other women gathered and took oaths, which dictated that what one did, they all did. Returning the next day, EAA negotiators, all men, met with colonial officials and failed to secure Thuku's release.[4] Upon the meeting's breakdown, these men returned to urge the dispersal of the crowd, now grown to eight thousand people. Dissatisfied, Nyanjiru pushed her way toward the front of the group and lifted her dress, revealing her naked body to the men and the larger crowd.[5] This practice, termed *guturamira ng'ania*, is where older women bare their nude bodies to younger men (typically their son's age) and has been long considered a curse, insult, or abomination within Kikuyu (and many other African) communities.[6] Other women followed suit, lifting their clothing and exposing their front sides to men whose power they no longer recognized and whom they saw as not taking Thuku's freedom seriously. Kenyan home guards or *askari* raised arms toward the protesters. Harry Thuku, watching from a jail cell window, remembered seeing the women "[pushing] on until the bayonets of the rifles were pricking at their throats."[7] *Askari*, threatened by the naked unrest of these older women, fired into the crowd. After the smoke and gathering dissipated, Nyanjiru, along with at least 150 other protesters, lay dead. Accounts emerged that depraved white settlers who were at the Norfolk Hotel eagerly participated in the massacre by shooting at the backs of running protesters. The *Kanyegenyūri* song and dance narrated grievances of Thuku's detention and celebrated Nyanjiru's activism; a version would become one of the songs during the Mau Mau resistance.[8]

Kamah raps, "Wa-shoot Muthoni wa Nyanjiru (They shot Muthoni wa Nyanjiru) / The same route wa-rape mama yetu Njeeri (In the same way or manner they raped our mother Njeeri)." Here, Kamah draws two incidents together: the 1920 assassination of Nyanjiru and the 2004 sexual assault of Njeeri wa Thiong'o, the wife of well-known writer and cultural scholar Ngũgĩ wa Thiong'o. This incident occurred after their return from self-imposed overseas exile.[9] The attack on Njeeri was widely thought to be a state-sanctioned hit against the returning elderly author, and the song sees little difference in the violence enacted against these two women. This song points to how underground rap can concern itself with how the body, in particular women's bodies, can be violated, raped, shot at, and killed. Moreover, hip hop locates itself within Kenyan social history, and here, it operates as a performative archive responsible for reminding people about those figures in an anticolonial struggle who may have been forgotten.

This single example of "Angalia Saa" shows the degree to which Nairobi hip hop takes account of Kenyan history and its complexities, which are its claims to Kenyanness and the music's seriousness. Underground texts like this understand the complex layers of the nation's history, not just as individuated events but as connected occurrences of violence and resistance. The song reveals a sophisticated awareness of how the history of musical suppression is indistinguishable from political violence. In 1986 and while in exile, Ngũgĩ wa Thiong'o published *Decolonising the Mind* and called for African literature to confront the "cultural bomb" of colonial rule, where the goal was "to annihilate a people's belief in their names, in their languages, in their environment, in their heritage of struggle, in their unity, in their capacities and ultimately in themselves."[10] Artists see their music as meeting the challenge of rectifying the damages of colonialism that Ngũgĩ precisely identifies.

We can use the engagement of "Angalia Saa" with history to further explore how the characteristics of the colonial state set the foundations for the content and meaning of rap and other music. Ngũgĩ's "cultural bomb" that detonated across the landscape was a slow, disjointed, and chaotic rollout of what would become Kenya's colonial state. This apparatus birthed twin forces that impacted music: the capitalist growth of music production and the state's squashing of public dissent—Nyanjiru's murder an example of the latter. Nairobi grew to serve as a cultural hub and "commercial nerve" of international styles for eastern and central Africa, helped by its status as a major city in the British-settled colony.[11] This music economy continued for some sixty years until its restructuring in the late '80s and early '90s. The Kenyan music industry started in the 1920s and was constructed alongside the colonial economic system, and then prospered during the post-WWII period.[12] Like other arms of a capitalist machine, such as agricultural production, the industry profited from African labor. While colonial authorities did not have a direct hand in the industry per se, the repressive state apparatus normalized and created pathways for exploitation and extraction from which the industry concretized.[13] From the start, the cultural positioning of music mattered; songs that were produced in studios and sold within the colonies, Europe, and India were regarded as entertaining. Conversely, work that dispossessed people created, especially expressing anticolonial sentiment, often received censorship and a mark of illegality.

Around the turn of the twentieth century and when Kenya was under British control as the East African Protectorate, colonial state workers, so-called explorers, and anthropologists traveled to various communities and recorded musicians and singers, just as they did in present-day countries like Uganda, Tanzania, Rwanda, Burundi, and the Democratic Republic of the Congo.[14] These recordings would end up in many European institutions, like the British Library Sound Archive and the Berlin Phonogramm-Archiv, which still hold many originals today.[15] By 1907, the Protectorate state had implemented "extra economic coercion" through the hut and poll tax, forcing Africans into an economy of labor where people worked for wages subject to taxation.[16] Concurrently, the global music companies scrambled to divvy up control of the music markets, each taking portions of the globe, in striking similarity to the 1884–85 scramble to divide the continent among colonial powers. The Gramophone Recording Company grabbed the region that would come to be known as Kenya and other parts of British-occupied Africa, and five other major companies participated: Victor Talking Machine Company (later RCA) (U.S.), the Columbia Phonograph Company (later CBS) (U.S.), the Edison Company (U.S.), the Lindström Company (later Polygram) (Germany), and the Pathé Company (France).[17]

The Protectorate became a colony in 1920, just two years before Nyanjiru's uprising and subsequent assassination. The colonial state took on the task of how to surveil and compel labor from Africans, like implementing the extremely unpopular *kipande* work pass, meant to limit movement outside of African reserves.[18] Also, around 1920, an emerging British and Indian consumer base began to buy American, Indian, and European records imported into the territory.[19] In the colony, institutions of power determined whether music was deemed acceptable or offensive. Africans who recorded in studios or learned European religious hymns tied to churches made acceptable music in the eyes of the state. These individuals were participating in how the state determined something as banal or impactful as musical taste, and as Achille Mbembé states, engaged in practices "designed to alter the moral behavior of the colonized."[20] Authorities viewed all other music suspiciously because of its potential to rally people against the colonial state.[21] From the 1920s, the Government Censorship Board (GCB) began to vet and ban any material, music, or performance undermining colonial domination.[22] For instance, the GCB targeted the nationalist Kikuyu Central Association and the associated Muigwithania paper.[23] Anticolonial uprisings drew strong responses from the state and ended in arrest, detention, or death. Beginning in the 1910s and continuing through the first half of the century, the state targeted people like Mekatilili wa Menza (sometimes written as Me Katilili) and prophet Ndonye wa Kauti, as well as the religious organizations of Mumbo and Dini ya Msambwa.[24] Colonial authorities also outlawed the supposedly seditious *Ituĩka* songs and dances, which celebrated and acknowledged Kikuyu traditional leadership. In 1930, under the Public Order Act, the British banned the Kikuyu circumcision song and dance, "*Mũthĩrĩgũ*," which doubled as a performance of protest.[25]

The presence of prohibited protest music came simultaneously with the growing industry's sale of commercial Kenyan sounds. By the end of the 1930s, the British company EMI had tremendous success selling records by local artists.[26] Several companies competed over the emerging star Shahir Sitti Binti Saad, a woman singer from Zanzibar, who sang the coastal *taarab* music. By 1928, she was in recording studios in Mombasa.[27] HMV, Gramophone, and Odeon all sought to profit from Saad and her band, who would go on to transform and popularize *taarab*.[28]

This incongruity, the state's squashing of sounds labeled subversive, and the industry's commodification of acceptable commercial music carried through the war, the State of Emergency, and into independence. The Mau Mau war for political independence ignited and continued the longer trajectory of freedom initiatives that began with earlier anticolonial movements. The sonic and dance performances of protest that blossomed were met with the state's swift censorship and banning. Authorities hunted and jailed those who refused to comply. After WWII, King African Rifles and East African Army Service Corps fighters returned from Burma, the Horn, and the Middle East Command and formed bands like the Rhino Boys and the Peter Colmore African Band.[29] Returning fighters also delivered their own messages of liberation, helping spur the subversive Kikuyu *Mwomboko* song and dance.[30] As Kenya's political climate intensified in the 1950s, songs continued to be censored by the colonial state or commercialized under the authority of music companies. To quell resistance, the forest fighters were regarded as an illegal group at the beginning of the 1950s, and a few years later, the almost decade-long State of Emergency began.[31] During the resistance, the Mau Mau composed a sizable catalog of songs that circulated orally. As mentioned above, at least one was about Mary Muthoni wa Nyanjiru's 1920s uprising.[32] Colonial authorities arrested then-activist Jomo Kenyatta in 1952, and about a year later, the state began to seize the land of the Mau Mau, others deemed terrorists, and people suspected of belonging to outlawed political parties. By 1956, 11,000 fighters were killed, with another 30,000 in detention camps.[33]

KENYA'S CONGOLESE PREDICAMENT

During much of this political upheaval, the music industry faced its most significant period of growth when the colonial state, benefiting from the economic upturn at the end of WWII, actively encouraged the expansion of mass media, forming more radio stations.[34] Wealthier "uptown" studios like Peter Colmore's HMV Blue Label and Charles Worrod's Equator Records attracted musicians from the Kenyan elite and artists from the DRC, Zambia, Tanzania, and Uganda. Colmore and Worrod, both British, promoted their music locally but also tapped into a wider regional and global market. HMV had great success in selling Afro-Cuban music throughout Africa, including in Kenya.[35] In the 1960s, Equator Sound Studios was also highly active, pressing vinyl and recording singers like Fadhili William and Daudi Kabaka, as well as South African Miriam Makeba and Beninese Angelique Kidjo. Smaller Indian-run labels in the working-class "downtown" River Road areas included Capitol Music Stores (CMS), African Gramophone Stores (AGS), and the Mzuri label owned by the still-operating company Assanand and Sons Ltd.[36] River Road in Nairobi became a popular place for production and performances during this time and still is.[37]

Political instability and violence in the Congo caused people to flee the region, resulting in an influx of musicians to Kenya, Uganda, and especially Tanzania.[38] Congolese music first made it to Kenya through 78 records and those coming for studio sessions and gigs in Nairobi. However, musicians relocating to East Africa helped solidify the long-standing presence of Congolese sounds in the country.[39] Artists recorded with multinational companies, like EMI, Polygram, and CBS, by the late 1960s and early '70s.[40] Congolese rumba included famous singers like Jean Bosco Mwenda, Losta Abelo, and Edouard Masengo, who traveled into the then-new country of Kenya to record and perform.[41] Jean Bosco Mwenda, famous for his fingerstyle, and other Congolese artists sang in Swahili and played versions of Kenyan and Tanzanian songs.[42]

Although Congo bands created a popular niche, Kenyan artists continued to make and perform music. Benga artists included Fadhili William, D. O. Misiani and Shirati Jazz, Fundi Konde, Paul Machupa, Jumbe, and Daudi Kabaka.[43] Performers played the guitar with a distinct finger-picking style, drawing on the traditions of other stringed instruments.[44] Even today, Kenyan guitar music is deeply popular and richly nostalgic. Both dry (acoustic) and electric styles are firm fixtures in the country and extremely popular, even though these sounds have never acquired the same status as Congolese tunes regionally, across the continent, or outside the African market. Kenyan musician Joseph Kamaru managed to engage in both popular music and subversive protest throughout his career, spanning both the colonial and postcolonial epochs. Beginning in the 1940s, he composed and sang the outlawed Mwomboko songs before his successful career in the '60s.[45] His high-pitched voice and diverse lyrical subject matter accompanied upbeat guitar sounds, and he sang in both Mugithi and Benga genres, gaining appeal in East and South Africa. Later, in the '70s, he composed a song condemning the state for the extrajudicial killing of activist J. M. Kariuki (mentioned below), and from the '80s until his death in 2018, he continued to record popular music.

The emergence of jazz bands in the '60s solidified Congolese music's influence. Franco Luambo Makiadi's OK Jazz / TPOK Jazz and Tabu Ley, who joined the band African Jazz, enjoyed popularity globally and in Kenya.[46] Nairobians frequented a growing number of bars and nightclubs that played the music. Although Benga enjoyed some international popularity in the '80s, it could not compete with Congolese jazz.[47] Congolese artists also sang in Swahili to connect with audiences while performing in Kenya. Some Kenyan musicians decided to sing in Lingala and play in the Congo jazz band style to remain competitive.[48] Paul Zeleza notes that "Congo music [is] perhaps the most recognizable form of modern popular African music across the world."[49] Given its status as a center of production, Kenya has felt the force of Congolese music's fame and appeal. Caleb Okumu, in a critique of the government and music industry, argues, "The yardstick of music performance in Kenya seems to measure how well one can sing in the foreign language, Lingala."[50]

Older artists with whom I spoke during my research have recalled the inequalities and unevenness of this early industry. In my conversations, this has cohered around one important story, that of Benga singer Fadhili William. His narrative highlights issues surrounding copyright, profit, and the exploitative aspects of global music production. Fadhili William is the first known singer of the famous "Malaika," the 1959 song with sanguine guitar riffs and cheerful and fast lyrics. The story goes that William was thinking about a woman he loved and called her *malaika*, Swahili for angel. The version that became popular in East Africa was produced in 1963 after William joined The Equator Sound Band. William claimed he never received royalties for the piece despite numerous covers of the song.[51] The grievance for many is that the song entered the world market with William's legacy obscured and forgotten. Miriam Makeba's serene and softer rendition of

"Malaika" has been the most internationally well-known. In 1966, she and Harry Belafonte won a Grammy Award for an album that included the song.[52] William's tale emerged when I asked reggae producer Jagero a general question: "So where do you think music is at right now in Kenya?":

> I'll start from way before, in the sixties. Kenyans are very talented when it comes to music. One of the most sampled songs comes from a Kenyan. It's called "Malaika." It's been sampled over and over and over, and the guy died a pauper.[53]

Jagero's sentiment about William's popularity and material poverty strongly mirrors hip hop artists' discussion of Kalamashaka and Ukoo Flani Mau Mau's inability to acquire wealth from the music they pioneered. The fact that hard work and talent cannot translate to economic wherewithal is a narrative that haunts artists in the industry. Gospel singer Mtawali also brought up Fadhili William. He expressed a similar sentiment of William dying penniless despite producing a globally recognized song: "Okay, he died a poor man; that is one. Okay, they said he was the composer of 'Malaika.' . . . That song is very controversial though no one knows who wrote it."[54] William dying in poverty is most significant for Jagero and Mtawali, illustrating the unfortunate realities of artists' powerlessness to profit from the music industry in Nairobi.

What is fascinating about William's "Malaika" is that the song works to dispute the claims made within the discourses of cultural anxiety, specifically that the lack of music is the fault of artists and consumers. William's saga is about how an artist came to be alienated from his own work, as the song reappeared as a foreign product and was consumable on the world market, where he could not receive the credit and recompense deserved. There is something interestingly relevant: even though "Malaika" still circulates in popular discourse and easily elucidates a broader problem in the structure of Nairobi's relationship with global capitalist economies, the story of William is not enough evidence to overturn widespread claims that Kenya has a dearth of music and fans.

Stories of Kenyan music exemplify how colonial power and exploitative global markets sought to regulate and relegate bodies in ways that increased profits and stymied the agency and self-determination of African peoples, as we see with the stories of Nyanjiru's unclothed refusal and the emergent Mau Mau songs referencing her, as well as Fadhili William's inability to gain in a 1960s market. The state set conditions by which the music industry profited while overseeing the active censorship of the creativities and subversions of African bodily performances, dances, and movements. At the same time, a flourishing recording industry emerged that benefited companies like HMV, EMI, and Polygram. These companies' preference at times for non-Kenyan sounds furthered the government's political aims (both before and after independence) of downplaying Kenyan music because of its inherent or potentially subversive quality. Kenyan artists in the industry struggled, while many Congolese artists experienced comparably more success from the expanding African continental and world markets. Yet, the impacts of the African music market in the country, including the rise of popular consumer taste in external styles at the expense of homegrown genres, has continued to engender soul-searching from Kenyan musicians and its devotees alike.

MUSIC IN THE POSTCOLONY

After 1963, Kenya faced nagging questions about whether music could operate as a tool of cultural self-determination necessary to move beyond colonial rule. At the beginning of Jomo Kenyatta's leadership (1963–78), the entertainment scene seemed to benefit from his policies. His openness to foreign investment attracted the Phonogram company, which then operated the only regional pressing plant for records.[55] Phonogram's role solidified Nairobi as a center of music production that promoted large amounts of Congolese styles, which coincided with Congolese jazz bands' explosive regional popularity. Kenyatta created pathways for small business owners, which, as Ian Eagleson states, "in terms of music, led to more production labels, music stores and studios, equipment owners, and venues such as bars and hotels."[56] However, Kenyatta also used music and performance to his advantage. Mau Mau songs of rebellion were transformed into presidential praise songs. Like so many African presidents, he utilized singers and dancers as a theater of admiration during official ceremonies and events, what Mĩcere Mũgo calls "coerced *waheshimiwa* orature" or "neocolonial ululation culture."[57] He oversaw the covert squashing of political dissent, the ethnicized consolidation of state power and resources to Kikuyu elites, and music's continued censorship. Kenyatta inherited and continued to use a censorship board, then called the Kenya Broadcasting Corporation (KBC) Censorship Board.[58] Joseph Kamaru's arrest and beating for the 1975 song "J. M. Mwendwo ni Iri" was one of the most high-profile bans.[59] The song excoriated the killing of the well-loved and dissident politician J. M. Kariuki. Kenyatta never admitted to the murder, though all evidence indicates his administration was responsible.[60]

Moi's presidency (1978–2002) profoundly impacted music culture. In 1980, Moi promoted his nationalist agenda by issuing a quota that mandated that 75 percent of songs played on Voice of Kenya (VOK) (renamed from the Kenya Broadcasting Corporation) must be Kenyan in origin and then reissued this quota in 1988.[61] Moi must have felt particularly confident that filling airwaves of Kenyan sounds would not be a conduit of protest. His directives showed how much the music culture had been emptied of its political potential. In other words, the quotas indicated the deep shift away from songs that challenged and liberated and toward a compliant cultural system. However, companies, radio stations, and the VOK intensely disliked this measure to promote Kenyan music. Companies paid radio stations to play the genres they were producing, mostly Congolese, and thus faced profit loss.[62] These entities falsely argued that there were not enough Kenyan songs, eventually causing the mandates to die.[63] In 1982, soldiers broke into the VOK to play East African pop and announced an unsuccessful coup d'état over radio airwaves.[64] These dissidents seemed to deliver the message of many past agitators—that music often accompanies, if not services, upheaval and revolt.

The failed coup shifted the climate by giving evidence to Moi that music must be under the state's constant review. The VOK's censorship board banned songs in ethnic languages and only played those in Swahili, English, or Lingala, and aired ones praising Moi, including "Rais Moi" (President Moi) and "Hongera Rais Moi" (Congratulations President Moi).[65] Odhiambo Osumba Rateng's "Baba Otonglo" and Joseph Kamaru's "Kenya ya Ngai" (God's Kenya) received censure.[66] Most patriotic songs had to contain the *nyayo* philosophy started by Kenyatta, which, among other precepts, asserts that following a leader is inherently African. Some Kenyan bands continued to play Congolese genres and/or sang in Lingala to secure gigs and avoid government surveillance. State-funded or supported groups like the Muungano Choir and traditional dancers were tasked to heap praises on the president, further muddying the waters about music's place within the nation.[67] Corporations created a market for Congolese sounds, then perpetuated beliefs about a shortage of Kenyan genres, and Moi banned ethnic songs in favor of those supposedly politically neutral. In addition to Congolese music, those tracks sung in Swahili were often considered unthreatening. At the same time, multinational companies like Polygram and CBS were pulling out of the country, their departure instigated by a thriving bootleg cassette tape industry, which meant that foreign music was sold unregulated and widely and cheaply available.[68] It is no wonder that people proclaim their dislike and suspicion of outside music in a setting where the spirit and vitality of Kenyan cultural expression have been perpetually cleared out. A large portion of Kenyan tunes during the 1980s and into the 1990s was co-opted for government purposes, censored and banned, and overshadowed by corporate and state preferences for Congolese and other international styles.

Yet, true to the defiant qualities of Kenyan art, musicians refused silence. Protest songs included Eric Wainaina's "Nchi ya Kitu Kidogo" (A Country of Bribes) (mentioned in chapter 4), Joseph Kamaru's "Mahoya ma Bururi" (Prayers for the Nation), Albert Gacheru's "Mucemanio wa Nyamu" (Meeting of the Animals) and his "Thina wa Muoroto" (Troubles of Muoroto). Artists felt the consequences; subversive sounds were not given airplay, Wainaina was sidelined, and Gacheru and Kamaru were briefly detained.[69]

It is within the difficulty of the Moi era that hip hop emerges. The 1980s were marked by his one-party and prebendal state benefiting the Kalenjin wealthy, where he eliminated opposition through imprisonment, extrajudicial killing, and exiles.[70] The '90s were not much better, as the impacts of structural adjustment programs (SAPs) and questionable election victories indexed by violence weighed on the nation.[71] Under- and unemployed urban youth, reeling from the poverty-inducing SAPs and the political climate, searched for another music to capture their disenfranchisement and found hip hop. Shortly after it gained momentum in the United States in the '80s, bootlegged products were sold alongside the hip and urban Jamaican dancehall in Nairobi stalls. By the '90s, U.S. rap songs and videos appeared on television, radio, and in bars and clubs. Kalamashaka and the related collective Ukoo Flani Mau Mau (UFMM) formed in the mid-'90s. Kenyan artists tried their hand on the mic with Poxi Presha's "Total Balaa" (Total Chaos, 1995), Hardstone's "Uhiki" (Wedding, 1997), and Kalamashaka's "Au Siyo" (Or Not, 1998) and the renowned "Tafsiri Hii" (Translate This, 1998–99). The bootleg industry would draw the attention of the state, multinational corporations, and the World Trade Organization (WTO), all of whom wanted firmer regulations. Furthermore, the liberalized airwaves opened up possibilities for music to be played on the radio, as up to that point, the media had been largely controlled by the influential reach of the Moi state.[72] While censorship abounded, Kenyan hip hop gradually snuck into media spots, and Kalamashaka hosted the country's first hip hop Wakilisha Show on the radio station Nation FM.[73] By 2000, hip hop was a mainstay.

THE MUSIC INDUSTRY: *HIYO NI TRICKY*[74]

Rappers who were tapped into the political climate argued that they were mouthpieces of the masses of angry and frustrated young people. Moi slowly capitulated to international and domestic pressure and held multiparty elections, making a pathway for Mwai Kibaki to win the 2002 election.[75] Like many people, these artists sighed in relief at the end of Moi's rule and desperately wanted to take advantage of the promises of a multiparty and neoliberal Kenya. Kibaki's presidency (2002–13) promised a new form of governance in the nation: "There was unheralded jubilation and heightened expectation that the change in regime . . . marked the dawn of a new era."[76] This apparent change was demonstrated poignantly by the appropriation and reproduction by Kibaki and his party, the National Rainbow Coalition (NARC), of Gidi Gidi Maji Maji's famous hype song, "Unbwogable."[77] During at least one political campaign concert, the group rapped enthusiastically alongside Kibaki. Wanting to convey change and attentiveness to a young populace, Kibaki crafted a positive image of himself to voting young people. He disrupted the Kenya African National Union's forty-year rule, symbolizing a break from the oppressive and hackneyed form of governance long associated with Moi, and he capitalized on people's hope, desperation, and unrelenting desire to see fundamental change. Extrajudicial killings, widespread and blatant corruption, and the tragic and hallmarked 2007–8 postelection violence dampened the aspirations that many had of a transformative Kibaki presidency. Initiatives like constitution reform and job assistance for the youth were marked by corruption and mismanagement.[78] These questionable schemes include the haphazardly created and enforced Michuki *matatu* safety regulations, with the overly punitive elimination of *matatus'* elaborate and colorful graffiti art and music.[79]

The Kibaki era saw WTO policies and the renewed Music Copyright Society of Kenya (MCSK) opening new complications. During the 1990s, Kenyan hip hop could be heard in some popular venues. Kiosks and shops along River Road sold inexpensive copies of Kenyan rap, gospel, and other popular genres. Yet by the 2000s, music in the informal sectors was no longer as widely available as it once had been. CD copies of African American rap like Tupac or 50 Cent and the underground Kalamashaka in cheap plastic sleeves were replaced by a hefty dose of U.S. music bound in hard CD covers displaying state-issued copyright stickers. These changes were due to the implementation of copyright legislation as part of the nation's membership status with the WTO and the Trade Related Aspects of Intellectual Property Rights (TRIPS) Agreement.[80]

On the surface, adhering to copyright standards and paying royalties is critical for mainstream and underground artists to earn profits. Yet the enforcement of TRIPS voided the informal practices and exchanges that much of the music industry was built upon and long depended on, meaning that many bars, clubs, *matatus*, and other venues did not play Kenyan music. Prior to the new Music Copyright Society of Kenya (MCSK) policies, music sales were an unreliable avenue to economic success for most artists, especially those who were noncommercial. But they were a marketing method and a way to book live performances on which most rappers have depended. After the new regulations, many vendors would not sell music that appeared to have a low production quality because the music looked bootlegged. News reports showed at the time how police rounded up music without the appropriate copyright stickers and publicly set fire to piles of CDs in the middle of the city center.[81] Especially during the Kibaki years, the MCSK used the police or private security officers to confront bar and restaurant owners, *matatu* operators, and other vendors for not adhering to policies. Some more high-profile encounters turned violent, made the news, and gave the MCSK a questionable reputation.[82] These stories of public destruction of music have waned over the years, but they still exist in public memory, and the threat of force remains, even if nominally.

I had several noteworthy interactions with street and stall vendors that spanned several years. Most of my fieldwork occurred during a shift away from CD copies to digital sharing via phone Bluetooth, and websites like ReverbNation and YouTube.com. One afternoon in 2011, a friend and I maneuvered our way through the crowded sidewalks and noisy streets of the city center with one steadfast objective: to buy Kenyan hip hop from the local street vendors in music stalls. I approached an eager vendor. When I stated what I wanted, she disappointedly about-faced and said softly and reluctantly that she only had a DJ mix for sale. I purchased the music for 300 KSH (approximately 2.50 USD), and my friend requested she play the CD to ensure its usability—a common practice. She looked shocked that we would ask and immediately refused, asserting that she could not play Kenyan music publicly because it was illegal. Her reaction to a simple request surprised me, yet I took the item and left. Out of a week of attempting to buy Kenyan rap from street vendors, this CD was the only one I could acquire. It had become increasingly clear that purchasing rap, or any other Kenyan popular music, was no longer an easy exercise but a painstaking process of chasing down vendors and following misinformed leads about where to buy music. The music we attempted to purchase would have been pirated or informally produced—that is, it was homemade or looked that way. Such music had become so commonplace that I thought nothing of buying it on the streets. Yet, unlike during my visit a decade prior, I could not acquire any Kenyan music. However, there were endless supplies of bootlegged Nollywood and American films, in addition to Congolese, Tanzanian, Nigerian, Ugandan, and other foreign albums. Even Kenyan gospel, which has been widely available and popular, was absent. The vendor's hesitance to sell me the music and her refusal to demonstrate the CD's usability are indicators of what I later discovered was her avoiding unwanted attention and fears of retribution resulting from the copyright laws and policies of the state.

I visited music stalls on Moi Avenue during a 2012 visit. After realizing that some Kenyan music had reappeared in stores, I requested hip hop, and a salesperson stated that he did not have it; instead, he had U.S. styles, which were bootleg copies. I pressed him as to the total absence of Kenyan rap music, and he told me that "they" did not want him to sell "pirated music." I asked him if all local rap was pirated, and he hesitated and thought for a bit before stating that the original copies were too expensive. Although he never specified who "they" referred to, at the time there were several factors at play, including the law enforcement's crackdown on noncopyrighted music and the MCSK, as well as the Kenya Copyright Board (KECOBO), which is the government body that gives licensing powers to the MCSK. I mentioned this interaction to rapper Evaredi, who responded:

> Basically, to tell you, I can say, like, the last albums that were being sold in Kenya for hip hop . . . you can say like the Kalamashaka [and] K-south. But up to date, I don't know what the problem is, but they believe, like, with hip hop in Kenya, it's like telling people the truth. So hip hop and the government are not on the same line.[83]

Evaredi's view that the state targets the music and prevents its sale is a sentiment I heard among many artists. However, there is little evidence that specific genres are subject to prohibition.

While not as aggressive with enforcement, the Uhuru administration (2013–22) simply continued the policies that began under Kibaki. As I wrapped up my fieldwork in 2018, I returned to Nairobi's streets, scouring the stalls for vendors selling Kenyan music. Someone told me, "We don't sell CDs anymore." This was somewhat true, as sellers still regularly cut American and Nollywood films onto DVDs, and a few still vend Tanzania's Bongo Flava music. During the same trip, I traveled to Eldoret to a shopping mall where someone was selling music in an entertainment store fitted with bright neon lights, video game consoles, and a young middle-class crowd milling about. The seller boasted of his expansive Tanzanian catalog, and when a friend I was with pressed him for Kenyan music, the vendor replied negatively, "Hiyo ni tricky" (That is tricky).

The MCSK is seen as an organization that steals money without reproach, uses force to implement measures, and threatens those it sees as not complying. Some rappers register with no expectations of getting paid; as Evaredi noted, "Basically, you'll be there [you'll register] because it's the only opportunity you can get."[84] Ndugus stated he is sent in circles: "I'm registered. I have my songs on radio, television. When I go there, [they say] come tomorrow. . . . They never pay us."[85] And many artists do not bother to register. Funzo Kuu stated, "They swindle money; they play your songs without telling you. They use your songs in advertisements. . . . You register for your royalties, but you have to go and ask for your cash. You have to ask and beg for your money."[86]

The MCSK adds much difficulty to an industry already racked with issues by fleecing monies that should be allocated for artists. The frustrations artists feel stem from a lack of structures advocating for them. Many could not afford the fees and did not register, meaning that their songs had no chance of being sold in stalls, played in *matatus*, or appearing on television or radio. Others faced bias on River Road when vendors, too fearful of reprisal, refused to sell their products. The copyright laws banned any pirated music, not any one genre. Underground albums also "look" pirated. Most do not have stickers, and the CDs are in inexpensive plastic wrap with a grainy copy of an image for the album cover. Because it looks unofficial, vendors do not want to sell anything that could be confused with being pirated. Most salespeople would rather refuse to sell hip hop and be assured they will not face reprisals from the state than vet music to figure out what is legitimate.

Artists, in turn, recognize and interpret this as a government dislike or prohibition on rap. What results is a *de facto* ban on the commercial sale of underground sounds. The government policies, MCSK practices, and the fear of retribution all create the implementation of a ban even when no such law or policy exists. It is effective and inconspicuous; it cannot generate outcry and disapproval in Kenya or internationally in the same way that a perspicuous law can. Following the logic of Giorgio Agamben, who wrote that "a ban is a form of relation," we may understand these artists as not separated from the law "but, rather *abandoned* by it."[87] The words of Agamben are the sentiment of artists; they believe the state both bans and purposely does not support underground hip hop, and thus, artists feel forsaken. Enforcement, or just force, can ensure that people in the music business, especially vendors, police themselves to avoid conflict with state or quasi-state actors.

Moreover, from the standpoint of fans and consumers across genres, it might appear that there is a lack of music culture, that venues dislike Kenyan sounds, or that artists are not interested in recording. Rappers want to see the MCSK function correctly; others long for the ability to make music without feeling coerced into a formalized economy, recognizing the bootleg industry's positive role in their own struggling careers. Those practitioners who advocate seeing it function to their benefit acknowledge that consumer sales are not the way to go but understand that the exposure might secure TV and radio slots, which could garner royalty collection. The new wave of MCSK policies that have hit the country in the past fifteen years has been inconsistent and corrupt, leaving musicians feeling that a state-like entity has squandered this hope of monetary gain. Replacing colonial and postindependence censorship, the implementation of TRIPS compliance has ultimately contributed to the absence of Kenyan music in many public spaces, which continues to ignite discussions of so-called consumer-driven cultural lack.

The noncommercial hip hop artists with whom I have spoken assert their biggest challenge is this restrictive industry created by the MCSK, the state, and the laws governing copyright issues. For many, these entities blur together. Recall Evaredi's comment above when I asked him why vendors do not want to sell rap, and he began talking about the state. While he does not discuss the MCSK per se, he believes that the government has a direct role in the industry. Several artists and producers I have spoken with have mistakenly conflated the MCSK and the state. Take graffiti artist Esen's comment:

> *RP:* How does the government view so-called underground hip hop? Do they care about it?
>
> *Esen:* I don't even know what the Music [Copyright] Society of Kenya does. So, if I must, I don't think so. I don't think they support [musicians] in any way cuz if they do, they would have created structures that would make it easier for underground artists to break even.[88]

Although I asked about the state, Esen answered by discussing the MCSK. His comment highlights how people have come to understand this organization through state power, and in essence, the MCSK has become an extension of the state through its practices of force. This perception has worked to the organization's advantage. The more people confuse the MCSK with the state, and the more they self-police in fear of reprisal or perceived powerlessness, the greater the power this entity wields. Mellitus Wanyama contends that the conditions for musicians are purposefully difficult to prevent dissent. He cites Susan Kibukosya, a producer and manager at Serenade Studio, who argues that "[one] way of perpetuating the huge gap between the rich and the poor is to censor the musician by economically immobilizing him. In such a state, he is 'tamed in order to remain submissive and toothless.'"[89] While there needs to be more evidence to support Wanyama and Kibukosya's claims that the government hinders musicians purposefully, their thoughts raise questions about who stands to benefit from policies. Of course, censorship still occurs in Kenya, but it is more likely that the difficulty musicians face is the result of ineffective policies and poor implementation that are not geared to help artists in the first place.

RADIO PLAY

In 2015, musicians protested in the streets of the Central Business District (CBD), outraged at the amount of South African, Nigerian, and Tanzanian music played. A collective known as the Kenya Musician Movement (KENAM) demanded that 70 percent of music on radios be Kenyan and called out the system of bribery that stands in the way of artists obtaining a spot.[90] Popular radio stations that these protesters cited also play a large amount of songs from the U.S., including KISS 100, Capital FM, Ghetto Radio, and Homeboyz Radio. Perhaps recognizing that the U.S. and U.K. slots were not worth fighting over, KENAM attempted to vie for airtime given to other African music. The protests sparked another round of debates over whether the system was unfair to Kenyan artists or whether other African music was better.

Radio stations have always played outside music. Historically, various components feed into this, like the lengthy presence and popularity of Congolese genres, the ban on Kenyan music deemed subversive in the 1980s, and radio stations that resisted a state-imposed quota to play Kenyan music. Christopher Okumu reported that in 2001, some programs on the KBC played 100 percent of music from other places.[91] Mellitus Wanyama cited a report that stated in 2002, 90 percent of songs played on the radio were from outside the country.[92] Currently, even Ghetto Radio, cited by many of the artists that I spoke with for having a good reputation for playing Kenyan underground rap, plays a large amount of non-Kenyan music. When Kenyan songs are played on most stations, they are primarily from the mainstream.

Musicians believe that the radio avoids paying royalties to artists by playing a hefty fare of American and other international music. "If you play like 50 Cent, here in Kenya," contended Judge, "it's really hard for that guy to come and start asking for their royalties here. But if you play like a lot of, let's say, J-U-D-G-E's songs (that's me!), I'll just be like, 'Hey!' You know?"[93] Judge asserted that these stations have an immediate money-saving incentive not to showcase Kenyan tunes. He may be correct, as Wanyama's analysis concluded that radio stations owed 68.2 million shillings to the MCSK in 2002 for the Kenyan music played.[94] Popular stations have always played a large amount of western music, even before the 2003 copyright regulations, and the MCSK claims that they pay remittances to foreign entities, though it is hard to ascertain if this occurs.[95] Regardless of the percentage of Kenyan music they play, stations must obtain a license from the MCSK and pay a flat rate annually.

Radio stations play American music and other international sounds, most likely to avoid royalty collection but also to appeal to advertiser demands because of the long-running privilege of western music. It is doubtful that the MCSK remits money to international entities. If the MCSK did pay royalties to global companies and bodies, there would likely be a dramatic decrease in the amount of copied and unregistered non-Kenyan albums, films, and television programs on DVD and CD that are sold in stalls. Since externally produced materials are still widely found, this suggests that the MCSK and KECOBO are mostly responsible for products made within the country. However, confusion and a disconcerting lack of transparency remain, which works to the MCSK's advantage.

Most actors in the industry argue that one must have inside connections to obtain radio spots. Many emphatically stress that knowing the right people helps to get onto the radio.[96] Reggae producer Jagero stated, "Most of the artists who are big names, they have a clique. When you deliver your music to the music station, only a certain clique gets frequent airplay. But if you are an upcoming artist and you are a broke one, for that matter, and you come from downtown [poor areas], you're in for a real shock."[97] Similarly, Judge asserted that bribing is so typical that many artists expect to pay, "because it has been a routine, they normally feel like, ah, they want to take their music there, they have to pay, even if . . . they haven't been asked or something. They normally pay automatically."[98] No one I interviewed admitted they had to bribe DJs, but the practice is widespread and unexceptional. DJ Adrian (Washika) supported this claim: "I think there is a lot of red tape at radio stations. I've heard a lot of artists saying that they went to a station, and somebody was asking for money, and you know, so I don't know what their policies are, but ours is kind of open door. So, you just bring your music."[99]

At the time of our interview, Washika worked at Capital FM and has since deejayed at several popular and wealthier locations, including Amboseli Gardens. His role has made him a gatekeeper in the industry. Washika affirms this by contending that he can choose what he plays and "within the first five seconds" decides if it is worth a radio spot.[100] The diverse actors contributing to the makeup of the music business play an essential part, whether DJs like Washika, desperately hopeful artists who come in ready with a bribe, or mainstream artists who are already wealthy and have an easier time navigating the system. The cutthroat industry and copyright policies do similar work to Moi's one-party rule and multinationals that once sought to exclude certain Kenyan sounds. The agents in the industry might differ today, but the results are the same. The radio's tradition of playing a base of outside genres has continued for a combination of the reasons mentioned and not merely due to one cause. Notably, every recent policy, mandate, and practice seems to have discouraged the growth of a diverse industry inclusive of underground artists.

Many hip hop practitioners, as well as scholars, hold conceptions that underground music is too controversial for commerciality. Hip hop researcher Halifu Osumare argues, "Kenyan radio is often reluctant to play socially conscious music typical of Kalamashaka because it challenges the status quo and often specific government officials."[101] In an above conversation with Evaredi, we discussed why hip hop is not sold in vendor stalls. I also asked him why some gospel is found in stores and hip hop is not. He responded, "After diluting your content in music, that's when basically you will get airplay, you get your music being sold in stalls. You see, like, that's what the government—that's what the media likes. Like you're supposed to do what the media likes for you to get paid. Or for you to sell."[102] For him, gospel is a more acceptable genre. His brief conflation of the media and the government is noteworthy because both operate as real and perceived barriers in artists' work. While the subversive nature of underground rap does not *wholly* explain why noncommercial songs are not played on the radio, especially given the presence of mainstream songs that seek to challenge the state, what does seem to be the case, as Evaredi noted, is that the state and the industry serve as gatekeepers and create settings whereby underground rap is marginalized. I did not ask Evaredi what he meant by "diluting your content," but his subsequent words suggested that "diluting content" involves eliminating songs that question political authority and producing palatable sounds that harmonize rather than disrupt in the way many underground beats do.

DJ Adrian cautioned that aspiring artists need to pay attention to production issues. "Production is very important. You find that sometimes they [the songs] are not mastered. So, the vocals are low [puts his hand down gesturing at a low level], the music is up there [and then puts his hand up, elucidating the disjuncture]."[103] DJ Adrian did not view the industry as restrictive:

> *RP:* One of the things that some folks say [is that] it's really hard to make it in the music industry because you always have to know people.
>
> *DJ Adrian:* I don't think that is really true because if you have a good product, I mean you don't have to really push it. Um, it will be acceptable. Like most of the time, you find that a lot of artists, mainly new artists, will come up with stuff, which is not really—I would say—quality. And ah, I guess they would have a hard time trying to push it. You understand? So, I really don't think you have to know . . . as an artist you just have to know the right producers.
>
> *RP:* So your track will be good?
>
> *DJ Adrian:* Yeah, your track will be good . . . your video will be good. Basically, you kind of have to bring money to invest in yourself as well. So, I think, ah, that is pretty much the disconnect people have.[104]

DJ Adrian believes that artists should be willing to pay to create good songs, a video, or an album. One aspect he overlooks is that some musicians lack the means to invest. Sentiments like his reflect the idea that most musicians cannot enter the business without wherewithal and expect to generate wealth. One must already have money to invest. These realities make it difficult for many artists to work their way into this system. DJ Adrian's perspective is not widely shared among many rappers I interviewed, as most view the industry as flawed and the obstacles as burdensome.

Recommendations for a national and standardized quota for radio and television have long circulated in public discourse. The Kenya Culture Policy (more recently called the Kenya National Policy on Culture and Heritage) is in place to facilitate and assist in creating a foundation for the acknowledgment and celebration of Kenyan musical and cultural traditions, following UNESCO's initiatives to honor and celebrate various ethnic customs.[105] In the past, the committees of the Kenya Culture Policy have set quotas for the amount of local music played on the radio—in 1980, at 80 percent.[106] The 2009 version notably cited colonialism's attempted erasure of practices and traditions as a rationale for a firm policy.[107] Musicians and nonmusicians agree with such conclusions and directives, believing that since consumers will not choose Kenyan sounds first and foremost, the government should intervene and execute the commitment to a flourishing culture. Even though quotas have not appeared in recent versions of the Culture Policy, many artists I interviewed often cited what they thought was the authorized percentage to demonstrate the absence of Kenyan songs on local airwaves. For instance, Mtawali referenced a 40 percent local / 60 percent foreign mandate, while Judge cited that DJs aim for 30 percent local / 70 percent foreign in clubs.[108] Nafsi Huru noted, "[Radio presenters] don't play a lot of local content. And according to our constitution, I think we are supposed to be like . . . I'm not sure, 70 percent local content, and the rest is from western places."[109] These artists' statements were always postulations; no one knew whether a current quota was in place or what it was. But, like KENAM's 2015 protest, they were committed to the idea of them as concrete measures that the government should take to correct the inequitable radio play. These conversations about quotas were always discussed within the context of a broader notion of absence and cultural lack, specifically how the government facilitates such inadequacies. Moreover, the deployment of the quota discourse was evidence that circuitously implies that left to the devices of consumers and musicians, other African and western music would dominate. The issue of quotas points to corporate radio decisions and perhaps the government's inability or disinterest to intervene in the industry for the actual material benefit of artists. And yet the entrenched discourses of cultural anxiety, including the frustration over the influx of U.S. country and pop in the '70s and '80s, hip hop and R&B in the '90s to the present, and Congolese genres throughout, will continue to point to people as responsible for the scarcity of Kenyan music.

Aside from the industry standards limiting possibilities, socioeconomic class also heavily determines the production and circulation of music. Most mainstream and commercial artists who sustain television and radio airplay are from the middle and upper classes; they already have cultural capital, connections, ways in the door, a method of favored communication, assumed legitimacy, and the privilege of everyday resources. Artists must have these connections to mainstream production houses and corporate performance venues to make it to the radio for any prolonged period. Baby T, for instance, has recorded with ATL Entertainment, which promotes her products. She has performed at middle-class venues like Tribeca Lounge and K1 Klub House. Most noncommercial rappers, however, do not have regular access to venues like this. Artists state that it costs about 20,000–60,000 KSH (160–490 USD) to produce one reasonably good song and up to 100,000 KSH (800 USD) to assemble a video with basic quality. Because of a lack of resources, it is common for songs to have low production quality, and some of their videos contain irregularities and mistakes. Combined with their frustrating tales of the MCSK, a collective experience of exclusion from the media, and their individual challenges recording, their working-class status contributes both to the music's marginal cultural location and to emergent political sensibilities, the latter of which the following chapters explore.

MUSICAL AGENCY AND THE IMPORTED BLACK BODY

Cultural anxiety discourses that produce the "Kenyans don't appreciate Kenyan music" statement work to formulate truths about people, human agency, and the postcolonial subject, even if the actual statement is faulty. The widespread sentiment of cultural anxieties promotes the idea that people do not appreciate Kenyan music and leads to the view that artists' work is so influenced by outside inspirations that it lacks relevance, context, and pride. Moreover, these beliefs posit that artists remain locked in a practice of always copying or imitating a culture that ultimately does not belong to them. Cultural anxieties about taste are rife within the material, economic, and political struggles of Nairobi. The histories of the music industry, the western imports of antiblack racism, and the 1960s call for cultural independence all bear responsibility for creating a discourse that vets and often jettisons hip hop. The lack of Kenyan music in many public or commercial spaces spoon-feeds this anxiety, and whether consumer taste can be blamed lies at the center of these accusations. If there is an overabundance of American hip hop and pop on radio, do the middle-class buying youth shoulder the burden of that circumstance? What about rappers who supposedly imitate African Americans? Should the musician participating in the long-standing borrowing of Congolese styles also assume responsibility if rappers are indicted? Whatever the answers, this remark—Kenyans don't appreciate Kenyan music—asks people to draw boundaries around what Kenyan music should be and holds people responsible for creating an accessible industry.

Hip hop enters a scene already marked by widespread perceptions that the available Kenyan sounds are derivative. There is a continued claim that the populace fails to vet pernicious outside influences and neglects to see the creative richness within their borders. Such ideas concern agency, self-determination, and the need to assess external cultural forces. The older artists, DJs, and producers who supported this allegation referenced its assumed historical accuracy, while younger critics spoke about how current artists uncreatively borrow from outside. I talked to Mtawali about the general state of the music industry. At one point in our conversation, I asked about what needs to shift for people to benefit. He responded by urging people to change their preferences:

> *Mtawali:* So, I think as a culture, we need to change. And begin appreciating our own music.
>
> *RP:* Why would you say that Kenyans don't appreciate their own music?
>
> *Mtawali:* Um, I think the reason is [it's] something that started a long time ago. We are like copycats. We really don't have a national identity. In every aspect. Look at the dress. If you go to Congo, now, you'll tell [that that is] a Congolese. If you go to Tanzania, you'll tell—if you go to Rwanda, name it. There is something that will tell you this is a Tanzanian woman; this is a Congolese man. Here, really, we don't have [the same]. So, musically, there has been a Benga [music], which is trying to come out.[110]

Mtawali argued that despite some shared histories, geographies, and politics, the DRC, Tanzania, and Rwanda have managed to carve out national identities and music cultures, while Kenya is stuck in constant appropriation.

The discourse of cultural anxiety constitutes a collection of ideas that obfuscates the state's role and mystifies the industry's powerful actors. Corporations and capitalist enterprises are let off the hook and their extractive practices muddied. While some artists acknowledge the presence of historical censorship bans and a current unfair industry, these facts are not used to explain the absence of music deemed Kenyan. Specifically, cultural anxiety discourses hail rappers, devotees, and others, thereby interpellating them as a particular postcolonial subject— victims of, rather than agents against, the onslaught of globally dominant cultural productions. Those who dislike the music are also hailed, particularly those willing to disparage hip hop in the name of challenging outside influence. Most practitioners understandably and swiftly condemn those who deride rap and assert themselves as people who resist subjugation, offer social and global critiques, and remain dedicated to Kenyan traditions. To give an example, consider graffiti artist Esen's comment about navigating mimicry claims:

> That's what they usually say; we are trying to imitate the west. So, to me, that's kinda messed up because it means these guys don't even have, you know, the right material to criticize us. So, when they see hip hop artists wearing earrings, they'd be like, "Hey, these guys are copying the west." Blah-blah-blah, but in a real sense, we've been wearing earrings even before the west knew what earrings were. All these Africans or Kenyan communities were wearing earrings, from the Maasais, the Kikuyus, and all that. We used to rock dreadlocks and shit like that.[111]

Here, Esen defended why rap is relevant and argued that the music is an extension of Kenyan cultural traditions, encouraging people to adopt an expansive understanding of hip hop's genealogy.

I have regularly watched television shows like Mseto, which showcases dancehall, Afropop, and some mainstream hip hop, and is aired in the evening, usually between 5 p.m. and 6 p.m. While doing so, friends and others who wandered into the room commented on whatever music video was displayed. Most people who were not fans of hip hop exclaimed, "See? This is a complete copy of U.S. music!" Shocked, I often wondered if we were watching the same program. I saw Afropop, dancehall, and commercial artists rapping in Swahili, frequently incorporating Congolese dance styles and with Nairobi and other East African urban backdrops. When I asked what they meant, responses were often vague: "I mean, their whole style . . . just everything is a copy." The signifier of apparent derivativeness seemed to be an aurally embodied performance: how rappers moved their bodies when they voiced their lyrics, how singers gestured as they sang the hook of songs, and how these artists danced to synthesized beats. Surely, some of these critiques must have been due to hip hop's usual references to nice cars, new urban clothing styles, and occasional ghetto backdrops. Yet, it seems that the corporealities interfacing with rap beats eerily similar to African American artists were fundamental to these criticisms. These decriers mapped African American embodiments onto Kenyan rappers, hoping that the indictments of mimicry would serve as enough warning to avoid the music. After all, what Kenyan artists do with their bodies in spaces is inevitably connected to the agentive ways they produce their subjectivity.

Contemporarily and globally speaking, rap continues to garner perhaps the most controversy of any other genre of music for its confrontational style and content and its deep ties to lower-class African American youth experiences: "The ghettoes of North America continue to be the primary cultural referent for hip hop around the globe."[112] Indeed, rap's critics often are older folks who accuse young people of succumbing to the appealing lure of American music and lifestyles. Underneath this disrepute hides antiblackness. For many nondevotees, hip hop is a monolithic genre that signifies misplaced Black American rage, sounding disturbingly illegible, often crass, and nihilistic. Most African countries have historiographies of cultural anxieties surrounding U.S. music, and rap appears as a focal point of youth interest and critics' disgruntlement. In formerly colonized countries, hip hop provokes debates about American cultural imperialism that easily slide into derision for African American people. U.S. rap is commonly regarded as the worst example of American culture, a signal of moral rot and urban backwardness commodified into sellable rebellion. Zine Magubane cites the beloved South African jazz musician Hugh Masekela, who once stated, "[Our] children walk with a hip hop walk and they think they are Americans . . . [they have] an African-American reject personality."[113] Bantu Mwaura acerbically writes that Kenyan artists "regurgitate Black American perversion of gangsterism and sexism."[114] Critics contend that American rap is only a cheap commodity meted out to the masses, void of cultural value or relevance in a Kenyan and African context. Many cite the gangsta rap of the 1990s, which traveled to the country in plentiful supply during that time. Gangsta rap supposedly embodies the worst of American excess and is the site of assumed personal failure, laziness, and violence. Overlooked in these conceptions are the interventions that gangsta rap makes. R. A. T. Judy (Ronald A. T. Judy) suggests the gangsta rapper, or the figure of the nigga, rejects a moral economy meant to keep Black bodies in place and embodies a "commodity affect" that sells "anger, rage, intense pleasure."[115] For its critics, detested American hip hop is the quintessential cultural example of empire decaying from within. The problem is not just that African youth listen to American rap; it is that they want to *make* hip hop, *become* rap artists, and *perform* rap embodiments, like Masekela's "reject personality" and "African American walk." Interestingly, the embodiment of rap aesthetics—the walk, talk, clothing, style, and the actual music—has agitated detractors. This harmful form of American racism is deployed to impugn American products, which then connects to more profound and historical apprehensions about so-called outside sounds in Kenya.

The historical and international circulation of African American genres also contributes to how people receive hip hop. Beginning during WWI, blackface, ragtime, and jazz helped create ideas about how aurality and corporeality were racialized. In African contexts like Kenya, Tanzania, Ghana, Liberia, Nigeria, and South Africa, jazz and ragtime bands blended with local styles and took off as popular urban genres. These performative styles carried with them discourses of *primitivist modernism*, to cite Louis Chude-Sokei.[116] The Black body was cast as still backward and subhuman but fused with the civilized sounds of sonic Americana and cosmopolitan urbanisms. In Kenya and Tanzania, the British and Germans put together military brass bands as part of their colonial projects and participation in the world wars. Stephen Martin remarks that the bands initially sounded "rough and unpolished . . . to the European ear" and cites German ethnographer Karl Weule's description, "Both bands are under official patronage... I cannot say much for the proficiency of the native performers; in any case, their music was accompanied by a great deal of noise."[117] Nonetheless, the ideological goal was to impress European military training and the lessons of musical time on the savage African.

The theme of the untamed Black body and its relationship to technologies surfaced in jazz's global popularity. As the music spread, highly desirable styles emerged that brought together ideologies of Black people's abilities to perform instrumentally and corporeally, combining the supposed "inhuman machinic accuracy of jazz choreography" and Black people's "supposedly innate ability to swing and jive."[118] The attractive duality of primitive bodily movement and obedience to the machine of the instrument came to typify the racial codes of Black jazz that would be transmitted and exported across U.S. borders. Jazz's presence did not exist without significant disputes about Americanization, even as early as the 1910s, in places like South Africa.[119] In this country, musicians like Hugh Masekela would later use jazz as a subversive, a protest against the apartheid government and in collaboration with U.S. artists and their struggles. Its evolution and white appropriation now mean jazz is respectable in the U.S., and in Kenya, it can confer a sophisticated cosmopolitanism. But the conversations it birthed about racial codes and Black people's relationships to music did not end and were spun into other genres like hip hop. Interrogations about hip hop have abounded: Would Black and Africana peoples use the sound system and computers to create music that inserts them into cosmopolitanism, modernism, and sophistication? Can Africana peoples use technologies to divest from their supposed atavistic and raw instincts and create desirable sounds? How much difference is acceptable as avant-garde innovations, and what difference exceeds the bounds of respectability?

In Kenya, colonial racism merged with U.S. globalized antiblackness to form racial codes. Carolyn Shaw notes how the British colonialists smuggled American ideas of blackness into the territory: "In colonialist imagery the Kikuyu and the Maasai form a contrasting pair similar to the black American slave and the wild Indian in American folklore."[120] For Shaw, colonist discourse identified both the Kikuyu and the African American slave as inherently "corrupt and corruptible," thus justifying the permanent subjection of U.S. Black people and Africans from Kenya.[121] In the postcolony, respectability politics attempt to save Kenyans from this abject status, purporting a Christian middle-class ethic that distances themselves from the savage Black figure. Relatedly, contemporary social bottom politics is extant, whereby groups of people are relegated to the underside of society, such as queer people, the poor, the mentally unstable, and those deemed lazy or permanently wretched.

Global racisms lie on one side of this discourse of cultural vetting, and on the other is a postindependence notion of what it means to resist cultural imperialism. In the 1960s, men scholars at the University of Nairobi interrogated the figure of the postcolonial subject and its supposed desire to remain in relationships of dependence.[122] Many like Ngũgĩ wa Thiong'o, Okot p'Bitek, Taban Lo Liyong, Eisha Stephen Atieno-Odhiambo, Bethwell Ogot, and others demanded that African culture should be the cellular unit upon which the nation should be built.[123] These scholars vigorously sought to shed the notion that Kenyans and other Africans were forever dependent and thus outside humanity. To be dependent means to be located at the bottom of society without choice, will, individual drive, or purpose. The solution was a return to and reclamation of African cultures. Ngũgĩ wa Thiong'o's famous essay "On the Abolition of the English Department" proposed, "If there is need for a 'study of the historical continuity of a single culture,' why can't this be African?"[124] The question did not stop there; culture was meant to be the imperative strand that stitched together and structured Kenyan and other African nationalisms. In other words, the role of culture is not just to provide subjects with pride and identity; it is also a means to build a nation of free-thinking and acting people.[125] Mbũgua wa Mũngai cautions that this moment also "[ran] the very real danger of instituting a nativistic project" through hardening notions of Africanness.[126]

The argument for cultural nationalism is circular: If people center their traditions and practices, they can create a sustaining nation, and if a country is built on prioritizing Kenyan culture, the people will prosper. In short, constructing a nation out of the ruins of colonial rule should not come at the expense of the cultural character of Kenya. Traditions and practices can supposedly resolve some of the country's most profound issues.[127] This line of thought for cultural nationalists delegates culture to carry out monumental duties, such as providing safety and security to the country, enabling human dignity, and operating as a framework for a functioning state. Cultural nationalism has shortcomings; it often locks women into being permanent carriers of culture and in servitude to the nation, and it effaces larger economic forces that structure societies and determine people's destiny while running the racist risk of implying the global south is poor because it lacks culture. Yet, the persistent demand to center Kenyan cultures has been imperative and critical for academics, rappers, and anyone else with an opinion on Kenyan society, and this is because cultural definition and freedom are fundamentally attached to human agency and self-determination.

CULTURAL ANXIETIES, CONSIDERED

The 2018 short documentary *Nu Nairobi: Inside Nairobi's Music Scene* explores several pertinent topics and debates about what it means to make Kenyan music.[128] Mainly focused on the lively dance-fused scenes in Nairobi's western and wealthier areas, the documentary begins by debunking the idea that Kenyan styles are statically "traditional" and only associated with drums and guitars. The narrators argue that colonialism disrupted the nation's lyricism and performances and assert that there is not one Kenyan genre, contending that a multiplicity of styles coexist, including hip hop. While *Nu Nairobi* credits Taarab and Benga, it centers on middle- and upper-class nightlife in Nairobi and focuses on Afropop, neo-soul, hip hop, and techno. The documentary turns anxiety discourses inside out, and musicians refuse to believe that there is a scarcity of Kenyan genres. Mainstream rapper Octopizzo argues, "We don't have, like, Kenyan music. It's not like Tanzania where there is one style of music, and you go to Nigeria, there's one style of music, which for me is a good thing because everyone can do their own thing." Immediately following this, radio presenter Patricia Kihoro of Homeboyz Radio argues, "We just want to make music, and it's Kenyan because we are Kenyan!" The sentiment from this moment is that while there may not be one coherent popular genre attached to the country, this is not a deficiency. Octopizzo and Kihoro instead identify how artists seize control of production in the directions of their choosing and that this is the definition of Kenyan music. The documentary pulls viewers into Nairobi nightlife; in between interviews with major industry players, there are synthesized background sounds interspersed with young people dancing near stages, large audiences moving to the flow of performers, and DJs grooving over their turntables while they spin. Clubgoers are framed as taking advantage of a wide range of genres as they participate in sonic embodiments of leisure and carefreeness.

No sooner are we taken in by the seductive imagery of beaming faces and lively crowds than the documentary takes a curt but necessary detour toward difficulties and disunities. Here, artists begin discussing class divisions in hip hop music, naming them "uptown" (wealthy) and "downtown" (impoverished) politics, with participants arguing that both sides perpetuate discord through "ego." According to interviewees, poorer downtown east Nairobi rappers arrogantly assume that English lyric-based rap lacks relevance and rich practitioners cannot know hood life. Likewise, west Nairobians supposedly condescend to their downtown counterparts for not knowing how to operate expensive synthesizing equipment. Attempting to cast these two sentiments as equally frictional elides how access to resources structures this entire conversation. These statements on divisions are unpleasantly insufficient in capturing class politics. Ultimately, what promises to be a hearty reading of the industry is a superficial and straw-person contention that leaves viewers wondering why so much of the film attends to wealthier participants. The documentary prioritizes more privileged musicians like EA Wave and Camp Mulla while almost entirely ignoring how poverty inhibits opportunities and makes life hard for artists from lower-class settings. In one of its more promising moments, artists speak to the cameras about what underground rappers have long been asserting: that a lack of policies that support musicians, weak royalty payments, the defunding of arts in education, and an oppressive political environment all bear down on practitioners. The political entities and figures implicated in this discussion are either edited out or assumed to be known. It seems that the documentary and its actors are willing to engage in conversations about the conditions of the industry because, while they do not live in poverty, they are not immune from royalty complications and an oppressive state. As quickly as the film pivots toward these problems, it returns to the hype and vibing millennials that make this documentary enjoyable to watch.

The ramifications of copyright policies, the difficulty obtaining radio play, and the hardships around royalty payments hamper music in public spaces and leave narrow pathways for artists. These realities only provide fodder for the discourse of cultural anxiety, which in turn encourages hip hop artists to enter studios and concerts keen on proving their worth and their music's value. The discourse continues to call on individuals, consumers, and devotees to drive Kenyan culture and create an affirmative set of diverse practices and beliefs. In a postcolonial setting, where echoes of freedom and self-determination still sound, people insist that consumers somehow have control over what songs the media plays. Congolese sounds are still the original foreign music that has set a fire of apprehension. Nowadays, hip hop seems to stand in the place Congolese genres had carved out, insisting on further questions about the role of culture that African nationalists and Kenyan academics fervently advocated for during independence transitions.

Chronicling cultural anxieties means piecing together the disparate elements that help comprise why music in Kenya is never just about the music but also about power and economics, postcoloniality, the state, and ideas of freedom. Recordings of African performances during the Protectorate era are still held in western institutions. Kenyans will continue to exclaim that Fadhili William received an unfair turn at success. The Kenya Film Classification Board from the 1960s still operates and continues to ban audiovisual materials that it decides are inappropriate to Kenyan culture, primarily films that contain explicit sexuality and queer content.[129] Music commodities, subversive embodied public performances, Congolese music, state bans and copyright policies, hip hop's Black body, the anticolonial war: these actors help write the script for how we understand cultural anxieties today. On the surface, statements like this from Bethwell Ogot, one of the University of Nairobi scholars calling for cultural nationalism, seem reasonable, "Foreign musical diet must be assimilated into the local cultural milieu, into a local popular musical tradition."[130] But questions of what music qualifies as Kenyan become knotty given the sixty-year presence of Congo styles and the almost thirty-year existence of rap within the country.

Debates over non-Kenyan genres continue, not because such genres have been outright rejected or relegated to television, but instead because artists, singers, rappers, and dancers insist these forms are relevant to their modes of culture and self-expression. In turn, hip hop artists continue to claim their work is African and Kenyan, pushing back against notions that would render their music mere mimicry. Rappers resist the idea that their songs have no place on radio and disavow the MCSK's excessive and arbitrary copyright enforcement. Underground rap challenges postcolonial anxieties that deem their music derivative by refusing the claim that they operate from a colonized mind. In response, they design and protect the creative boundaries of hip hop. When artists state that "underground hip hop is serious," they also mean that *it is Kenyan*. The music's innovation and dynamism are deeply connected to Kenyan sociality and are extensions of African culture. Hip hop speaks to all Kenyans and prioritizes the urban poor, exemplifying how a music can unite everyone, which responds to the call that African cultural nationalists and anticolonialist writers made a half-century ago.

So much of cultural anxieties are about how bodies create and perform certain types of artistic expressions. Anticolonial writers have conjured the body, mainly relying on normate-centric parameters as the marker of agency and culture. For Ngũgĩ wa Thiong'o, returning to African languages can combat "producing a society of bodiless heads and headless bodies."[131] Léopold Senghor similarly asks, "But what of a headless body, and an arm with no soul?"[132] For these writers, the disarticulated body indicates one's alienation from their culture. Ableist tendencies in tow, these writers conscript postcolonial subjects to appreciate their culture and throw out any lasting impacts of colonialism. Perhaps these words also portend why hip hop's performing, unruly, and disruptive body unnerves critics, as it too quickly represents western cultural imperialism, even if it is subversive. The idea that culture can serve as a balm to the irregularities and injustices of society neglects significant and often violent forces that work in people's lives. When the failures of the state and economic instabilities materialize, people want to know that their culture is intact, even if that culture is multiplicitous and adaptive. Rap music and its performances betray any neat confines and solutions to the political and economic chaos of postcoloniality.

2

———

Play and Gender

"Can I freestyle for you?" L-Ness asked me at the end of our interview as we sat on the steps outside of the Kenya National Theatre, a site that has always been a space of tension, possibility, and contradiction.[1] The theatre opened during the war for independence and hosted European plays, and even after 1963, many Kenyans were excluded from producing works due to the state's fear that they would incite dissent. In 1976, Ngũgĩ wa Thiong'o and Mĩcere Mũgo managed to put on *The Trial of Dedan Kimathi*, much to the ire of the Kenyatta government and the white expatriates who held sway at the theatre. Ngũgĩ reported that at the close of the performances, the police stood ready down the street in protective gear for battle at the Central Police Station.[2] Some fifty years earlier, it was home guards, or *askari*, who gathered and slaughtered Mary Muthoni wa Nyanjiru and her fellow protesters in front of that same police building. The theatre has distanced itself from its troubling past, holding various events, including Kenyan and African dramaturgy and music and dance performances. In the early 2000s, it was common to see gatherings of young people outside on the grounds smoking weed, playing drums, or freestyling, often there to perform at or support an occasional hip hop event. However, by the 2010s, the theatre's high fees pushed planners to seek other venues. That, in combination with the increase in security, gating, and anti-loitering spikes on the perimeter sitting walls, means that hip hop practitioners view the space as catering to a more affluent crowd unfriendly to a working-class underground culture.[3]

On the day of our conversation, L-Ness sat as she rhymed, moving energetically from one line to the next. One hand was extended, with her fingers and palms flatly horizontal with the earth. Her hand moved briskly and sharply from side to side. This common rap embodiment resembles the DJ's gesture of spinning a record. L-Ness extended her hands in the air, creating a space for the lyrics and building hip hop liveness. These days, it seems like there are very few performances that manage to occupy the thick present unscathed by reproductive technologies, even if it is a cellphone camera lens.[4] Indeed, L-Ness's performance was subject to some form of technological capture, for I used a digital voice recorder for dictation. Archived or not, rappers use their bodies to create a temporal spatiality for words to exit their mouths. For L-Ness, each hand and arm movement might appear without meaning, though taken together, these styles signify and create hip hop culture. There, on the steps of the theatre, L-Ness created hip hop without a studio, musical instruments, a stage, or a microphone, and through orature alone.

L-Ness can rap and rhyme at incredible speed without pause or hesitation. Her rapping is clear and firm; she enunciates her words with precision, using crisp and sharp bodily movements to match. L-Ness's movements demonstrate the creativity and indecipherable wit of hip hop embodiments. At times, she raps so fast that she passes the beat by, almost as if she expects the beat to keep up with her stamina and excitement. While she gestures in ways expected of rappers, her hard and fast rap style is often at odds with societal notions of the feminine.

L-Ness's performance is a primary example of the ludic in hip hop. This ludicity consists of several interlocking components. First, ludicity is a part of orature, performed and embodied, spoken and verbal, and often sonically influenced and produced. Ludic embodiments found in much of global rap culture encapsulate the quotidian and formalized ways that artists use their bodies to deliver creative, often indistinct disaffection and unorthodoxy. I draw from Victor Turner's discussion of play as containing the potentials of disruption. For him, play is "a volatile, sometimes dangerously explosive essence" that "cultural institutions seek to bottle or contain in the vials of games of competition, chance, and strength."[5] Creative corporealities allow rappers to participate in the urgencies of lyrics while preventing societal circumstances from informing their perspectives in totalizing ways. Ludicity is never divorced from the political surroundings, and hip hop play is not just a performance that produces a hollowed-out area of pleasure devoid of meaning or intention. Rather, at its core lies a constant shifty and trickster ethic that refuses obedience and contains inherent defiance of social norms. To cite Turner, it is the music's political seriousness that "bottles" ludicity, framing it as a part of the substantive strength of the music.

Next, the ludic is based on intentional unreadable alterity, or what Turner would note as "recalcitrant to localization."[6] Here, I additionally root the hip hop ludic in what Édouard Glissant terms opacity/*opacité*, which occurs in the illimitable interpretative qualities of alterity, like those found in literature and poetry.

FIGURE 5. L-Ness (*left*) and Baby T (*right*) fist-bumping with other artists. Image by L-Ness.

For Glissant, cultures at large, especially those marginal cultures, need not be bound to larger social forces. Glissant understands that opacity is a right that all cultures should have, which avoids an "enclosure within an impenetrable autarchy" and can yield freedoms.[7] Further, this notion of freeness is fundamental to hip hop ludicity. These performances hold indefinability as an articulation of the aesthetic, and such bodily gestures articulate brief notions of freedom. In further thinking about how play produces epitomes of freeness, Jayna Brown notes that music-making breeds what she terms a "utopian impulse," which is an "ineffable connection, a collective space free of possessive individualism."[8] Brown notes that musical experiences, specifically in the Democratic Republic of the Congo, involve the sonic and the embodied to make spaces of utopia that intervene in a society and world filled with crisis, war, and unsustainable transnational capitalism. Nairobi's rap performances respond to a similar volatile social context and gesture toward something beyond on-the-ground specificities. Hip hop finds spaces of creativity as it rejects and responds to the economic crises of poor youth, state-sanctioned violence and corruption, and the siphoning of resources toward foreign investments. Moreover, play's alluring and pleasurable elements are an intensely local production, as well as radically located in hip hop's Black diasporic politics. The opacity of embodiments and the creativity of music-making allow for openings and possibilities because this art is political, imaginative, and expansive.

Lastly, far from flawless, playfulness is indeed masculinized. Ludicity is about opening a space of creative movability and freedom, and so, too, is masculinity. To perform masculinity, especially one that is cishet, is thus to hold privilege and authority. When women like L-Ness utilize play as a way to move and spit rhymes, they are often read as acting like cisgender men, whereas men who flow are more easily granted validity as rappers. Cismasculine rappers are, furthermore, the direct beneficiaries of hip hop, while for those of marginalized genders, there is no uncomplicated way to access benefits from engaging with the trope of masculinity. Cismen can play more spaciously, as these rappers structure and define the music and have the social power to set the parameters. Women and many other marginalized genders, alternatively, are often caught in a trap between the performances of perceived feminine oversexualization and masculine tomboyishness.

This chapter investigates the cogency of hip hop flow like L-Ness's, which occurs as performed and often indecipherable masculinized freeness. To conceptualize how ludicity fits into Nairobi's underground world, I first articulate its cityspace as the focal point from which artists make music, arguing that they draw from the city's masculinized tenets, music culture, and the long traditions of protest and dissent. Next, I provide a section that discusses how rappers draw from the masculinity already present in Nairobi and Kenya, as well as practices from global hip hop, to produce what I call the *armor of gender*. Artists draw from local Mau Mau characteristics and the global culture of the music to perform the armor of gender. Such embodiments work to interrogate local conditions and assist in asserting rappers' presence in the transnational hip hop game. Through an engagement with two songs, Black Duo's "Rap kwa Mic" and "Looking Up" by Udita, Alisha Popat, Sugar, L-Ness, Baby T, and Taamic, I situate ludic embodiments within the city's gendered space and gendered discourse.[9] I investigate "Rap kwa Mic" as a text where cismen's performative participation in armored gender is comparably more straightforward; they steward masculinized toughness in notions of play, earnestness, and subversion. Ciswomen, however, maneuver unfairly around an intrinsic trap of gender, caught between supposed oversexualization and excessive masculinity. To escape this snare, women insist that they, too, own the right to play with space and sound, thus staging versions of political seriousness. In an extensive analysis of "Looking Up," I explore how women's performances of play and modalities of seriousness manage to breach power, both creatively and radically, even when the music promotes some of hip hop's pernicious gendered traditions. Lastly, I investigate how rappers use ludic orature to find joy and intimacy within the context of play and how such performances have existed within spaces like the Sarakasi Dome. Within these explorations, ludicity appears as both locally bound and consistently diasporic. In this respect, this chapter introduces how ludicity is inherently tied to how artists cite a U.S. hip hop blackness. Taken together, rappers fashion creative disruptions and modes of compliance through play and gender and *play as a mode of masculinized gender* to facilitate artistic self-making unique to Nairobi that is also globally recognized.

PLAY AND POLITICS IN NAIROBI STREETS

Hip hop practitioners of all genders engage with the politics of Nairobi to make music. Many craft ludic embodiments, which though diasporically instantiated, are localized interactions with the material conditions and discourses of Nairobi. Women rappers stage their way out of gender constrictions through a political seriousness that draws on a tradition of protest, activism, and a refusal to be repressed by the city's strictures. Their work in the underground indicates an engagement with the confinements of the city, the vibrancy of street culture, and the long traditions of dissent. Alternatively, men reiterate the gendered dynamics of the cityspace as one made for men even as they speak out against injustices like poverty and state corruption. Masculine artists' playful resistance to the city's politics is from a place of relative privilege and fundamentally distinct from women's place in hip hop.

Nairobi has a thriving street culture from which rappers are influenced. Heavy foot traffic births a complex economic and cultural life. Street musicians occasionally play drums and sing. Magicians perform card tricks. Preachers yell about the end times. Men and boys shine shoes, *jua kali* workers push loads through town with trailers, and women sell books and clothes.[10] Street boys get high on glue to chase away symptoms of hunger and disenfranchisement. Pickpocketing duos and triads band together to slip their hands into pockets, snatch a purse or watch, or peruse surreptitiously through a backpack. Workers take long breaks to sleep on the grass and smoke cigarettes in the now-designated areas of the city. Just outside the city center and along footpaths, men sell roasted maize. The further east one travels toward the birthplace of Kenyan hip hop, Dandora, the more poverty there is, the more cramped the housing, the more visible the trash, the bumpier and dustier and muddier the roads, and the more heavy-handed the police. Conversely, in the cleanliness and spaciousness of Westlands, there are high-end stores, fancy nightclubs, malls, cafés, closely guarded apartment complexes, and well-manicured lawns and bushes.

Matatus (public transportation minibuses) help construct the classed and gendered spaces of Nairobi life. *Matatus* offer movement around the city while at the same time serving as culturally complicated and masculine-defined spaces. They are Nairobi hip hop's symbolic and official vehicle occupying the streets in a sonically and visually brassy fashion and are seen as representative of street culture. Before the restrictive Michuki regulations in 2003, touts (workers who take money and find passengers) regularly crammed people in, hooking, swinging, and hanging out of moving graffiti-stained and bass-emanating *matatus*.[11] These days, the culture is not forgotten, as graffiti has slowly returned to the vehicles, and one still sees touts engaging in this persistent, playful practice. The touts have cautiously begun to perform this reckless defiance again, which can earn them a ticket from the Nairobi City Council if caught. Touts can be women but are mostly cisgender men. Their work is hard, but it is also spirited, whipping their bodies in graceful, controlled movements, attempting to catch the ear of potential customers by shouting the cost of the ride or the vehicle route. They laugh and argue with other touts, catcall, chew *miraa* (khat), buy cigarettes on the street, skip out of their *matatus* to run alongside them, and return to their vehicles before their speed increases. Those heading into the city center call out, "Tao! Tao! Tao!"—a Swahilinized word for town. There is a difficult underside to this space as well; passengers and touts alike have accosted and assaulted women on *matatus*.[12]

Nightlife bustles throughout the city. Night-shift hawkers and those not exhausted from their daytime schedules maneuver through traffic on Nairobi's major thoroughfares to pawn cheap Chinese goods and sometimes recorded music, depending on how they perceive the threat of selling bootlegged CDs. Cisgender women and men, and some transwomen, sell sex for survival and means. People gather at bars and clubs after work. In poorer areas, some might gather around *changa'a* (illicit brew) spots and purchase a cup of alcohol to socialize and unwind. In other places, patrons listen to live music in small bars. The Westlands hosts middle-class college students and those with well-paying jobs just off work, and both groups find their way to higher-end establishments. On the weekends, Kenyans in their late teens and twenties (and some even older) go out for a night of leisure, drinking, dancing, and clubbing until daylight creeps up on them. New venues pop up regularly, but places like Carnivore and K1 Klub House are long-standing. Spaces often host themed musical nights. James Ogude writes that Nairobi's venues host popular "traditional" music nights for genres like Mugithi and Benga. Ogude contends such music nights dislodge the genres from their ethnicized rural locations, allowing for the consumption and appreciation of a range of music: "It is the openness of the city—its fluidity—that allows for the creation of spaces within which a projection of fantasies rooted in popular cultural memory could be performed."[13]

While the city's music venues open possibilities, Nairobi's public spaces have historically operated as exclusive. It has all the characteristics of a former administrative colonial center. Racial and class apartness has been a key feature of the city since colonialism, as the wealthiest parts are to the north and west where the white settlers resided, while the south and east, once confined to Africans and Indians, are poorer and more working class.[14] Although women take up space in commercial and public areas and work in most professions and at every economic level, the city is a masculine and heterosexist space. In the city center, men regularly snatch women's purses and sexually harass women in the streets. Just like in other cities, women and gender-expansive people, especially those who are poor, are more susceptible to violence. Mobility, wealth, able-bodiedness, and masculinity make it so that abled men can easily move and occupy public space without the same fears of unwanted attention that people of marginalized genders face.

Kenyan official histories privilege cismen, which is profoundly evident in the structural makeup of the city. Kenyan cultural nationalism proffered African traditions that centered men and encouraged governing women's bodies as foundational to build the new nation. These views paradoxically borrowed from colonial beliefs that insisted urban spaces corrupted migrators. Women have long been the targets of urbanity's perceived degeneracy, resulting in the conviction that women should remain subservient to men and only occupy domestic spheres so as not to be tarnished by the city's offerings.[15] Besi Brillian Muhonja states that after independence, Nairobi architecturally archived an exclusive history of men freedom fighters through monuments, street naming, and landmarks.[16] For Muhonja, this action built on and revealed how the city space masculinized itself by removing women from contemporary public histories. After all, and as she notes, the road outside where Mary Muthoni wa Nyanjiru lost her life protesting Harry Thuku's detention is named Thuku Road.[17] These gendered elisions correspond with anxieties about Nairobi women that continue to populate television, social media, and the radio. According to popular heterosexist beliefs, urban women make disadvantageous partners for men because they are unruly, assertive, educated, and untrustworthy. These supposedly disobedient city women are said to have affairs with married men regularly, refuse to accept their duties of unpaid house labor and childrearing, and hold opinions assertively and to the disdain of men.[18] Caroline Mose also reminds us that hip hop is not immune from participating in this discourse. Mose argues that rappers attach those viewed as obedient and politically conscious African women to the struggle and troublingly juxtapose them with the unruly urban and promiscuous femme figure.[19]

The femme sex worker, the young university woman, and the educated urban single woman are held up as examples of how Nairobi corrupts those who supposedly cannot refuse the lure and temptations of urbanity. Men regularly comment about how rebellious city women are and how wife prospects, domestic and docile, are to be found in the countryside. When these tales circulate, men are rarely characterized as culpable for buying sex, courting young college students, having extramarital affairs, or even leaving their families for mistresses or second wives and families. These stories, whether fact or fiction, are often told from masculine perspectives, lamenting how city women betray their supposed rural roots and African upbringings. Gendered narratives and other interlaced discourses and the city's spatial politics weave together Nairobi's character. Keguro Macharia simply terms this ideological and material violence as the "unhoming of Kenyan women," where through juridical, discursive, and physical means, women are dislocated from a society from which they are supposed to belong.[20]

Amid the city's constraints, people regularly take to the streets in protest. These gatherings attack corruption, call for election reform, and decry both legal and illegal evictions, to name a few. Political parties sometimes curate these uprisings, specifically those opposed to the ruling party, and many times receive the support of people from across class divisions. There were organized protests after Kibaki's questionable victory in 2007 and amid the postelection violence.[21] Boniface Mwangi led the Occupy Parliament protest in 2013, where he and others marched a pig and piglets in front of the Parliament building. There, Mwangi and others spilled buckets of blood onto the sidewalk where the pigs furiously licked the *damu,* all of this to represent the MPs as vociferously greedy swine who were then voting to confirm yet another raise for themselves.[22] University of Nairobi students, often unhappy with unreasonable school fees, many times have organized public demonstrations, set up blockades on roads, and thrown stones at cars and police who fired tear gas at them. Kenyan feminists have long protested rape culture, inheritance laws, reproductive rights, environmental concerns, and education and job training.[23] In 2012, 2015, and 2021, sex workers, often alongside LGBTQ activists, protested the illegality of both prostitution and queerness. Those who have taken to the streets don bright red masks and carried banners that read *mwili wangu, chaguo langu* (my body, my choice), decrying violence against and murders of sex workers.[24] Beginning in 2014, a movement called *#MyDressMy-Choice* began to confront the culture that enables men to assault women wearing skirts physically and sexually in public.[25]

Many of these protests contain chants and collective jogs of dissenters moving through public space. These performances can quickly turn into a subtle and rhythmic dance, with participants grabbing tree branches and pointing them toward the sky as they perform slowly and methodically through the streets. Not all these examples are situated within lower-class agitation, but many are often influenced by economic precarity. These are instances of orature, incorporating song, chants, movement, and just the slightest dance steps in order to inspire the collective energy of the crowd and any onlookers. Hip hop practitioners situate ludicity and political seriousness inside many of these Nairobi realities: the performances of life's regular hustle, the charged discourses of gender, the vibrant music culture, and the embodiments of political urgencies. Hip hop play is deeply involved in the sociality of Nairobi life, and since the music so profoundly engages with street life, it enmeshes itself within the city's gendered codes.

THE ARMOR OF GENDER

The masculine elements of ludicity include movement-based gestures and stances of armor that are common in hip hop, such as the stiff body, wide-stance posture, and hardened facial features. These practices are globally circulated but also interface with Kenya's history, the city of Nairobi, and its hip hop spaces. The performances found in Nairobi rap are similar to Tricia Rose's early observation that "ghetto badman posture-performance is a protective shell against real unyielding and harsh social policies and physical environments."[26] The *armor of gender* is a series of performances that practitioners enact that hold hardened, creative, and underclass-based masculinities as an available set of actions within the culture.

Men, almost all cisgender, use this performance to assert their privilege as a broader set of resistance practices that centers lower-class experiences. Such performances draw on Mau Mau tropes used by the Nairobi underground.[27] Mickie Koster notes that the histories of the Mau Mau army and the war with the British are not seamless stories but often contradictory and up for debate. Nonetheless, the Mau Mau moment bred a singular question about the concept and notion of freedom for Kenyan people that continues to exist in many hip hop spaces.[28] Koster notes that the question of liberation remains "unresolved and painful histories like Mau Mau that go untreated carry visible scars in the present."[29] Rappers, in turn, have picked up and developed these pervasive questions about whether Kenya is free and, if not, what a liberated Kenya would look like. I add that these sentiments of liberation, fighting, and masculinity meet similar global themes within hip hop that converge to form an outward-looking Nairobi rap culture. As I mentioned in the introduction, rappers have largely moved away from the confrontational and effective ways that Ukoo Flani Mau Mau incorporated the Land and Freedom Army into their videos and lyrics, and what has remained is a warrior-inspired, toughened masculinized resistance.

Kenyan practitioners use the armor of gender regardless of their actual gender, though there are critical differences between women and men artists. Those who are masculine people use the armor of gender to construct and maintain the culture. In contrast, women and others of marginalized genders adopt carefully fashioned performances within this framework so as not to jeopardize their legitimacy. Imani Kai Johnson explores this practice in her notion of "badass femininities" and considers how U.S. Black women practitioners constitute their subjectivities through histories of slavery, colonization, and anti-Black class marginalization.[30] Johnson argues that badass femininities should not be called masculinity per se, but rather be thought of as the assertive and bold characteristics that can and do constitute femininity. My analysis is slightly different in that I insist that the women I follow in Kenya negotiate and embody an existing masculinity even while they identify as women and with femininity, thereby pushing back against the masculinizing presence in the music.

Jessica Nydia Pabón-Colón in *Graffiti Grrlz: Performing Feminism in the Hip Hop Diaspora* is vastly helpful in this regard because she provides a thorough examination of global graffiti culture and its community of women and femmes, most of whom are white, Latinx, white-passing, and otherwise non-Black or African. She identifies a "feminist masculinity" at work for these artists, which is "a gender performance characterized by the utilization of recognizably masculine traits."[31] Her study is helpful in that she demonstrates that women and femmes enact a recuperative feminist method of performance that fashions a hip hop diaspora and uses masculinity to articulate a viable subjectivity. While Pabón-Colón recognizes a U.S. Black and Afro-Caribbean origin to hip hop and graffiti, she does not necessarily factor such characteristic roots into how artists construct feminist masculinity in graffiti performance.[32] I contend that the armored gender I study is subversive, masculinized, and historically situated within Kenyan contexts, and in addition, it also uses a U.S. blackness as a cultural throughline to create diaspora. Pabón-Colón also distinguishes between the conventional performance of masculinity found with cismen in hip hop and the feminist masculinity that seeks to redo constructs of power in performances. My observations of Nairobi rap culture differ from her study of graffiti culture because, in Nairobi rap, all artists navigate a similar gender dynamic. While women do not have the same privileges men do and may use armored gender to assert space in the culture, they also make music and perform alongside men, as well as understand their work as pulling from the same traditions as men. For these reasons, I use one term, the armor of gender, to describe how all artists navigate masculinity.

Women, both feminine and masculine, use able-bodied toughness in performance to create a culture where they prioritize themselves. Armor allows artists to perform impenetrability, which is a necessary tool to protect oneself from social marginalization. Here, Pabón-Colón's notion of feminist masculinity is particularly salient. She writes, "I locate feminist masculinity in how graffiti grrlz perform their gender, but it is a performance of self available to any body. Feminist masculinity does not come at the cost of femininity."[33] She observes how not all graffiti artists identified with the term "feminist," but most understood the stakes centering women's work. In the performances of Nairobi's armor of gender, femme and masculine women incorporate armor to perform their subjectivity. Just like the artists in *Graffiti Grrlz*, not many women I spoke with identify as feminists, but most understood the critical task of taking up space and making music using themes of political seriousness.

The *armor of gender* helps to compose hip hop's playfulness. While "armor" may imply a rigid set of bodily conscriptions, the opposite is true, and it unfolds with the theme of playfulness to produce willful rebelliousness and shifty subversiveness. When I discussed embodiment with Sue Timon, her response indicated a marked commitment to ludicity: "There's the bounce. [Laughs hard.] There's that bounce. [Although she is sitting, she gestures a bounce using the upper part of her body, while laughing.] You know, the way someone walks, the 'don't care' attitude. The N.W.A. thing, you know. [We laugh.] You just know."[34] Sue not only gestured expressively and excitedly when I asked her questions, but she also referenced the hip hop group N.W.A. (Niggaz wit Attitudes), the Compton gangsta rap group from the late '80s and early '90s. While Sue did not identify as either a feminist or a tomboy, her more masculine performances demonstrated that hip hop offered embodiments that worked with the music she then made.

I asked several rappers to discuss embodiment, and many stated that performance was another element of the culture, similar to breakdancing, DJing, rapping, and graffiti art. Others noted that bodily corporealities are found in all hip hop elements. When I asked graffiti artist Esen what bodily postures convey, he smiled, lifted his arms a bit, and proclaimed, "Whatchu sayin, nigga?!"[35] Here, Esen responds with a rhetorical question that translates into a protective readiness that is confrontational, playful, humorous, and U.S.-originated. Additionally, Eva-redi noted that hand gestures are also meaningful: "I can say, basically, the body language of hip hop is crazy, like, the throwing of hands, the sign of the fist."[36] While he explains this, he puts one hand up slightly and raises his fist to illustrate his point. A part of this fist-raising is a vestige of how early conscious hip hop in the U.S. sought to continue the mission of the Black Power movement of the 1960s. During the same period, the thrown fist became an anticolonial and anti-apartheid symbol as it spread to places within Africa, especially South Africa. Eva-redi, Esen, and Sue cited the U.S. in their discussions of embodiment and hip hop play, which did not convey a sense of alienation or foreignness to their work but rather a closeness and familiarity. These embodiments that convey elements like a defiant "attitude" or Black power aesthetic point to how the ludic is a diasporic proposition, rooted in U.S. Black music, that has been localized and reformulated to work in Nairobi rap, illustrating that citational practices are also exercises in indigenization.

Artists use ludicity, masculinized and diasporic, to perform freeness even as they feel restrained by the industry and its lack of real opportunities. Women participate in the larger social project that hip hop offers, and they continually challenge the dominant masculine culture of the underground scene. Further, ludicity allows cisgender men to apprehend performances of cool and subversion to move their narrations of hood life to the forefront of Nairobi's chronicles. Taken together, the *armor of gender* is a diverse set of embodiments that draw on and reinforce the masculinity present in the music.

SOMEWHERE IN NAIROBI

Artists' rhyme schemes, lyrical critiques, and demonstrations of rap skill all depend on them using their bodies in defiant, cool, and stylized manners. Practitioners find inventive techniques of masculinized play to confer knowledge about an analysis of Nairobi life. On the surface, it may seem that the ludicity of bodily performances enables the potency and effectiveness of the political seriousness of lyrics and sound. However, play can still be found in the lyrics, and armored gender encapsulates both play and seriousness. This unpredictability makes the music innovative and pleasurable while also allowing artists to find small moments of sonic and bodily liberation. Notably, many cismen practice embodiments to create spaces of freedom where their voices and raps gain legitimacy. In music videos, these gestures of self-determination often materialize through physical movement and one that mirrors the privileged mobility that men enjoy in the city.

"Rap kwa Mic" (Rap on the Mic) by brothers Judge and Mo Phat of Black Duo dropped in 2009 and illustrates how masculinities are formulated and how they are in conversation with the spatial politics of the city. The song was an instant hit. When I spoke with Judge about this, he lamented that bootlegged singles were so rampant that he hardly made any money from the song. He held no hard feelings, as he understood that such economic practices were part of the hustle. "Rap kwa Mic" samples from U.S. musicians Talib Kweli, Hi Tek, and Bahamadia's 2008 song "Chaos" from the album *Soundbombing Vol. 2*. Talib has gained mainstream exposure, and his dedication to underground and noncommercial music has earned him some fame among artists in Kenya. The fact that Talib has an established career but remains committed to politically conscious music makes him appealing to many Kenyan rappers.

"Rap kwa Mic" uses computer technologies to create an ample range of divergently assembled noises exuding a solemn and cautionary tone about hood life in Nairobi, building on the already established serious nature of "Chaos." We hear piano keys, a violin, a saxophone, and eventually a horn, which is retained from the original. The standard kick drum gives the bass, and after the beat drops, there is a noted transition to softer and subtle horn sounds that fall into the background to provide room for the lyrics. It is not just the raps that provide the vocal presence. Just like U.S. hip hop from the '80s and '90s, there are chuckles and improvisational sounds that make the song unfold like a conversation that is firm and advisory. Also retained from the earlier version is the "la-la-la-la-la" ad-libbing, which appears in the beginning before Talib begins his lines. In "Rap kwa Mic," the *la* ad-libs exist throughout the song, creating an aura of impending or imminent danger. The chorus is sung in staccato, with several overlapping high and off-pitch voices laid on top of each other. At one point, the chorus's *la's* bleed into the verses and are met with the rappers speaking "la-la-la-la-la" in lower registers. These vocal sounds meet one another and vie for respect, creating a sounded compilation of Nairobi life that produces "reconstituted echoes" of "Chaos," to cite Glissant.[37] These differing clatters organize "Rap kwa Mic" as a polyrhythmic diasporic text located in the specificity of Nairobi.

The video opens with grim music and grainy, sepia imagery with the words "Somewhere in Nairobi." Viewers are never given a full view of the city, and the majority of the scenes are from the working-class area of Ziwani, near Eastleigh.[38] The scenes are gritty and harsh, matching the serious and contentious words, and there are few markers to locate where in Nairobi this was shot. Viewers see buildings and children playing and dancing on top of metal structures, along with Black Duo's crew walking through the neighborhood. Judge and Mo Phat are constantly in motion, walking deliberately through the streets as they laugh and communicate with their crew of men and masculine individuals, as the performance of mobility is a common theme in many videos. Listeners only hear voices sonically read as masculine; therefore, we encounter a text specifically about the experiences of cismen. The song progresses, and more men join their casual and slow walk, the strut of collective cool. Their movements are slow and carefree, not labored or swift. In this way, the rappers represent themselves as not being exploited, nor are they fearful of or worn down by their neighborhood, where underemployment and insecurity are rife.

Throughout the culture, the playful and the serious reside alongside one another, and armored gender fits into the presentation of both the ludic and thematic earnestness. Songs like this are never about complete social ease—the ludic is indexed within a conversation about the importance of assuming tough bodily postures that can withstand economic marginalization. As Black Duo raps, their crew performs hip hop's hand gestures in the air as if they are rhyming. Performances like this, which are easy to overlook, are part of the shared diasporic orature that combines the themes of play and earnestness. Michael Jeffries names embodiments like these as "complex cool," which shapes "a publicly conflicted discourse of black masculinity" and "[affirms] black cultural practices and black collective identity."[39] When Black Duo's crew walks and then suddenly dodges and darts toward the camera or provides solemn stares and then outbursts of laughter, they demonstrate their relationship with the ghetto, that within the unjustness of their lives resides a space of something spirited and playful. Jeffries describes such interactions as a mutuality: "Rappers represent the hood, while the presence of the hood . . . makes them seem both powerful and authentic as representatives of a neighborhood constituency."[40]

Jeffries explores people like Jay-Z, T. I., and Lil' Wayne, analyzing how performances of thug masculinities in gangsta rap are the toxic and creative methods used to express vulnerabilities and connections, deliver social critiques, and position themselves as skillful artisans. He identifies how, for instance, nihilism in Tupac's music "should be seen as a force ripe with possibility," understanding it as a meaningful exercise in perspective.[41] Jeffries stops short of concluding that these performative presentations equate to political progressiveness or radicality, given investments in misogynism and capitalism. He ascertains that what occurs in subcultures does not have enough strength to shift Black people's lives: "The symbolic work accomplished by hip-hop practitioners and fans is insufficient for structural change."[42] The U.S. rappers Jeffries studied may not be able to make effective political interventions, but the ways listeners and fans use the music in their daily lives is essential. Furthermore, evaluating hip hop in terms of its direct ability for structural reform could limit our understanding of what music does in society and what it should do. In thinking through the vast differences between the mainstream U.S. hip hop that Jeffries analyzes and the underground Kenyan music I discuss, we should not overlook the cultural force of play, pleasure, and joy present in both musics, especially as they are tied to contributing to the social discourse that rejects systems of policing and economic exploitation in both places.

Robin D. G. Kelley makes this often-referenced point in his discussion of gangsta rap and infrapolitics in writing that listeners use the music to make claims to public space.[43] Drawing from James C. Scott, Kelley argues that infrapolitics are the regular forms of working-class, subtle resistance and defiance, or the "seemingly innocuous, individualistic acts of survival and resistance [that] shape politics," like "footdragging to sabotage, theft at the workplace to absenteeism, cursing to graffiti."[44] In hip hop music, it is critical we identify how artists and devotees employ methods of defiance through orature, both the commonplace and the rehearsed. Sonically embodied performances have everything to do with how the force of imagination meets quotidian subversion.

Infrapolitics in "Rap kwa Mic," like in much of the Nairobi underground, is orature that is habitually indecipherable and elusive, issuing a defiant sensibility and social critique. Judge and Mo Phat's performative repartee is catchy and styled, and their fleeting performance of freeness meets lyrics that exude struggle and seriousness. Mo Phat opens the song by comparing music to prayer, and he invites his listeners to participate: "Muziki ni kama kusali / Wee piga magoti / Ni tamu tu kama sukari" (Music is like prayer / You, get on your knees / It's sweet like sugar). In the middle of the song, Judge states that rapping helps to feed and sustain him: "Na hii rap 'taweza kuniekea dish (With this rap I can get myself a dish/some food) / Ama niimbe tu kenye wote mna (Or I only sing about what y'all have)."[45] Lyrics, like embodiment, blur the categories of the ludic and the earnest. Mo Phat japes: "Ndio maana unapigwa na butwaa[-twa-twa-twa] (That's why you are hit by surprise) / Hili kichwani ni kama Doom (In the head, it's like Doom)."[46] At the moment of this rhyme, Judge and Mo Phat walk in front of the crew, and Mo Phat draws out the word *butwaa* (surprise): "but-twa-twa-twa!" Just as we hear the words/sounds "twa-twa-twa," overlaid with the sound of gunshots, Judge confidently steps forward and provides the final "twa," while pointing his hand in a quick upward formation as a finger gun toward the camera and takes a shot. Firing his weapon, Judge surprises his opponents and cynics and does not diverge from the beat, and he continues his rhythmic gait.

According to their words, when a devotee meets Black Duo, they are hit in the head as if with Doom, the popular cockroach spray. Being struck with Doom for roaches means instant death if they cannot dodge the liquid. Similarly, if listeners are not attuned to their rap skill, they will also receive a blow resulting from these practitioners' overpowering verbal confrontations. The artists' creative banter leads to a grave warning to their rivals about the depths of their flow.

Even with its specific detailing of Nairobi in "Rap kwa Mic," this song is not just about the capital city; it is also about the transnational globality of hip hop blackness. It asserts the city is a grim and unforgiving landscape where men rappers eke out survival. They walk but start and stop in the same place and never end up somewhere physically different, wanting viewers to know that Nairobi is the focal point. However, there is a marked global element. Michael Jeffries calls this hood-making, "building the universal hood through affirmation of local hood experience."[47] While he cites places like Brooklyn, Chicago, and Atlanta, Black Duo adds to this by staking a claim in a global hip hop scene outside of only U.S. cities, thereby rejecting the cultural geopolitics that relegates African music to the margins.

The combination of the performative, the visual, and the sonic characteristics in the video effectually emits a global tone worth noting. Specifically in this song, the shrill and admonitory overlapping *la*'s, the contentious boast-style raps, the firing of a warning shot, and the full instrumentalities work together to announce how people must clamor for recognition in the limited spatial realities of the hood. Mark D. Morrison's notion of Blacksound is helpful to evidence this, a theory that describes how racialized performance, sound, and mimetic scripts are foundational to American popular music. Tracing the origins of Blacksound to blackface minstrelsy, Morrison contends that music's historical commodification constructs notions of race, relying on the flexibility and fungibility of blackness. Morrison states that it is inherently transnational and global simply because Black music is.[48] Thus, the practices of sampling found in "Rap kwa Mic" are a part of how the politics of mimicry are tied to the fungibility of blackness. The song's connection to the U.S. through Black sonic characteristics is not derivative but is instead part of a cultural system of citations. What surfaces is a long tradition of borrowing that is deeply dependent on how diasporic sameness is forged and how U.S. blackness and its cultural productions remain reliably appropriable. It is not that the gunshot, the *la*'s, or the ominous sonorous qualities are intrinsically Black, but rather that together they signify a recognizable hip hop blackness. The video creates urban blackness through its connection to "Chaos," using rappers' embodiments and visualities, and the narrations of lower-class youth in Nairobi. The song and video produce Blacksound, which "amplifies these low frequencies by directing attention to how the sonic and material histories of race continue to resonate."[49] These sonic qualities are generalizable to any ghetto, and therefore listeners and viewers encounter both the Nairobi hood and the global hood.

Pairing the diasporic travel of the sample with their motility and rhymes, this song is a text about play, movement, and freeness. The "Somewhere in Nairobi" framing exudes an anonymizing element in that these rappers do not wish to make known where they are in the city. In this way, rappers perform untraceability and indefinability, which are central to the ludic themes of the music. Their playful, dodgy, and shifty gestures add to the idea they resist being fastened to any modes of surveillance that would undermine their project. Judge, Mo Phat, and their crew perform a type of movability to walk, exercise leisure, and find instances of joy within their movement. By the end of the video, the conditions of the hood have not changed, but the artists have found space to implement their ludic contentment. These practitioners move on their terms and create a conversation that is not about a desire to leave the hood behind, Ziwani or otherwise, but rather for them to author their stories of movement within the places they live.

<h2 style="text-align:center">LOOKING UP, PERFORMING FROM BELOW</h2>

Women use the armor of gender to move through the difficult bind they often find themselves in when making music. Along with gender-expansive people, many in the Nairobi rap community argue that their performances are separate from the tomboy/hypersexed trap that permeates the music. The armor of gender operates as both limiting and capacious, allowing these rappers to adopt fraught embodiments to explore their subjectivities and move toward notions of freedom. Mwenda Ntarangwi hints at this in *East African Hip Hop: Youth Culture and Globalization* when he writes that practitioners of all genders use hip hop to explore their place in the culture and the world at large and that it "expresses . . . the fluidity and performative nature of gender, revealing how normalized gender identities can be reconstituted to gain new meanings."[50] As Ntarangwi notes, the music can also affirm societally established gender, and thus, any fluidity that exists should not be confused with a free-range set of gender expressivities.[51] Focusing on mostly commercial artists like Wahu from Kenya and Zay B from Tanzania, Ntarangwi observes that women artists primarily challenge their marginal position in the culture in several ways, including by unsettling the commercialization of their bodies and critiquing men's dominance in hip hop. In underground music, these elements are present. Women rappers also constantly navigate performances of masculinity, which are always available tools for all rappers. They often "reorder the existing gender normative values without changing the existing structures that define them," as Ntarangwi observes, but this altering in hip hop occurs as these artists work through and enact masculinity.[52] These masculinized sets of performances are practiced and made into a "user-friendly" armor for all to implement, even when real exclusion is evident within the culture.[53]

Rappers work through structural, ideological, and societal politics that inform hip hop spaces. Women's navigations reflect what Mary Njeri Kinyanjui terms African feminist "fireside knowledge," referring to the everyday ways that Kenyan women activate methods of solidarity, shared expertise, and modes of survival. According to Kinyanjui, women in the kitchen or cooking hut produce significant feminist ways of knowing.[54] This "anti-patriarchal frame which does not position women as 'add-ons' to a masculine framework" so aptly describes how women rappers create and apprehend sonic space as central actors in the culture.[55] She refers to how *jua kali* traders, peasant farmers, and other working women develop systems of knowledge that confront the constraints that sexist capitalism delivers. Like the working-class women Kinyanjui references, women rappers also advance musical interventions meant to defy the cismen-dominated industry.

The 2015 "Looking Up" music video is particularly exceptional because it brings together a large group of women Kenyan rappers and singers. In this video, two singers provide the hook, Udita and Alisha Popat, while Sugar, L-Ness, Baby T, and Taamic all take turns with verses. This song is a remix of a track by the collective Dandora Music. While the original song includes predominantly masculine rappers, the artists in the remix sought to create a song centered around the skill-set and perspectives of Nairobi's "femcees," a term women artists call themselves. In a conversation about the video, L-Ness informed me that they chose to shoot the track in the informal settlement of Kibera in an effort to not always focus on Dandora.[56]

The video exemplifies how women authorize themselves as rap's knowledge producers through embodied and sonic orature. Daphne A. Brooks names such works "Afro-sonic feminist noise," which are the ways in which a collage of competing, refracting, and conducive vocalities by Black women are often found in musical and performative texts. Brooks calls us to consider how Black women's musicianship interfaces with sonic musicalities, sometimes in tension with each other and other times in tandem, producing a fertile engagement with and fervent disassociation from structures of power.[57] A deluge of sounds builds throughout "Looking Up" and collaborates with the disparate voices of the six performers, working to create a type of sonic fullness that refuses women's silencing. Along with pronounced piano sounds and a subtle bassline, the song contains a violin motif that creates themes of perseverance and urgency to which the lyrics add, thus creating a conversation about women's firm tenacity in the culture. While it is polyphonic and clarion, there is no heavy bass sound. The presence of the boom and rattle of basslines are regularly gendered as masculine, as Shanté Paradigm Smalls notes, and while such characteristics can be found in other songs by women, here such elements are absent.[58] As each rapper and singer moves through the text, they embody its aural intensity and perform an announcement of their sustained presence within underground culture. Their performances are articulations of their agentive subjectivity but also ones that must be fought over within the thorny field of masculinities that organizes rap.

The song begins with rapper Sugar emerging from a couch over railroad tracks that cut through Kibera. Donning large gold rope chains and a red jumpsuit, she walks down the middle of the tracks toward the camera. In her hip hop version of Mary Njeri Kinyanjui's fireside knowledge, Sugar steps over debris and through small, enflamed piles of trash while her raps grant homage to her mother's resolve. Through smoke, Sugar rhythmically moves her arms and hands in and away from her body through her verse, which creates a site for her lyrics and verifies her rap skill. She lays down bars with strength and certainty, exemplifying how William Cobb describes hip hop flow: "[It] is not about *what* is being said, so much as *how* one is saying it."[59] Ending with a customary nod to Kenya, she raps, "2-5-flow! To the death, killing 'em!" before passing the song on to her five collaborators.[60]

Sugar's saunter toward the camera illuminates how motility and armored gender converge. A styled gait allows rappers to establish ownership over the spaces that they occupy, just like Judge, Mo Phat, and their crew's movement through the hood in "Rap kwa Mic." In "Looking Up," Sugar is the only rapper to perform this strut; L-Ness sits and paints, Udita and Baby T are also seated, and Alisha Popat sits, stands, and dances in place. The last artist, Taamic, rides a bike through the neighborhood, but she hops off and heads toward a group of sitting children to stand before them and spit her bars. The summations of these gestures symbolize how women often unconsciously navigate their feminized bodies within hip hop's gender performance. In the frames, the women use poses, stand, and interact with others, yet none walk toward the camera as Sugar does. However implicit and without specific intention, it is essential to highlight how these women artists' bodily enactments of relative immobility reflect the gendered realities of the underground and that moveability is often an attribute of cismen. Furthermore, the presentations of these women rappers as largely stationary reflect how the city does not enable the safe movement of Nairobians of marginalized genders. These performances articulate a political problem because while cismen can marshal masculinized gestures to create hip hop more easily and to navigate their presence in the city forthrightly, women are left wrestling on two fronts: how to be a woman in the culture without being dismissed and how to participate in an authentic hip hop Nairobiness. Therefore, we must recognize how Sugar's embodied reframing of this normally masculine script aptly indicates how women use gendered codes often set against them to uphold their abilities as creative producers.

At times, one's decisions to perform gendered armor may be directly personal or situational. In other performances and videos, Sugar performs very feminine attributes. She is an example of an artist who straddles the class demarcations of the mainstream and underground worlds. In chapter 4, I mention Sugar's appearance in the song and music video "2-5-Flow," in which she teams with commercial rapper Bamboo and sings the hook to that song. In "Looking Up," however, she is centered in the video as the first rapper to appear. And unlike her traditionally feminine positionality in her video with Bamboo, she wears a tracksuit and Timberland boots, walks, and gestures insistently. Yet her collective movements are not exactly the firm, masculine performances that rappers like L-Ness or Sue Timon produce, as her embodiments adopt more feminine signifiers. In an interview with *Pulse*, a youth and entertainment magazine in *The Standard* newspaper, she states that she was concealing a pregnancy at the time of filming. When asked why she kept her pregnancy a secret, Sugar revealed that she wanted to continue working on her music without being sidelined for her "condition" (her words) because of some of the stereotypes that run in the music industry.

> I wanted to run business as usual. There was no missing studio recording sessions and concerts for me. I was also afraid of the pregnancy going wrong. This is because Brian and I suffered a miscarriage before we were blessed with Sabira. The emotional trauma was a bit too much to handle, therefore I wanted to keep [the pregnancy] a secret.[61]

Sugar's experience as a woman in an industry that can often be hostile, as well as the personal pain of a miscarriage, informed her performative inclinations in the video. It makes sense that she thus dons baggy clothes as a protective shield guarding her temporary secret. Her gestures add to her armor by protecting her body from viewers who would notice her pregnancy and perhaps also safeguard her from the internal pain of miscarriage. The way she stands and walks down the railroad tracks, rapping and using her gestures to emphasize her lyrics, all serve to celebrate her as a rapper and detract from her status as an expectant parent. For better or worse, most would not associate her flow with pregnancy, and thus, she successfully uses the performance to keep her personal life closed off from public view. Considering this video, the one with Bamboo, and her comments on pregnancy, Sugar ultimately puts forward a marked adaptability of performed gender. She thoroughly understands that different idioms of gender change her stance, and as much as she operates within the constraining settings of the industry, she also asserts personal and artistic decisions about her body.

Women embrace armored gender carefully and by not fully endorsing masculinity, but rather by engaging in a tactful balancing act rooted in socially gendered expectations. Many recognize that they must perform around modes of masculinity for them to be taken seriously while also understanding that treading too close would not be sexually desirable and would ultimately draw indignation. Msia Clark remarks, "[African] female MCs can be labeled troublemakers (because of hip hop's confrontational nature), lesbians (because of hip hop's masculine culture), and whores (when female artists do not express their sexuality in socially approved ways)."[62] Thus, being too masculine and too feminine both carry pejorative associations, so women must sacrifice something to be accepted. The tomboy persona on one side and the hypersexual figure on the other are both hip hop's versions of the rogue urban woman who defies the contrived categories of gender. Although an analogous dynamic is found in U.S. versions, the trap that this binary produces is also particular to how postcolonial discourse relegates African and Kenyan women's corporeality, which is regularly absorbed into rap. In the "Looking Up" video, despite the differences in navigating femininity and masculinity, none of the rappers buy into conventionally regarded femininities, such as seductive vulnerabilities or heterosexual availability, nor do they advocate fully for the tomboy.

Women practitioners often measure their performance against the rather disparaged tomboy. For Baby T, she has rejected more masculine or tomboy identities. She stated:

People think that all female artists are gangstas, tomboys, and bad girls. Not all of them are so hard. *Some of us are shy.* Like basically, I'm shy, that's why people call me Baby, cuz ah, I don't think we all have to go hard. And ah, [be] gangsta, and wear shorts and baggy pants. People think that all female artists are gangsta.[63] (emphasis mine)

In this discussion, Baby T finds it difficult to design her hip hop presence outside the trap and therefore uses shyness. Although shyness can be rendered feminine, she uses it to place herself outside of the music's binary. She is not unlike other women who try to articulate some other way to be a rapper aside from masculine and femininely sexy and ultimately find it challenging.

In the video, she is seated with Kibera's informal settlement housing, which appears in the background. She wears a hoodie, a ball cap, red lipstick, and over-sized hoop earrings. As she raps, she moves her arms slightly in and away from her body, with less emphasis than L-Ness or even Sugar. If masculinity is about movability and the taking up of space, Baby T's gestures only mildly make use of such availabilities. Her words coincide with her physicality of creating a gendered armor, albeit distanced from associations of tomboyishness and women gangstas. Her performance is confident and affirmative, adding to the gravitas of the song. She raps:

> I know life ain't easy, teenagers in the streets tryin to make a living /
>
> Society mistreated by the leaders they believe in /
>
> No work for the youth, kids dying, no food /
>
> But I keep on looking up because the streets need hope /
>
> We've been down for too long /
>
> now we tryin to move on cuz /
>
> shida za dunia, ka sabuni zuisha (the problems of the world, like soap, will get finished) /
>
> mi najivunia kwa hii maisha, yeah! Baby! (so, I am proud of myself in this life, yeah! Baby!)[64]

Considering her performances, lyrics, and interview statements together, Baby T articulates what Daphne Brooks describes as "black women's sonic performances and phonic expression[, which] are dialectically and dialogically engaged with black women's discursive and dramaturgical acts."[65] Baby T's corporeality attends to the compromise between what are two impracticable poles of masculinity and femininity, creating a footing for her words about the unfair lives of poor youth.

Cisgender men also express uneasy sentiments about the tomboy and proclaim that hip hop women should not feel boxed into what they regard as an imposed assignment. Judge states, "If you're a chick [they say] you have to be like . . ., for example, a tomboy . . . . Naw. You can still be sexy, and you are doing hip hop. You know?"[66] Similarly, Agano argues that one does not have to be a tomboy to make it, though many are. I asked him if this was acceptable, and he said, "Okay,

FIGURE 6. Rapper Baby T in the "Looking Up" video. Screenshot by author. Source: Dandora-Music, "Looking Up Rmx X 254 Female Rappers (Official Music Video)," YouTube, November 6, 2014, https://www.youtube.com/watch?v=w6PoSkSuDqU&t=2s.

there is [*sic*] no rules there, but I think they can do what they are doing. I think it's cool. But not every girl should be like that though."[67] These statements imply that women do not *have* to be tomboys and should be free to choose their identities, deducing that the tomboy is unsuitable. Judge's notion that women *should be able* to be sexy seems to imply that women simply *should be* sexy in underground spaces. Judge and Agano solidify the cultural mores, implying that for women, the available genders are either one that resembles masculinity or something desirable to normative masculinity. There is an unresolvable exclusion that women face: that rap skill level is read through a masculine sieve, but also that the nonheteronormative subjectivity of the tomboy is inherently pejorative because it does not fulfill cismen desires that are encouraged in hip hop's heteronormative spaces.

L-Ness, of all the people I interviewed, most identified with the tomboy label, though she stopped short of calling herself one. L-Ness believes that women should not make themselves desirable to masculinity:

> Most female hiphoppers are just tomboy. I don't know, it just comes. . . . But ah, the other performers, they want to go an extra mile to be sexy. They'll want to appeal to the men. You know? There's a difference. If I'm rapping, I want to touch everybody. But there is someone who will go on stage and start singing, and maybe they want to appeal to the men. You know, they are dressing in something short. Even their moves, they have to be sexy moves. . . . It's not necessary. Women shouldn't be portrayed like that. If you look at many videos, you feel sorry for most of the models, because it's not just about that. . . . But it's just a westernization kind of thing.[68]

For L-Ness, this is an inauthentic method of rap subjectivity. Like Baby T, L-Ness recognizes the bind, but unlike her, L-Ness's way out is to avoid the conditions that make women objects of sexual attention. From an outsider's perspective, these women may all sound the same. However, they have unique and differing methods of creating themselves as artists in this music video. How they navigate gender elucidates the imperfections of the Nairobi underground. However, these comments also allude to how variegated the artists' performances and subjectivities are and how differently they choose to position their bodies within the culture.

The politics of the Nairobi hip hop tomboy feed into larger ideas about notions of imitativeness and mimicry that circulate within Kenyan discourse and the histories of sonic technologies. Alexander Weheliye reminds us of the historical situatedness in which practices of mimicry in music-making occur: "Not surprisingly, unmediated mimetic listening was most habitually ascribed to 'others,' such as native subjects, women, and black people. The mimetic dimensions of recorded sound were also highlighted in scenes depicting the ascription by 'primitives' of paranormal powers to this machinery."[69] The notion that social others can only hope to copy and imitate carries over into the figure of the tomboy. Although a large part of disavowing the tomboy label is a refusal to be read as lesbian, queer, or nonfeminine and thus disregarded, what is also at play is ciswomen artists' refusal to be assessed as only parrots of their cismen counterparts. L-Ness, Baby T, and Sugar eschew claims that their embodiments are inauthentic while steadfastly asserting that they articulate an imaginative and inventive method of rapping. At the center of gender politics in Nairobi are anxieties that ciswomen artists are inauthentic rappers because of their propensity to copy. A large part of the social anxiety over hip hop is due to claims of copying the west and not having the informed capacity to make cultural or musical choices that reflect Kenyan culture. If mimicking is the worst characteristic of a non-U.S. rapper, to be a woman or femme indicted for mimicry of their men colleagues is a judgment that aims to cast women outside the bounds of the culture. The tomboy serves as the quintessential imitator of both U.S. hip hop and Kenyan cismen practitioners, solidifying the otherness of women artists. While cismen might only be accused of a single U.S. imitativeness, women supposedly doubly mimic both men and U.S. rap at large. This dual spotlight is the essential dilemma for many people of marginalized genders whose actions are constantly up for review and attempted dismissal by cultural gatekeepers. This intra–hip hop dynamic, then, in turn, serves to accuse femme artists within the space as the "actual" imitators. In other words, it is not Kenyan rap at large that is guilty of mimicry, nor are the men who dominate it; it is women. Hence, anxieties over postcolonial subjects wanting to parody western culture seep into the underground and surface as conversations about whether women rappers have the capacity to express the complexities of an urban, globalized hip hop Kenyanness.

Women rappers combat this snare in two ways. First, their mere presence in the culture disrupts the field of hegemonic gender, and thus, they shift and reconfigure spaces. While women rappers recognize that there may not be a way out of masculinization, they problematize the music through their performative participation. They disrupt men-only spaces and masculine music practices, even if nominally, and their performances and songs in concerts and videos force the music into a more inclusionary politics. Women recognize that men gatekeep the industry side, as men are the most likely to be producers, own studios, and have labels. However, men MCs, as a collection of artists, perform embodiments in hip hop culture through nonnormativity and rejecting social categories. Cis-women performances compel artists to question gender through an interrogation of society's figures: the tomboy, the lesbian, and the promiscuous woman. Tanya Saunders writes on Cuban underground music that regardless of one's subjectivity, "it is a queer act for a woman to enter into hip hop and make an intervention into non-normative behaviors" and that "the female presence within hip hop is a queer presence in and of itself."[70] Building from Saunders, Kenyan women's embodied performances queer the space of Nairobi rap and thus queer the performing body that helps constitute the hip hop diaspora. These rappers do not explicitly advocate for queering spaces, but instead their embodiments unsettle a cismasculine dogma. Such disturbance opens the door for the culture to question itself and further decipher its values, impelling many men artists to confirm their support for women rappers, even if that support comes with guidelines and policing. In so doing, and however imperfect it might be, these artists of marginalized genders communicate embodied knowledge about how hip hop is a space to affirm the outcast while jettisoning the idea that they should be marginalized. Above all, women's performance practices make spaces that insist they have a place in the music. The fact that women use normative standards to discuss gender means that such interventions are never forthright but murky and imprecise.

Secondly, the women use this song to participate in the commonly mentioned "hip hop is a way of life" axiom. This concept is a celebrated and globally embraced ideal that asserts that dedicated practitioners recognize the music as a method and set of practices for engaging with the world. Michael Jeffries writes that practitioners state that "hip hop is more than just art . . . and the subjects insist that hip hop is something they live, not just listen to," concluding that it "is something that allows people to tell the world who they are."[71] Usually, Kenyan artists espouse the "way of life" adage to combat accusations of U.S. imitation by responding that they cannot mimic this art form because it is how they live. The video contributes to the "way of life" philosophy by framing the music as a quotidian exercise while also staring down the idea that only men can live hip hop.

In the underground, the artists reclaim the culture for poor youths and exemplify that it can be performed in everyday settings, contesting mainstream rap's regular representations of wealth and excess. For example, during L-Ness's part, she raps with her standard speed and grit, which adds to the song's sonic surges. Although she remains sitting, her rhymes take up performative space, along with how the sound saturates the video. She sits in front of a picture and paints, wearing a graffiti-style half-mask respirator. Her body moves quickly and assertively, implicating her viewers in listening to what she has to say by repeatedly pointing directly at the camera. Even though she does not use spray cans, she sports the mask, framing her painting as a part of graffiti art. Toward the end of the song, hip hop is transformed into a class when the last rapper, Taamic, displays her lyrical skill to an audience of children sitting in an outdoor classroom, eagerly absorbing the knowledge she imparts. Though the chalkboard she stands by is not entirely shown, enough is there to gather that her lyrics have been written onto it, transforming her verses into actual lessons. By insisting that they have something to contribute to the culture, these women demand that their music is how they live.

POLITICAL SERIOUSNESS IN "LOOKING UP"

In "Looking Up," the rappers exhibit a critical claim to political seriousness and utilize it to respond to their marginalization. Women's usage of the "way of life" adage and the intentional centering of their spatial and sonic presence are examples of political seriousness. This section explores the multiple other ways this framing occurs in the video, including through social critiques and affirmations of their work. These women rappers demonstrate that despite being stymied by gender constructions, they still retain creative control over how they represent themselves as critics of Nairobi, which for them is a place containing layers of social and economic dispossession.

The serious elements within the lyrics are extended through the various performances in the video. The rappers' words induce an earnest, normative "feel good" logic. The verses and chorus are generally about never giving up, not succumbing to poverty, and always remaining positive, all while the artists acknowledge the precarity and vulnerability of poor people's subject position. Throughout the video, people from various backgrounds, ages, genders, and races hold up a sign with the words Looking Up. It is passed from one to another, including three white people in succession, a young child in a school uniform, and another child living on the streets. One woman carrying firewood on her back also has the sign affixed to the wood. The message leans toward promoting a hip hop bootstrap capitalism as a response to poverty. At the beginning of the video, Udita sings, "Just keep on, looking up / Keep on, keep on, looking up." With these words, the song participates in the hood narratives of perseverance that have long pervaded underground rap. By asserting that one's good outlook on life will result in upward mobility, the song's political seriousness utilizes common neoliberal messaging of human worth as defined through positive attitude and affect.

However, the embodied performances in the video rescue it from being solely and unpleasantly aligned with a normalized economic ethic. Children in the video skip with makeshift jump ropes, hula hoop with wire, and participate in collective breakdance battles. The activities exist as similar practices, framing rap as a part of the life of marginalized people in the hood. Applying "hip hop as a way of life," the video suggests that all these actions are the same. Furthermore, such imagery mirrors those early days in the U.S. when practitioners used discarded records to scratch on, made sound systems from whatever resources were available, and fleeced electricity from light poles. Hip hop theater scholar Daniel Banks calls these practices making "something from something."[72] Rather than calling these innovations "something from nothing," as the adage goes, these children make "something" and interrogate notions of what is considered outcast waste within an economy that manufactures easily discarded and obsolete products in order consistently to market what is new. Such a shift, regarding children making things from other things, also allows viewers to see children as who they are: innovators and inventors. This moment in the video thus is not just about seeing hip hop as a normal part of children's lives but also about seeing the children as actors in artistic technology. Rap culture becomes a part of these inventions, an example of the technology that rejects capitalism's insistence on consuming goods and new products. These scenes demonstrate how children's fun, leisure, desires, and knowledge production can exist outside of consumer culture in affirmative ways.

Themes of defiance and compromise with an economic status quo often occur in the same contexts. In "Looking Up," this happens when Alisha Popat sings the hook to a young boy: "You got the power, just use it / Make a difference with what you have / Don't ever think that you're not worth it," and continues with "Believe in you / Dream that dream." The young child nods in affirmation, walks away, and performs a basic freeze, which is a breakdance move in which a dancer boosts themselves into a position and holds it, usually to the beat of the song that is playing. The dancer then returns to a standing position or transitions to another move. Here, the freeze occurs when the child does a handstand and bends his legs upside down, holding his body in an L position before lowering back down. Lyrics like Popat's commonly relate to how one can accomplish goals related to acquiring financial means, education, and a career.

Therefore, this moment could be read as hip hop's investment in capitalism. Popat is a Kenyan Indian with more racial and class privilege, and her instructions could be seen as insultingly and patronizingly informing a young African person with less access to resources to develop their potential agency. Before this specific scene, the boy is shown attempting to breakdance and then falling to the ground. Other taller (seemingly older) boys around him laugh and push him out of their way so that they can have their turn dancing. The older youths have an easier time hitting their moves than the smaller boy to whom Popat eventually speaks. The faulty implication here, too, is that the older boys represent the obstacles this young child faces in his life. A common discourse in Kenya puts forth the idea that youths without privilege need good role models in a context where gangs and other impoverished men are simply "bad examples" who encourage laziness, crime, and dropping out of school. This classist argument, of course, erases the larger systemic issues that all marginalized people encounter.

In addition to the problematic dynamic between Popat and the young child, this scene also encodes dance as an act of resistance. The young boy's breakdancing is a performance that seems to refuse the false logic of "work hard, get ahead." In this sense, breakdancing is a rejection of the status quo. In his defiance, hip hop embodiments become his answer to poverty. He and other abled children breakdance on the dirt, which yields no immediate benefit within a productive frame of labor, meaning that the space is seized and created for the playful and the performative. The children dance, smile, laugh, and move because they find joy in doing so. The excerpt illustrates that these embodiments offer a space to depart from the mainstream discourse on individual economic wealth subsequent to hard work, even when that discourse is found inside rap culture and, indeed, the song itself. The dynamic between the youth and Popat is yet another instance where the music can display the troublingly conformist and compellingly disruptive in the same scene, which, in this case, is the commitment to capitalist philosophy alongside its disruption of that same code.

Situating activities like Taamic's teaching and L-Ness's painting inside women's hip hop are instrumental to resisting the faulty perceptions that the music cannot be an appropriate life for women. For instance, several cismen artists told me that women have it hard as rappers because of their duties to raise families, which is supposedly their primary responsibility. For them, men do not have to share in the unpaid childrearing duties and can thus have time and space to make music. Rapper Ndugus laid the blame on society, family, and husbands/partners:

> [Women] face a lot of challenges, *like trying to convince people that this is what they live by*. Because in Kenya, when we were starting hip hop, our parents were like: . . . Will it really pay you? Will it help you feed your kids in the future? It's also complicated for females. Let's say at night they need to go to shows. You also find that a female is a married woman, and she has kids to take care of. They have a lot of challenges.[73] (emphasis mine)

Ndugus reaffirms the idea that women artists encounter the regular pressures to make money from hip hop and that their primary responsibility is supposedly to care for their families. In the video, instead of rejecting the label of women as caretakers, they embrace it. The beginning of the song has Sugar producing a gracious ode to her mother for her childrearing, and such practices also transpire when Alicia Popat encourages the breakdancing child and when Taamic educates the children in her outdoor class. This type of caretaking is usually not seen in videos of artists who are men and can easily slide into the gendering of labor. The women's presentation of motherhood-like care alongside rap lyrics and breakdancing suggests that these acts need not lie in juxtaposition. Rather, rappers can be parents and custodians of children as well as be cared for, as Sugar demonstrates with her gratitude toward her mother, all of which are exemplary of living hip hop.

"Looking Up" represents how women artists push for radical inclusivity in underground music, thus expanding who might be included in the "way of life" philosophy. While many cisgender men vocalize their acceptance of women, they often imagine themselves as hip hop's lookouts who determine who is accepted and who is not. Alternatively, women's ingenuities manage to intervene in and push up against the fabric of Nairobi's underground culture. For example, "Looking Up" shows parts of the hood that are often rendered too "abnormal," even for hip hop tales. In the middle of the song, a street child or boy, or *chokoraa*, holds the Looking Up sign. Street boys have notorious reputations in Nairobi. To stave off poverty and hunger, many buy shoe glue from street cobblers and inhale it. It is common to see street children affix glue bottles between their teeth as they walk, stand, or sit along busy roads and in lower-class neighborhoods. They often beg for money from middle-class people who walk within the city limits and are chased away by *askari*. When they are high, they can be aggressive and violent. For the most part, the lack of social nets, intergenerational poverty, and systemic disenfranchisement account for the pervasiveness of children who must live and survive on the streets. In Kenya's imaginary, the figure of the street child is the dirty, abject, and outcast, located outside of the boundaries of parental concern and societal welfare. Empathy for these young people is often in short supply from wealthier (even slightly well-off) Nairobians, and children who call the streets their home are often the focus of bile or apathy. In the past, there have been several governmental attempts at reform. In 2003, during Kibaki's rule, the administration reinstituted the National Youth Service, designed to provide education and job training to young people, especially street children.[74] This was welcome news in Nairobi, and in other urban areas as well. During one 2008 trip, I noticed a marked absence of street children in the city center. But by Kibaki's second term, this program ran ineffectively and, at times, not at all. During the Kenyatta presidency, two high-profile corruption scandals broke in 2015 and 2018, and reports indicated that huge amounts of funds were stolen from the program.[75] Relatedly, the World Bank–funded Kazi kwa Vijana (KKV) (work for the youth), headed by Raila Odinga, was a youth training program implemented after young unemployed men were blamed for the 2008 postelection violence. The World Bank pulled funding from KKV after it determined a misallocation of funds.[76] Many young people have since visibly returned to the streets, and their problems remain.

In this video, the street child's abject subject position does not preclude him from possessing enough humanity to appear in and participate in the music's narrative. During his scene, while he holds the Looking Up sign, he clutches a glue bottle in his mouth and gets high (or performs the act of doing so). Through his intractable intoxication, he, too, is afforded the ability to grasp onto a hope that, although unreasonably inequitable, most would see as unavailable to him. However, he stands alone in the video, like the other nonrapping adults who hold the sign. This child appears slightly older than the other small children who play and run throughout the video, breakdancing and hula-hooping. He is not afforded the space to play or explore these freedoms, presumably because his life is solemn and severe. If we consider Taamic's teaching to be a form of gendered care, he is excluded from that as well. The video situates him within the context of neoliberal, able-bodied adulthood, and he is positioned as someone who should take responsibility for his economic mobility. Though he does not receive nurture nor the opportunity to participate in leisure, as the other children do, his inclusion in the video is fascinating, given the reviled status of *chokoraa*.

In another embracing of the abject, flying toilets are also referenced. This occurs in the scene when L-Ness paints a large and colorful checkerboard of abstract shapes. Like the other artists, L-Ness's lyrics relate to the urgency of personal change and the basic understanding of class oppression. The following is a portion of her raps:

> Step up, stand up, rise up, sky's your limit /
>
> Badala ya kublend gizani light up a candle (Instead of blending in the dark, light up a candle) /
>
> Na look up kulingana na jinsi tunafinyanzwa (And look up in regard to how we are oppressed)[77]

In the upper left corner of her painting, the words Toilet with Wings appear in large lettering. This statement is a reference to the phenomenon of "flying toilets" in slum areas, where people who lack sanitation dispose of solid waste by wrapping it in plastic bags and throwing it onto rooftops.[78] Here, she participates in the many existing campaigns to end the practice, which can only be dissolved when people's lives change, including adding widespread sanitation infrastructures to residential areas. Nevertheless, she inserts the most uncomfortable truths of the hood experiences in this video.

Taking cues from L-Ness's painting, "Looking Up" operates as a performative bricolage that assembles those things that would not normally appear side by side: images of trash, references to waste, outcast street children, white people, and women rappers from a range of backgrounds. In much of this text, what is often repudiated exists alongside the artistic elements of the music. The performances of the street boy and references to flying toilets articulate how these artists embrace those things outside the bounds of what should be visible. These women artists do not present the hood in standard, often hackneyed ways, that is, by convincing viewers that the hood should be exhibited as a romanticized place of perseverance for only strong-willed and abled men. Instead, the video elucidates the unsavory and unspoken facts of people's marginality. While many men artists claim to speak for the dispossessed, these women artists have created a text that steps beyond the

FIGURE 7. Rapper L-Ness in the "Looking Up" video. Screenshot by author. Source: Dandora-Music, "Looking Up Rmx X 254 Female Rappers (Official Music Video)," YouTube, November 6, 2014, https://www.youtube.com/watch?v=w6PoSkSuDqU&t=2s.

rap canons and elucidates themes of the ghetto experience that have many times been rendered too uncomfortable to explicate.

In this video, the rappers understand that hip hop is a place of possibility for their expression and a site where they need to assert their agency as practitioners. Most women MCs will defend the culture while deliberately marking out a place for themselves. Woman hip hop artist and poet Amora made this point when I asked her if women face undue obstacles in rap settings:

> But that's everything. When it comes to men and women. Men always have a higher hand. Like if I give an example with Kenyan culture, back in the coastal region, they believe that a boy child should be educated to a certain level, very higher [*sic*] than a girl child. A girl child will reach like primary six, and that will be it.[79] And ah, a boy child should go to the university. A boy child should be the president. So, it's not only in hip hop. So everywhere, if you are a lady, you have to fight your way, yeah. You have to walk the extra mile to get what you want. It's not only in hip hop.[80]

Amora does not want the genre to bear the responsibility of societal sexism. Marcyliena Morgan correspondingly writes: "Most successful female MCs recognize that for them the only place where they can navigate race, class, gender, and sexuality with relative freedom is the hiphop world. It is not an ideal space but rather one populated by those searching for discourses that confront power."[81] Women make use of these far-from-idyllic spaces even when the music and culture are imbued with power inequalities that directly impact them. "Looking Up" and the women that perform it accomplish an expansive list of feats by using armored embodiments to activate knowledge while embracing the outcast, insisting that hip hop is life for women, interrogating sexisms, mucking through the tomboy figure, and offering a subtle challenge to wearisome neoliberal values. This cultivation of fireside knowledge "preserves and transfers women's logic, norms and values of nurturing, care, [and creates] solidarities and commons," which, for women rappers, allows them the space to make music.[82] The probing and imperfect practice of play is the centripetal force underlying and actuating most of these interventions, and rappers of marginalized genders insist upon the space to explore and create innovatively.

PLAY AND INTIMACY

Practitioners enact ludicity collectively with others. Tinkering with words, embodiment, space, sound, and diaspora produces a shared politics about rappers with similar musical and cultural goals. These embodiments of play can be the rehearsed intentional actions in front of a camera in making a video or the unprompted and subtle performances at events. Hip hop corporeality, which is both planned and banalized, intentional and impulsive, constructs a set of intensely and aesthetically powerful practices. Artists create culture alongside each other in intimate ways in attempts to locate themselves both inside and outside of economies of production and commerce. Jayna Brown notes the importance of intimacy in the Congolese music spaces she studies: "I stress the importance of music's connection to physical response, the utopian articulations of the body we find enacted in dance. It is our bodies as much as our souls that we seek to reclaim, or recover, despite the impossibility of restoration."[83] She writes of dance here, but this explanation could easily be applied to any bodily movement alongside musical sound. Moreover, the experiences referenced in this quote indicate contact with others aurally and physically in methods that are profoundly meaningful. Working from Brown, I want to stress that practitioners engage with each other to produce corporeal interventions that are collective as well as individually affective. Nairobi rap orature, which is ludic, masculinized, and serious, occurs in public spaces but produces sites of closeness and familiarity that artists and fans depend upon for evoking pleasure, subversiveness, and freeness.

Hip hop corporeality is in conversation with the city of Nairobi and wider society, as well as in specific spaces. One of the crucial sites artists have used to try out their shared embodiments and lyrical skills is the NGO Sarakasi Dome, where events have been highly competitive ecosystems. Most artists within the space toil amid adversity; only the few privileged and lucky move to the mainstream and formulate careers. There is a hustle-like work ethic at Sarakasi, and one must be quick and always prepared to take advantage of often fleeting and precarious events. Sarakasi is located just east of the city center and in the working-class area

FIGURE 8. Sarakasi Dome at the Hip Hop Fest, 2012. Photo by author.

of Ngara. Venues like this can serve either as the primary place where artists navigate their careers or as transit stops where the fortunate ones move on to radio and television airplay and receive endorsement deals. At these events, organizers, rappers, graffiti artists, and other participants receive small stipends through funding from Sarakasi. There are often vendors selling jewelry and occasional aspiring rappers selling CDs between performances and outside by the walls where graffiti artists are sanctioned to paint. Most artists cycle in and out of spaces like Sarakasi, using their learned skills to acquire other careers, perhaps remaining in the underground or sometimes leaving altogether. They will not readily admit that they have left the scene if asked; they just stop making music and showing up to events. The fact that not many artists leave the underground (or admit to departing), except when they make more money and move into the mainstream, works to solidify the sacredness of the underground.

Impermanence does not mean that rappers write off spots like Sarakasi or withdraw their participation. It is the opposite; artists make space and exploit any opportunities with the full knowledge that the events could be short-lived and their contributions fugacious. Within this space of transience, rappers develop a culture that is prepared, enduring, and potentially mobile, always ready to move to different physical sites. In the midst of such conditions, the opacities of play exist, and artists make do with what they have, which often generates evocative and nourishing interactions. During the open mic portion of the Hip Hop Fest in 2012, I observed two young men standing in the back of the performing hall. The audience had their attention on the freestyling performer rapping to a predetermined generic beat, and these two men stood together, one facing the other in proximity, while he rapped to the beat. As he rapped, he moved his body back and forth, his

FIGURE 9. Sarakasi Dome at the Hip Hop Fest, 2012. Photo by author.

hands performing an angled gesturing while his head bobbed to the music. Since it was an open mic, he could not have been rapping along with the performer's improvised lyrics. He, too, was freestyling, or perhaps he was rehearsing a song he had written. The other listening man stood facing the stage and bobbed his head to the music and his friend's raps. Occasionally, the rapper would briefly place his hand on his friend's shoulder, still rhyming. Neither of these two men ever took the stage to rap themselves during this event, never assuming rap's authoritative position as the live onstage performer. Perhaps this rapper was working up the nerve to perform during the open mic session; perhaps he was attempting to prove his deftness to secure a future gig, or maybe he was simply sharing the space with another person.

These participants exercised the ludic by hewing space out of an event that already welcomed the spirit of artistic freedom. They fashioned a moment of intimacy, even during the competitive spirit of the event at Sarakasi, which included rap battles. Additionally, the two individuals took ownership of whatever musical spatiality was available. The rapper held the self-assurance to refine his acuity somewhat publicly, and the listener stood supportively, moving slightly to the voiced montage. This interaction illustrates that the hip hop live show can operate as a portal for other types of performing, listening, and participating. Such an instance of sonic closeness, where only the comrade gazing upon the stage heard the rapper's words and where the rapper made listening demands upon the other, calls for our recognition. Inside of the on-stage freestyle was another space of independence where this practitioner made art on their own terms outside of any governing body, even the likeminded planners of the event, demonstrating a brief example of what Jayna Brown calls the "repossession of bodily freedoms."[84]

Hip hop intimacies also occur in planned performances. During another visit to Sarakasi that same year, I witnessed Sue Timon, who stood to the far left side of the hall and bobbed her head back and forth to the music. Again, rappers free-styled and tried out new songs during the open mic session, the Sarakasi Acrobats performed, and a talented beatboxer showed off his skills to a crowd that was awed by his abilities. Judge MC'd the event with impressive talent and an energy that kept the crowd meaningfully engaged, even when some of the actual performers were either beginners or lackluster. The atmosphere shifted when the group Washamba Wenza took to the stage. Although the hall had filled up, it was not exceptionally crowded, and people started moving and dancing more energetically. There were about seventy-five people in attendance, including the hip hop heads, vendors, and a few shoppers and devotees meandering around outside. Sue also became more enthusiastic, and even before the beat dropped, her body began to move back and forth to the rhythm of her head sways. Her arms lay to her side at one point, and she moved rhythmically to the raps, relying on her back-and-forth head-bobbing to communicate her connection to Washamba's performance. As she moved, her body pivoted around with expressions of intensity, looking at other audience members for affirmation of the collective experience. At one point, Sue put her arm up and moved it up and down rhythmically to encourage and pay respect to the performance. This is a familiar gesture in rap music culture, the moving of one's arm vertically as the rapper displays their lyrical abilities, and it communicates the audience member's knowledge of the song. The sound system was not equipped to handle the acoustics, and the space swallowed the lyrics while magnifying the music's heavy bass. The muffling of their wordplay did not stop Sue, nor the other audience members, who simply rapped along to the song's then often incomprehensible lines.

Sue is tall and slim, and her hair at the time was cut into a Mohawk surrounded by a close fade. She was one of the few women in attendance. Washamba transitioned to different songs, and Sue moved close to the stage to be right under the duo, grooving to the beats and moving excitedly. The climax of the performance occurred when Judge transitioned from MC to rapper when it was time to perform "Shupavu," a song that he collaborated on with Washamba Wenza, who includes Flamez, Smallz Lethal, Kev Mamba, and later Frank West (I analyze this song in chapter 4). A large crew of men rappers then gathered on the stage, showing support by dancing and gesturing. Washamba rapped and moved to the music, bending toward the crowd below them. Sue and others danced and grooved to the beat, allying themselves with the message. The crew onstage and the audience members right below them drew in close and built a sort of cypher as the rappers spit into the mic, shooting their lyrics into the speakers and beyond the huddled crew. Their stage energy was hardened and masculinized, with the audience producing energetic and rhythmic responses to the rappers' calls. Being one of only a handful of women did not faze Sue. Her presence differed vastly from the few others of marginalized genders and many other men who stood by, conversing with each other or observing quietly without offering any overt gestural presence.[85] Sue's shared experiences here, and with Flamez in their music video "Ulimi" (discussed in chapter 4), demonstrate how tough and playful performances often pull participants together in a shared space. Her moment with other cismen practitioners exemplifies the contradictory nature of gender in the underground. In conversations with me, some men vocalize their uneasiness about the role of masculine-performing women like Sue, while many have collaborated on work with such women.

The two men fans standing in the back of the hall sharing a close moment, as well as Sue Timon's participation in Washamba Wenza's stage act, are exemplary of how rappers insist on their subject positions by making or practicing hip hop through embodiment even when they are not central in the rap performance. These practitioners participated in the culture's exercise of gender by both disobeying and affirming the well-etched social codes within music-making processes through performances that, though particular, are also constructed as unremarkable. The ludic in these contexts involves making space through performance within a site that is contested but also relatively welcoming. Embodiments that are playfully dissident also comprise small and unconscious decisions about what rules rappers will cleverly forsake, resist, and infringe upon. These two stories about the ludic serve as evidence of how Sarakasi participants realize themselves as practitioners who are creating systems of knowability that are deeply dependent on their commonalities with others. Both instances illustrate "underground hip hop's capacity to blur distinctions between musicians and fans" through the sharing of a singular space.[86]

To return to Jayna Brown's discussion, musical sites do not simply put aside society's ills; instead, they take them on and make a space that cohabits with society's flaws in facilitating a sonically utopic vision. Her remarks about how music spaces in the DRC are not far removed from authoritarianism, bloodshed, and late capitalism are instructive for the Kenyan milieu because these Nairobi practitioners are unable to reckon with large economic forces that impede their music lives but find space within Sarakasi's walls for something different and new. Many are disillusioned by intergenerational underemployment and lack of access to the resources that some wealthier Kenyans take for granted. In turn, these rappers facilitate spaces where those urgencies hover and occupy but do not subsume them, employing the performative ludic and what Brown calls "bodily utopias, the rehabilitation of the body as a site of joy and exultation."[87] Hip hop culture uses ludicity to engage in the boundaries and borders present throughout Kenyan society. The music creates critical commentary about the wealthy and poor, women and men, the global and the local. The ludic orature of practitioners, fit with armored gender, engages with these dichotomies in both compliant and resistant ways. They exercise musical freeness through play and, in so doing, are able to enunciate their critiques of society while ensuring that their bodily performances remain dislodged from conformity, thus preventing them from wandering too close to officialdom. Even when this orature is short-lived and couched in the inequities of Kenyan settings, rappers use this persuasive modality to participate in expressive self-making.

3

Diaspora, Love, and Limits

When Sue Timon and I met, she greeted me with a pound hug. She grabbed my right hand and swung her left around my back, and I did the same, feeling a bit compelled. At the end of the shake, our fingers met and hung tight while our hands quickly moved downward before release. This gesture, known as a pound hug or a pound and a hug, is an embrace of familiarity between friends or comrades and is typically performed by masculine people. I possessed a certain type of bodily unaccustomedness since I do not typically perform this gesture, although I am familiar with it. Timon would later state during my interview with her that how artists greet each other is significant: "The greetings. 'Yeah, what's up?' Ah, there's this [U.S. rap] Southern thing, I don't know how they put it. 'How *we* do?' [Laughs.] There's that greeting part of the thing."[1] The phrase "How we do?" is not known to be associated specifically with Southern hip hop in the U.S., especially given West Coast rapper The Game's song of the same name. It is possible that Timon could have been referring to "What it do?," which is a phrase that emanates from the U.S. hip hop South. Nonetheless, Timon's references to U.S. Southern rap culture represent a larger and more significant pattern. Her embodiments displayed styled joviality and the seamless coupling of U.S. blackness with her understanding of the world as a Kenyan person. The coalescence of her words and performances demonstrates one of the many ways rap culture in Kenya and Africa produces ideas of diaspora. Kenyan artists use U.S. hip hop blackness to realize themselves as artists, to make music about Nairobi, and to produce notions of Africanity and Kenyanness.

In this chapter, I piece together the elements that constitute diaspora, Pan-Africanism, and love in the Nairobi underground, inspired by Sue's brief interaction with me during our conversation. These elements help rappers negotiate through divisive social conditions within the country and connect to hip hop's transnationality. As I laid out in the introduction, within African hip hop studies, many scholars explore how artists indigenized the music by abandoning English-only lyrics for rap bars in indigenous languages and by disavowing gangsta rap for politically salient sounds. There is more to be said about hip hop's engagement with what is largely referred to as the "global" and what I identify as a Black diasporic performance politics. For example, Caroline Mose observes that Nairobi rap draws on globally practiced traditions, like swag and street cred. Drawing from Murray Foreman, she briefly writes of Nairobi's connectivity to blackness within hip hop: "The city is seen through an expanded vision of Blackness, where an international Black tradition is manifested in the local space; local and national borders are erased, and the city becomes an extension of a global Black experience."[2] Though she mentions street cred and swag as performances, most of her instances asserting Nairobi's formations of blackness are lyrical, and it is from here that I build on Mose through my attention toward orature. This chapter explores how diaspora is profoundly evident in the orature of artists—how the linguistic, the embodied, and the sonic converge with other characteristics contained within music videos and live performances.

A hip hop diaspora in Nairobi is made up of four key points. First, I identify that a collective and public political love is a dominant theme in the music that undergirds diaspora. This political love does not fit neatly into a local-global binary and occurs in hip hop flow throughout the lyrics, sounds, and movements. Political love serves as a framing device and creates space for how ideas of diaspora circulate throughout the culture. It is most readily identifiable through lyrics, community initiatives, and the way rappers discuss why they make the music they do. Political love is both a local production of Kenyan sensibilities and a participation in a larger imagined global culture. When Sue Timon greeted me as an old acquaintance, she enacted an assumed commonality of love for and devotion to the music. Although we had not met before, that did not matter to Timon because she felt compelled to communicate with me through an embodied language of hip hop blackness (although the pound hug exists outside of the culture as well). The affection she presented to me was not just individualized (between us) but a broad gestural nod meant to identify the commonalities between two devotees from different parts of the world. In essence, her brief action demonstrated the local practice of a globalized music culture.

Second, Nairobi hip hop diaspora is composed of interpreted notions of U.S. blackness, which may be explicit references to the U.S. or more subtle citations. As previously stated, diasporic blackness operates as an indigenizing force by allowing practitioners to root the music in their own localities. Like Sue Timon's gesture, it is often embodied performance, materializing as ludic and masculinized. Furthermore, hip hop diasporic blackness dynamically draws in other forms of Afrodiasporic cultural characteristics. I depart from scholars like Marc Perry, who identifies the ways that artists perform the culture through lyrics and aesthetic bodily style, resulting in the specific creation of an Afro-Atlantic diasporic blackness. He references South Africa, Cuba, and Brazil, noting, "Blackness, as such, becomes a transnational site of identification and self-making; one made most immediately tangible for many diasporic youth by way of hip hop."[3] Perry argues that this music diaspora draws on multiple sites of blackness throughout the Atlantic world: "Diasporic rather than U.S. understandings of blackness are in the end instrumental in fashioning critical expressions of black Brazilian self."[4] I contend that hip hop diasporic blackness is fundamentally rooted in U.S. notions, even while artists draw on and devise modes of blackness and Africanity that digress from the U.S. Perry notes how rappers use figures like Malcolm X, baseball caps from American teams, and baggy pants. He states that Brazilian rappers Consciencia Urbana drew on how U.S. rap used Malcolm X's radical positionality and reconfigured him to be a global and diasporic figure in their project, thus exemplifying its diasporic blackness. However, such moves by Urbana depend upon recognizing that American hip hop first engaged with Malcolm X, a dominant figure in the U.S. Black struggle, even as he turned his politics globally outward. While we must recognize the diverse ways artists play with notions of diaspora, hip hop, no matter where it is located, always contains a persistent, originary U.S. blackness.

Third, Nairobi's hip hop diasporic blackness lays the foundation for profound notions of Pan-Africanist sensibilities that draw significant cultural connections within Africa and places outside of the U.S. Nairobi artists recognize and celebrate their Africaness not in opposition to a ubiquitous blackness but because of it. Moreover, the music's Pan-Africanism allows Nairobi artists to celebrate uniquely Kenyan musical contributions alongside other African cultural elements. Both the diasporic blackness and Pan-Africanism in Nairobi music are always a gesture back to the local, and, in fact, these characteristics say more about on-the-ground politics and realities than they do about anything beyond Kenya's borders. Through examining two songs, Nafsi Huru, NJE, and Kevlexicon's "Still Strong" and Mic Crenshaw, Khusta, Ran-D, Judge, and MC Bagol's "Amandla," I identify how ideas of diasporic blackness and Pan-African sensibilities appear through Kenyan lenses, which grounds the music as a local and indigenized production of the global. Specifically, relying on Nairobi as an international city of commerce, rappers paint it as a place of economic, political, and cultural motion, where they imagine themselves at the center of this motility. Inspired by Soyica Diggs Colbert, who discusses that movement is about not staying in one place, whether physically, socially, or politically, I contend that rappers align hip hop's physical motility with the various political movements they may reference throughout the African diaspora.[5] While these songs seek to transcend national boundaries through diaspora and Pan-Africanism, they use the globality inherent in hip hop to respond to the local and closely felt state violence and repression in Kenya.

Last, Nairobi practitioners do not accept all forms of hip hop blackness they encounter. Most position their work as separate and oppositional to gangsta rap and thug subjectivities, which both fans and critics widely reference. Artists understand the figure of the gangsta or thug as incompatible with their versions of diasporic blackness, Pan-Africanism, and political love. For most artists, this figure is antithetical to the objectives of social change and wades too far outside of political seriousness, and many see it as a way to be further discounted by critics. In the U.S., the gangsta or thug has been seized by hip hop and is rendered a masculinized and romanticized antihero who participates in illicit economies and eschews societal hatred of Black men.[6] In Kenya, the thug is not necessarily glamorized, emerging during colonialism to name Africans as unruly and criminal and continues to the present day to label them as intrinsically and ferociously lawless and violent.[7] Nairobi rappers, thus, depend on this figure and its meaning in Kenya to state affirmatively what work they do *not* do, and criticism and dismissal of the gangsta or thug helps artists define their music. The widescale jettisoning of this trope in the underground means that not every characteristic of the U.S. suffices and that artists vet what is functional to produce their aesthetic interventions. Marc Perry is informative to this point, demonstrating how early South African rappers, looking to defy apartheid's racial categories, employed the music to create a "recuperative notion of a black Africanness."[8] Despite the significant racial and ethnic differences between South Africa and Kenya, the notion that rappers produce African formations of blackness—which, I argue, cite the U.S.—applies to the Kenyan scene, as these artists do not abandon affiliation with their ethnic communities or their identities as Kenyan and African, but rather incorporate modes of blackness into their embodied performances. If at all, artists rarely and briefly integrate notions of the gangsta or thug into their work. Here, I rely on conversations with several artists and a reading of Evaredi's video, "Ukweli," which briefly references the thug persona. I contend "Ukweli"'s overarching themes of Pan-Africanism and the art of the struggle work to undo the troubling histories of the term thug and participate in creating masculine-centered notions of diaspora.

For the final section, I do a close read of the 2010 Kenyan documentary *Ni Wakati*. The artists profiled from the U.S. and Kenya are invested in arguing that hip hop has African roots and thus is fundamentally African. However, in attempting to put forward this concept, they inadvertently affirm how U.S. blackness is an unremitting signal for the music, upholding my central point that all hip hop is rooted in a negotiated U.S. blackness, however slight or abstract. Using this film, I maintain that artists engage in an ongoing citational practice with the U.S. that grounds the ways they imagine and perform a masculinized underclass diaspora. Taken together, the examples laid out in this chapter articulate how cisgender men are the unspoken appointed drivers of a diasporic transnationality in the music.

POLITICAL LOVE

Political love is an indispensable theme in Nairobi hip hop on its own terms and through its connectedness to diaspora. It serves as a staging ground for articulations of diaspora because it moves artists past boundaries and creates openings for them to connect with others outside of socially constructed categories. Rap's continual references to love are not just about fondness toward the music; rather, they are about a deeply entrenched affection utilized by rappers to prove their innate and undying commitment to the music culture, to Kenyans, and often to Africana peoples at large. Such sentiments mark out connections that allow artists to produce various subjectivities about what it means to be Black, Kenyan, a part of their respective ethnic community, and African. Therefore, this political love operates in two ways: to attend to local realities in Kenya about how to create a culture and to connect artists to a global imagined hip hop community. Such a sentiment mirrors Keguro Macharia's insistence on a type of love that enables transformative ideas and actions. He writes that love can be holistic: "an embedding, a valuing, a possibility, a 'risking,' a demand."[9]

Political love serves to indigenize music and locate it within Kenyan contexts while also allowing artists to create music outside of the bounds of a society that often rigidly defines difference. When artists delve deep into their neighborhoods, critiquing poverty and inequalities, love is applied as a guiding principle. This enthusiasm and commitment solidify the authenticity of practitioners and espouse a basis for music-making that claims to better Kenyan society. During the emergence of the genre in Kenya, Ukoo Flani Mau Mau (UFMM) established love as a guiding element in their music, as their name stands for "Upendo Kwote, Ole Wenu Ombeni Funzo La Aliyetuumba Njia Iwepo," meaning "love everywhere, woe unto you, seek the teachings of the creator for there to be a way." Mickie Koster observes that UFMM's notions of love are tied to social change: "The group [aimed] to help use love and the power of the Creator as a force for equality and justice."[10] Many artists have come to reference *upendo kwote* (love everywhere) in songs and everyday speech, so much so that it has become a cliché. The phrase's wide reach has led many to rely on the well-worn theme to provide homage to UFMM's work. During interviews, several artists phrase-dropped *upendo kwote* in casual speech as a basic way of describing how their music is in conversation with the culture of the underground. In so doing, these practitioners both acknowledged UFMM as the inventor of political love and established *upendo kwote* as a guiding principle that has created a sustaining culture.

Artists additionally use ideas of love for self-making, seeing themselves as part of a larger global community. Woman rapper and spoken word artist Amora insisted, "You don't have to be Black or white to do hip hop. You don't have to be a certain tribe to do hip hop. Hip hop itself is a culture of its own. . . You're a chick, you're a dude, you're gay, you're not gay; it doesn't matter. As long as you have the culture in you."[11] The music's connection to U.S. blackness does not mean that artists of other races are excluded, as many rappers envision a culture informed by blackness, but that can and does comprise people of different races. Statements like these exemplify how affiliation and devotion to rap music and culture allow artists to transcend how the state politicizes ethnicity and identity. Furthermore, hip hop investments emerge from the artistic soul, causing a love dedicated to resistance, artistic creativity, and enlightened consciousness.[12] Self-worth is often measured in terms of how authentic an artist is, which may appear limiting, but the impactful feelings of adoration that artists have for the music reflect their value as people who make culture. Amora's sentiment seeks to address, but does not settle, the problems that women face. Nevertheless, many share her opinions and recognize how hip hop earnestly attempts to reconcile unequal social differences. Rappers root their enduring honor of music in their souls and then move beyond the self toward community and diaspora.

Political love articulates political seriousness, creating credibility and legitimacy within the terrain of Nairobi music. To dispel the constant criticisms, they proclaim, "I do it for the love." With this phrase, along with *upendo kwote*, artists disregard the claim that they copy American music, allowing them to insist on their place within an imagined global music community. Some rappers attempt to fight off imitation claims by stating that it is impossible to imitate an inherently African style. Even for those who root hip hop as something that arrived externally, love is an indigenization device that allows them to argue that the music is now Kenyan and is situated in the creative soul of artists. Many recognize that they are viewed as imitators and mention their intrinsic affection for and participation in transnational rap culture to buffer themselves from outside criticisms. Such self-making is more than resisting disapproval; it is also tied to how one sees oneself within larger social categories of Africanity, blackness, and Kenyanness. Sue Timon raps in her (and Flamez's) song "Ulimi," that love is the basic element that undergirds hip hop's cultural mobilization: "Mi naifanya juu ya mapenzi /na hii silaha mdomoni / kama kijana mkoloni" (I do (hip hop) out of love / with the weapon in my mouth, this tongue / like a colonized boy/girl/youth).[13] Timon sees herself as a force resisting the legacies of colonial rule. Not wanting to ingest the harmful ideologies of the remains of British domination, Timon fosters political love to develop rhymes that resist. Lyrics like this undergird how rappers understand their place as cultural practitioners in a postcolonial world.

Artists realize themselves as legitimate actors and employ love to counteract claims that Kenyan rap is unimaginative mimicry and to reinforce their authenticity and authority to enter and help create a global diaspora. The culture's cultivation of love is used to solidify Kenya's participation in revolutionary traditions that exist within hip hop's diasporic music. Underground rap is also juxtaposed with the intentions of commercial music, which many rappers believe is void of meaning. Evaredi explained the following in my discussion with him:

> But underground hip hop, I can say, is like when *you do it for the love.* You do it from your heart. Like you are doing it for the people. You're doing it for the correct way. Not basically because of the money. . . . But when you say commercial music, it's like you'll do it for some time, get your money, move on. Yeah.[14] (emphasis mine)

To make his point, he compared his reasons for rapping to the motivations behind mainstream music. Of course, artists in underground settings still need to make money, which Evaredi acknowledged when I pressed the issue. Still, most rappers do not want to abandon the principles of social change and activism to acquire economic mobility. According to underground rappers, commercial artists are vacuous and money-driven and cannot hold *upendo kwote* in their hearts. I also asked many artists about the regular presence of commercial songs with socially conscious messaging, which they laughed off, proclaiming that such songs do not stifle their critiques. Instead, mainstream artists who rap or sing about societal problems are seen as fleecing from the culture's core values and are thus considered inauthentic, a topic that I address in chapter 4.

Hip hop's ethic of love serves as a very localized answer to the continual reiterations of polarizing notions of ethnicity in Kenya. Ethnicity is not the problem, but rather the ways state actors have historically hijacked it to consolidate political power, and this dynamic has long plagued the country. In the recent past, for example, the postelection violence in 2007–8 should be seen as a culmination of fracturing and enflamed tensions rather than as a unique moment in time. This violence marked the second term of Mwai Kibaki, who was sworn in amid a highly disputable victory in December 2007. That night, Kalenjin, Luo, and Luhya groups, supposedly funded by Raila Odinga and William Ruto, began to attack Kikuyu businesses in the Rift Valley.[15] These events started a series of retaliatory attacks, whereby Kikuyu groups fought against Kalenjin, Luo, and Luhya militias, committing acts of violence and killing people from those communities. Likewise, Kalenjin, Luo, and Luhya militias and informal youth groups hunted down and killed Kikuyus and burned houses and other buildings. Uhuru Kenyatta went on trial at the ICC, charged with giving resources to groups like Mungiki, which is a largely Kikuyu organization and street gang, to retaliate against Luo and Kalenjin communities. Likewise, Ruto's allegations included funding Kalenjin groups to purposely hunt down and kill Kikuyus.[16] All charges were eventually dropped due to witness intimidation and lack of evidence.[17]

After the bloodshed, artists famously came together to form the Hip Hop Parliament, using a call for love as the solution to how the country had been torn apart.[18] Angela Wainaina, Muki Garang, Judge, Buddha Blaze, Mwafrika, and Roje Otieno were among the artists who convened and held concerts calling for reconciliation and ending all brutalities. When former UN Secretary-General Kofi Annan arrived in Kenya to mediate a power-share between the two presidential candidates, Mwai Kibaki and Raila Odinga, the Hip Hop Parliament wrote and delivered a Declaration of Unity to Annan.[19] This action solidified how the artists envisaged themselves as legitimate political actors whose power rested in their separateness from the treacheries of the Kenyan state. The declaration espoused that while leaders have fanned ethnic flames, rappers have long used their voices to inspire commonality, equity, and welfare for others. Their solution was not to privilege one ethnic language over the other but to promote Sheng as the official inclusive language of hip hop culture. Though spoken throughout the country by people of all ages, there are neighborhood-specific Shengs in Nairobi, and lower-class urban young people are responsible for its consistent production of new words.[20] Sheng has come to signify poor urban youth, and its use in the document affirms its presence in hip hop culture. The document disdained violence of any kind, stated that women and men stood as equals, and denounced what is regularly referred to as "tribalism," which is the pernicious manipulation of ethnicity for political and economic benefit. Bluntly stated, the group's campaign was "Ukabila ni taifa killer" (Ethnicity is a nation killer), which may seem like a strong statement. However, these artists responded to the crisis of the moment and how political leaders have historically woven ethnicity into the practices of manipulating its populace. Like songs and music videos, the declaration was another hip hop text originating from the underground, demonstrating the culture's political seriousness and exemplifying how rap practitioners offer solutions to social problems.

Rappers' incorporation of their personal ethnic affiliations in the music is a careful project, especially because of the politicization of ethnicity. While many use notions of Africanity and hip hop blackness to produce the commonalities of love and diaspora, most rappers only reference their ethnic communities in their music if doing so does not challenge their overall mission to promote lower-class solidarities. Artists have long been aware of the volatile climate that surrounds ethnicity and power and are careful to ensure that their content does not contribute to the politicization of difference that has become too regular. Many often avoid discussing their identificatory markers if explicitly asked, as Esther Milu recounts in her study. Rappers often told her they were "Pan-African" or Mkenya (Kenyan) or would not say.[21] I did not ask this question in my research, yet many rappers volunteered to state their ethnic community. In addition to seeing me as an unknowing outsider, I attribute their openness to the fact that I did not explicitly ask about where they were from, which may have led them to believe that I was unbothered or unconcerned with the topic. It is possible that Milu's direct questioning gave the impression that she was attempting to form conclusions about artists based on this social category, which caused the artists to avoid answering. Nonetheless, Milu's accounts highlight that artists want to be acknowledged for their contributions to Kenya's music culture, as well as a larger Pan-African ethos, rather than be enclosed in a set of historical indicators, especially given the tense ethnic climate that waxes and wanes around elections and other political moments.[22]

Since ethnicity can often be seen as a marker of privilege or, alternatively, as an indicator of disempowerment, celebrating an ethnic identity is a tricky, but not impossible, task in the underground. One imperative that a shared diaspora calls for is not the elimination of difference but rather the expulsion of ethnic particularities that can fracture a community. For example, artists from Kikuyu communities are much less likely to reference their ethnicity in music, due to the history of state power. Out of five presidents and the over forty ethnic groups in Kenya, Jomo Kenyatta, his son Uhuru, and Mwai Kibaki are from Kikuyu communities. Daniel arap Moi and newly elected president William Ruto are Kalenjin.[23] Since independence, presidents have created ethnic blocs of power, monopolizing resources and placing allies from their communities in high governmental positions. Jomo Kenyatta's Kikuyu nationalist state enabled politically connected elites to buy former white settler land and take government positions, arguably resulting in what Jeni Klugman calls the "kikuyuization" of the country.[24] Kibaki created what was termed the "Mount Kenya Mafia," a small group of politicians he turned to for support from the Kikuyu, as well as the related Meru and Embu communities.[25] Uhuru Kenyatta grew his family's secreted wealth by solidifying monopolies on milk and creating opportunities for income generation in timber, banking, and construction.[26] It should be known that Moi conducted a similar practice by enabling land sales and providing government posts to connected and loyal Kalenjins. These exercises of ethnicized state power bleed into social and economic spaces, as evidenced by several instances of violent ethnic clashes and conflicts.[27] Therefore, what it means to be Kikuyu in public space and the historic and politicized meanings of such identification can be fraught, even for those from working-class backgrounds, and this translates to many artists avoiding the mention of Kikuyu ethnicity. Moreover, regardless of the community that rappers hail from, many avoid this topic because of the divisiveness it engenders and the possibility that it undercuts both an aspired egalitarianism and a political love.

To promote love, artists must find a workable balance in which the celebration or naming of ethnicity does not feed into the destabilizing ethnic atmosphere that often materializes in Kenya. In some circumstances, they are willing to use ethnicity in their music. For example, Judge's song "Mad Jaluo" references his Luo identification, and he also has drawn on blackness, as his former group with his brother was Black Duo. The duo Wakamba Wawili, of which rapper Agano is a part, named themselves after their community, as the name means "two Kambas." Rapper Ekori often raps in Turkana and seeks to resolve entrenched conflicts in the northeastern region. Many of his songs have addressed struggles over resources among Turkana, Pokot, and Daasanach communities.

While some artists do identify as Black or African *and* as a part of their ethnic community, I believe that spending too much time on *how they identify* does not give credence to the more accurate and imperative questions of *what they do, how they perform*, and *what they rap about*. Underground Nairobi rappers often seek out ideas of blackness and Africanity, typically alongside their respective ethnic identities. These explorations can be described as what Jennifer Nash calls "affective politics" or how "bodies are organized around intensities, longings, desires, temporalities . . . and how these affects produce political movements."[28] Nash uses affective politics to enunciate the "Black feminist love-politics" that have long been present in the U.S., similar to the deep collective sentiment of political love found in Kenya's hip hop. Both focus on what culture workers do rather than on how they identify. The motivation to recognize people as makers of serious, creative, and subversive works allows one to see artists beyond their identities, often not the artists' focus. Instead, concentrating on what practitioners do allows one to regard them as holistic producers of music culture.

DIASPORA MOVES

In Nairobi hip hop, diasporic blackness enables the flow of music from the U.S. to Africa, and then from Kenya outward. It is the fixture that artists use to tell stories about the specificities of Kenyan cultural life. Embodied performances that exude diaspora are often indecipherable, unpredictable, and rhythmic, allowing rappers to do their part to create an imagined global community. Here, I bring together Soyica Diggs Colbert and Paul Zeleza to consider how the music actualizes diaspora. Zeleza proposes that the musical relationships between Africa and its diasporas are best described not by a dynamic and contemporary (western) diaspora and a fixed and always borrowing Africa but as historically multidirectional cultural exchanges within the continent, between diasporas and the continent, and within diasporas.[29] Zeleza's argument that Africa participates in developing dynamic and diverse musical styles in conversation with other continental music and those outside Africa allows us to consider how diaspora in Nairobi hip hop appears as a vigorous performative method, not a passive recipient practice. Soyica Diggs Colbert explores how various U.S. Black culture workers use embodied performance in the post–civil rights era to contest the ways that blackness marks social and physical death and to create notions of freedom and political sensibilities.[30] Colbert identifies how performers and writers foster "webs of affiliation," which draw on past performances to articulate desire and liberation. Colbert's theory of "webs of affiliation" is useful in thinking about how hip hop embodies ideas of diaspora. While rappers facilitate musical networks that connect themselves with Kenyan history, they are also invested in contemporary meaning-making that pulls from U.S. blackness, past and present Pan-Africanism, and a variety of the culture's signifiers, places, music styles, and artists. Placing Colbert and Zeleza together, I identify how embodiments in Kenyan underground music reveal a vibrant assertion

FIGURE 10. Rapper Nafsi Huru in the trailer for the "Still Strong" music video. Screenshot by author. Source: Kevlexicon, "Still Strong—Musa Aka Nafsi Huru and Kevlexicon," YouTube, January 22, 2012, https://www.youtube.com/watch?v=aMQSVPP8g4c.

of ideas of freeness through movement by proffering paradigms of diaspora and African agency.

The movement-based themes in "Still Strong" create Nairobi as a global city that artists use to demonstrate diaspora and Pan-Africanism. This song is by Nafsi Huru, white American rapper Kevlexicon, and Kenyan R&B singer NJE. The music video displays scenes outside the Kenyatta International Conference Centre (KICC), which sits on Harambee Road near Jogoo House, the Kenya National Archives, Jomo Kenyatta University of Agriculture and Technology (JKUAT), and the upscale Stanley Hotel. The building's architecture is slim and tall, with a lid at the very top. Several governmental offices are located at the KICC, but it also symbolizes Kenya's internationality, often hosting concerts by African artists, entrepreneurial events, and academic conferences. The KICC is located in the middle of the Central Business District and is a symbol of Kenya's participation in the global economy. In the music video, the structure is the backdrop to young people roller-skating in circular formations, hanging out, smiling, laughing, sitting together, and bouncing back and forth as Nafsi and Kevlexicon rap. There are several other artists in the video, for example, Judge, Amora, and Karpchizzy. When I spoke with him years after the project, Nafsi fondly mentioned that watching it reminds him of a family reunion.[31]

The "Still Strong" video is comparably more leisured than other texts about hood life, and even still, it pairs the necessary political seriousness with the vitality of ludicity. When artists make music videos demonstrating harsh realities, their embodiments, in turn, appear comparatively more hardened and armored, conveying that they are equipped to navigate the streets and to say something meaningful through lyrics about life in poor settings. In the "Still Strong" video, however, the rappers are not in the hood, and their embodiments appear more leisured and carefree, but their creative objectives continue to exist within the lexicon of underground activist-themed music. At the beginning of the video, a flash of light appears, and the scene transitions from a color setting in front of the KICC to a black-and-white blurred shot with five or so men throwing up Black power fists, which summons a history of activism that is still marshaled for present-day confrontations of injustice. The men's faces are indistinct and grainy, but the gesture is clear. The juxtaposition of roller-skating and clenched fists indicates that the force of the song and the playful themes belong alongside each other. While Black power fists evoke a focused solemnity, these clenched hands appear within a context of ludicity. The raised fists are reminders that playfulness is always indexed within the intensity of struggle in the underground. In this video, resistance resides within the context of joy and pleasure, with its momentary and fleeting reminders of a more expansive and transnational struggle for the freedom of Afrodiasporic peoples.

"Still Strong" tells the story of how Nairobi holds unique diasporic elements. It has a smooth melodic flow and does not contain the sense of urgency that we hear in other songs that visually, performatively, sonically, and orally recall the inequalities of ghetto life. NJE delivers synthesized reggae vocals, and together with Nafsi Huru and Kevlexicon's raps, there is a harmonic union of different voices. Nafsi adds to the diasporic tendencies in verse: "Dunia nzima utazunguka kwote utatupata tupo tupo, pale pale, mambo yetu, yale yale! Irie! Irie!"[32] Some of the force of this line is lost in the English translation. For instance, the last part has alliterations and rhymes and is best appreciated when listening to the song: "tupo tupo, pale pale, mambo yetu, yale yale! Irie! Irie!" Nafsi raps quickly using the rhyming words *pale* and *yale*, participating in the African diasporic practice of repeating words for emphasis. The lyric roughly translates to "You'll go around the whole world and find us at the same place! Our stuff! Same stuff! *Irie! Irie!*" The repetitive, alliterative nature of *tupo, pale,* and *yale,* along with the quick delivery, makes the lyric difficult to understand, almost indecipherable, yet it is also a creative and witty moment in the song. *Dunia nzima,* which translates to "whole world," appears in the same line as "Irie! Irie!" *Irie* is a well-known Jamaican or Rastafarian word meaning "I am at peace with myself." It is also a greeting that means "I am fine/well/cool." It is similar to several Swahili responses to greetings used in Kenya, such as *poa, fiti,* and *mzuri / nzuri.* Nafsi's use of *irie* is a signifier of Jamaican music's long influence in Kenya and the similar cultural position of reggae and underground rap.[33] Both genres are known as types of hood music that signify working-class people and experiences, and artists occasionally do collaborative work with reggae musicians and the genres share venues in Nairobi.

During his raps, Nafsi rhythmically shifts back and forth to the beat of the song while rotating around the camera to promote his affirmative confidence and disaffected coolness. His movements are rhythmic, engaging, and energetic, wherein the embodiment exudes an unfazed deportment from any external pressures seeking to criticize him. He confidently proclaims "Mi ni mtemi!" (I spit, or I flow).[34] The force of the moment is in the way he articulates "mtemi," placing the emphasis on *te*, following Swahili grammar.[35] As he says the phrase, he lunges slightly at the camera with his chest out and then bobs quickly back and forth before moving to the next lyric. Nafsi's legitimacy is born from and within his oratured rap flow, wherein his mastery of style connects him to a community of rappers in Nairobi and an imagined diaspora. He maintains a cool control, putting *irie* into action. He draws on similarities between *irie* and Kenyan words, thus making *irie* local and a part of the local and global formations of hip hop. The music video's camera moves around Nafsi, allowing him to own the space that his lyrics and performances produce. At times, it is more important for the lyrics, rhyme, or beat to induce affective pleasure than for the song to embody a set of complete ideas. Nafsi's lyrics transmit the common objective in rap culture, which is not to be comfortably legible but instead to create artful expressions open to interpretation. The use of different elements like Sheng, Jamaica's *irie*, and Black references creates what Glissant calls Creolization, which is "a perpetual movement of linguistic interpenetrability."[36] This intentional untranslatability, whether in the body or lyrics, is not the same as unknowability. Instead, these enactments of clever sharpness converge Pan-Africanism and hip hop blackness and demonstrate the capacity to use rap bodies in tune with music, thus authorizing themselves as cultural producers.

These performativities are globally recognizable in and out of rap communities, with their meanings not easily describable. Imani Perry writes, "incomprehensibility is . . . a protective strategy" in hip hop, stating that "the lack of clarity . . . represents struggle against the repressiveness of traditional literariness in terms of content, censorship, and more important, in terms of the limitations tradition imposes on structural innovation."[37] When the power of corporeality appears inside the music, these performances open possibilities that perhaps defy straightforward description. Practitioners aim for this incomprehensibility by inserting hidden meanings, rapping quickly, or shifting the meanings of words. This intentional obscurity appears in gestures and stances, whereby most rappers seek to dodge the normative mechanisms that are in place in Kenya. Bodily movements that aim for intentional obscurity, such as Nafsi's, allow practitioners to resist, counter, and avoid repressive political and economic conditions, if only temporarily or symbolically.

The motility of diaspora is put forth as a solution to state corruption and violence and the poverty the artists attribute to inept governance. Its commitment to educating listeners about social issues that impact vulnerable communities is never far from oratured ludicity and the diasporic articulations in Nairobi rap.

The pleasure that Nafsi finds in his movements exists in the context of societal difficulty. Kevlexicon raps the following:

> Robbing the Ministry of Education is dumb and politics is get a buck and run /
>
> *MPs wana mashilingi mingi lakini wananchi broke* (MPs have a lot of money while the citizens are broke) /
>
> *Nje ya mtaa watoto bila hope, kuna stress kwamba tunavuta cess for re-cess* (Outside in the hood, children are hopeless, there is stress, we smoke cess [taxes] as we are taxed again and again)[38]

Kevlexicon's lyrics are meant to speak to the locality of incompetent Kenyan governance, used as a basis of political solidarity across boundaries. Halifu Osumare names lyrics like these "connective marginalities," which exemplify the "reality of extant social inequalities that link youths internationally through hip-hop culture."[39] The need for diasporic connections often begins with a common dissent about local governance, poor economic conditions, and the state's apathy toward disenfranchised youth. Throughout the video, Kevlexicon's lyrics are accompanied by footage of beaming and laughing young people who demonstrate freedom and joy through diasporic movements that work to counteract the realities of a failed state polity and their economic disempowerment. Joy in the midst of struggle is not a less mighty form of seriousness; it is instead one more way rappers forge a method of love and diaspora within harsh conditions.

Diaspora does not mean the space is always exclusively Black or African. Kevlexicon is a white rapper, historian, and filmmaker from New Jersey who has collaborated with other underground practitioners.[40] For instance, in the music video "Tumechoka," he teamed up with several Kenyan artists, including Ekori, L-Ness, and Skobo. It is notable that in a cultural cityspace where rappers are regularly tagged as imitators, Kevlexicon, as someone who is not Black or African, is never labeled as such, which is a testimony to how privileged whiteness allows him to escape the identifier of mimic. Daphne Brooks, who writes about U.S. Black women's music, is instructive in identifying this dynamic: "That which is 'authentic' and 'original' is made by white men. That which is mimetic and lacks innovation is made by everyone else."[41] Kevlexicon's place in hip hop reminds us how the marker of cultural mimic is leveled toward those who are already rendered marginalized or othered and rarely toward those who sustain or embody power. It is also important to note that white, light-skinned, and racially ambiguous people are regularly present as extras and collaborators both in mainstream Kenyan music videos and in the underground world. In songs such as "Still Strong," what comes through most forcefully is a spirit of collaboration and an understanding of shared politics among artists. They all uphold the powerful testimonies conveyed through love and political seriousness, and for these artists, the fact that Kevlexicon is white and American is less important than a set of mutual political beliefs.

The song and video "Amandla" illustrate a transnational collaboration that articulates a hip hop Pan-Africanism, affirming the same diasporic articulations of movement and openness in "Still Strong." "Amandla" accomplishes several objectives: it highlights the dynamic linkages of diaspora by explicitly recuperating U.S. blackness as a part of Africanity; it sees Kenyan music traditions, often regarded as static and fixed, as part of the globality of hip hop; and it presents diaspora as a symbolic remedy to the conditions of the poverty of informal settlements. These are instances of what Nadine George-Graves calls "diasporic spidering," expressed as "the multidirectional process by which people of African descent define their lives [and] the lifelong ontological gathering of information by going out into the world and coming back to the self."[42]

The song's artists are Mic Crenshaw from the U.S., Khusta from South Africa, and Ran-D, Judge, and MC Bagol, all from Kenya. The song is part of the Afrikan Hiphop Caravan, a collective of artists from South Africa, Zimbabwe, Senegal, and the U.S., among other countries. One of the founders of the Caravan is Soundz of the South (SOS), a collective that describes itself as antisexist, anarchist, and anti-racist. Beginning in 2004, SOS, along with other activist groups in Africa rooted in resistance to neoliberalism, consumer culture, and authoritarianism, poured these philosophies into various phases that worked to provoke their hip hop activism. These artists have traveled around the continent, providing concerts and producing music videos, exercising "horizontal organising based on principles of direct participatory democracy."[43] In Nairobi, the Caravan put on shows in 2013 at the Goethe-Institut and 2014 at the British Council. In 2017, the Caravan released an album that cited several social issues: the xenophobic violence in South Africa and Mozambique, U.S. police brutality against Black people, the disappeared anti-Mugabe journalist Itai Dzamara, and the charges against the rappers and activists who have come to be known as the Angola 15.[44] The Nairobi rappers' alliance assists the Afrikan Hiphop Caravan in spreading awareness about themes of political seriousness and diaspora. The music video's shots are mainly from Kenya, but the lyrics and the rappers' embodied practices work to display the Caravan's Pan-African sentiment. To emphasize cross-continental comradeship, the artists also proclaim in repetition "Amandla Owethu" (or "NgaWethu"), the widely used anti-apartheid South African Nguni phrase, meaning "Power to the People," "Our Power," or "Black Power."[45] The continued usage of this term across southern African states marks the relevance of the morphing struggle for Black rights in a post-apartheid and racial capitalist context.

Diaspora appears in "Amandla" by negotiating Kenyan societal conceptions of blackness. Mic Crenshaw raps during his verse, "Black American, I'm Afrikan (African)! I'm on the caravan!"[46] Black American is a term often used by Kenyans and other Africans to describe African Americans. Many Kenyans have explained to me that "Black American" is an intentional term meant to exclude U.S.-born Black people from the category of "African." However, hip hop refuses

FIGURE 11. "Amandla" music video, featuring (*left to right*) MC Bagol, Ran-D, and Mic Crenshaw. Screenshot by author. Source: Nomadik Studio, "'Amandla' Ft. Khusta, Mic Crenshaw, Ran-D, Judge and MC Bagol," YouTube, December 14, 2015, https://www.youtube.com/watch?v=usamqjWxtyk.

such designations, and Mic Crenshaw turns the term on its head. While in wider Kenyan society, U.S. blackness may be antithetical to Africanness, in the culture these two terms can overlap, touch, and come together. Mic Crenshaw leans on a shared commonality of hip hop love and political seriousness that allows artists to address the claim that Black people are not considered African in Kenyan society. Instead of avoiding the term "Black American" to proclaim his Africanness, Mic Crenshaw uses it alongside "African" and "caravan" to announce his ideological and physical travel. Because "Black American" is flexible enough to acquire new significations, he easily flips the phrase's meaning to include it within the framework of caravan politics.

"Amandla" addresses how what is regarded as Kenyan or African traditional music is also constitutive of a Pan-Africanism and hip hop diaspora. The *nyatiti*, a Luo stringed instrument, can be seen and heard throughout the song. It is common practice for Kenyan practitioners to embrace elements of Kenyan culture that are deemed "traditional" and "ethnic" to exemplify the flexibility of both hip hop and other types of Kenyan music. Here, the video accomplishes what Paul Zeleza calls for: "not to freeze [African music] in temporal boxes in which Africa's influences on diasporan music are confined exclusively to the past."[47] Not only is hip hop rendered African, but so is the *nyatiti* made contemporary and active, disrupting the notion that noncommercial and ethnicized music is static and permanently localized. Stringed instruments in rap can also be heard when artists freestyle over guitar sounds. In the film *Ni Wakati*, analyzed in the last section of this chapter, and in Michael Wanguhu's other film on the underground scene,

Hip Hop Colony, artists are filmed rapping or freestyling to guitar music. Firm beats and weighty bass traditionally mark hip hop. In Kenyan music, while computer-generated beats are widely utilized, rappers regularly use the guitar. As discussed in chapter 1, guitar music, such as Benga and Congolese rumba, has a long history in Kenya. Additionally, other chordophones, such as the *nyatiti* and *litungu*, have been used in Kenyan music both before and after the introduction of the guitar. In fact, East African knowledge and usage of these and other instruments have made the guitar a beautifully viable source of music-making.

The presence of the *nyatiti* demonstrates Kenyan hip hop's indigenization practices, also exhibiting that the project of diaspora is not always transnational and outward-looking. Often, the reclamation of African and Black humanity in diasporic projects means that artists must draw lines, or webs, according to Soyica Diggs Colbert, in a multitude of directions. Some connections are made intercontinentally, others are made across oceans, and still, other critical lines are drawn within Kenya itself. The *nyatiti* is positioned near the artists on the ground when they are rapping, and MC Bagol plays the instrument intermittently. Given the history of string music and its frequent incorporation in rapping, the video expresses that hip hop owns its place within the many genres of Kenyan music. Because the music is viewed as a consistent other, linking it to various genres is one way it sturdily asserts its presence within the catalogs of Kenyan sounds. This othering appeared during a television interview on the show *Culture Hub* with MC Bagol. Halfway into a short conversation about MC Bagol's life, *nyatiti* musicianship, and career goals, the presenter asked a platitudinous question comparing American and Kenyan styles: "What is your message to the other young folk that we see, especially here in Kenya, who are imitating a lot of the hip hop that is in the west?" MC Bagol, partly refusing to fall for the trap of setting Kenyan music on a moral high ground against western (i.e., American and therefore African American) forms, replied:

> Well, okay, I don't have anything against hip hop. Hip hop is a powerful music. It is about the African man in the diaspora. The Black man. He is expressing the issues that are affecting him in the diaspora. So hip hop is a positive culture. I can say it is a good culture. So, we have to enrich it more. We have to enrich it more. So, my message to all the young artists that are coming up, the hip hop artists in Africa that are coming up, I just like to say, they can do hip hop, but let's enrich it. Bring it to the motherland. Bring it back to the roots and have some conscious messages.[48]

Bagol continued to note, nodding to Haile Selassie, that artists must focus not only on economic empowerment but also on spiritual fulfillment.[49] Though Bagol's comments partly fold into the notions of a flawed American music, he also recognizes the cultural sameness and commonality of struggle that exists among Black peoples, or, specifically for him, among Black men. Like Mic Crenshaw, Bagol briefly places blackness alongside Africanity in a unifying gesture. Black and

FIGURE 12. "Amandla" music video, featuring (*left to right*) MC Bagol, Ran-D, and Mic Crenshaw. Screenshot by author. Source: Nomadik Studio, "'Amandla' Ft. Khusta, Mic Crenshaw, Ran-D, Judge and MC Bagol," YouTube, December 14, 2015, https://www.youtube.com/watch?v=usamqjWxtyk.

African may be two opposing subjectivities in Kenyan society at large, but here, in the underground, the concepts are brought together in a gesture of sameness. In hip hop, Black and African are not necessarily synonyms, but they are still two similar characteristics whose nets are cast in differing directions and meet for a common purpose.

Espousals of diaspora forge a mutual recognition of the similarities that Africana people share across various borders. Jean Muteba Rahier and Percy C. Hintzen write that "white supremacy is . . . at the center of black misrecognition," and if this is so, then diaspora works to "[render] the 'space' of collective self-recognition and self-consciousness."[50] A hip hop diaspora produces a relationality: an imagined camaraderie wherein Africana people do not render those who look like them as "other." In this version of diaspora, artists resist the disarticulating regimes of colonialism and slavery as well as their afterlives while also speculating on unity based on shared perspectives. The idea of diaspora, of seeing others as not dissimilar to oneself, is a mutual recognition that the other is not an other after all.

The traversal of this musical African convoy of the Caravan from hood to hood, from South Africa to Zimbabwe, and then to Kenya and beyond, allows for the growth of a music-based activism that sees the hood as a diasporic site. Ran-D rhymes in "Amandla" and contributes to the idea that the moving caravan is an answer to a seemingly inescapable social confinement:

Jamii iko locked ndani ya poverty, maisha mabaya (The community is locked in poverty, bad life) /

Wamebow down to pressure, domestication (They have bowed down to pressure, domestication) /

The slave master kupitia Intimidation Avenue kufunga (The slave master through Intimidation Avenue closes [to close]) /

Kuwafanya wajinga, wameziunda concentration camps ndani ya mtaa (To make them stupid, they have built concentration camps in the hood)[51]

Here, Ran-D states that powerful forces, referred to as "the slave master," have domesticated or held down the oppressed, who are forced to accept their positions. Some artists refer to the downtrodden as being unknowing or, in this case, stupid. Ran-D positions himself as knowledgeable and capable of providing answers to those who are miseducated. Normalized ableism does appear in hip hop music. For example, the 2019 King Kaka song "Wajinga Nyinyi," meaning "Y'all stupid," which is examined in the next chapter, encourages people to hold the political system accountable. Rappers place themselves as responsible for lifting a veil that those in power have placed over the impoverished populace. Calling for political consciousness is reasonable, yet the accusation of stupidity does not exist without an ableist and elitist indictment of the working class and poor persons as being unaware and naïve.

The settings of the "Amandla" video also mark the ghetto as a project of social confinement. The video was shot in the middle-class area of Hurlingham. In one part, there is footage just south of Hurlingham from a moving vehicle capturing a scene from Lang'ata Road. Kibera, known to be Africa's largest informal settlement neighborhood and where the "Looking Up" video was shot (see chapter 2), can briefly be seen in the background. Rather than heading away from the city and hood, the caravan heads toward both because the hood is one stop that it will always make. In some traditional ideas of diaspora, homeland, and motherland, Africa is portrayed as ahistorically positive. Far from the land of queens and kings or collective village life and animals, the hood is a marker of hip hop diaspora and transnationality. The space and visual sight of ghettos operate as an indigenizing mechanism that locates the music inside Kenya, and with the help of the caravan, the ghetto functions as one stop along the Pan-African path.

The caravan-as-*matatu* is quite apposite given the vehicle's sturdy connections to rap music culture. Songs like Nazizi and Wyre's old school classic "Kenyan Girl / Kenyan Boy" (2004), Baby T's playful and upbeat song about sexual pleasure, "Dandiwa" (Jumped On, 2015), and Tunji's flashy song "Mat za Ronga" (*Matatus* of [Ongata] Rongai, 2017) are just a few ways the *matatu* figures prominently in songs. Octopizzo's proclamations of "Namba Nane" (Number 8) in his music as a nod to the *matatu* route line to Kibera and Evaredi's use of the 33 *matatu*

FIGURE 13. Graffiti artist in the "Amandla" music video. Screenshot by author. Source: Nomadik Studio, "'Amandla' Ft. Khusta, Mic Crenshaw, Ran-D, Judge and MC Bagol," YouTube, December 14, 2015, https://www.youtube.com/watch?v=usamqjWxtyk.

route line in his clothing and music as a marker of the way to Embakasi are other examples. Working from Evan Mwangi and Wanjiru Mbure, who call the vehicle a "fugitive institution," I see the *matatu* as symbolic of diaspora through its propensity to transgress borders in hip hop.[52] In "Amandla," what is important is the *matatu*'s symbolism of a Pan-African caravan that joins people together across geographic space.

The complicated interventions of "Still Strong" and "Amandla" echo Paul Zeleza's note that "movement, it could be argued then, in its literal and metaphorical senses, is at the heart of the diasporic condition."[53] This theme of movement shores up how hip hop prioritizes bodies that are able-bodied, whether in dance or rhyme. Unlike "Still Strong," where only skilled roller-skaters participate in the performance, using the *matatu* figuratively makes the caravan available to those who cannot walk their journey. The *matatu* conveys the possibilities of an inclusive caravanned diaspora, wherein one is not required to be physically able-bodied to partake in the transit. Moreover, "Amandla" and "Still Strong" illustrate that representations of diaspora are produced mostly by cisgender men, resulting in its masculinization, however unintentional.

Although the diaspora in "Amandla" only includes men, the translocal articulations are dynamic and still unfolding. In fact, in the larger project of the Afrikan Hip-Hop Caravan, women rappers such as Mama C (who I profile in the last section of this chapter) are on the album in other songs. In "Amandla," Ran-D,

Khusta, Mic Crenshaw, and Judge can be seen spitting their verses in front of the mic in the studio. As they rap, they hold up their recently completed and "not-yet-memorized" bars, reading from either cellphones or paper. During Judge's rap, there is a cut to shots of a man graffiti artist painting a collage, which includes an open book with a tree growing out of it and an image of an African woman on the mic. These practitioners are all in process, embodying their purpose while remaining open to the possibility of something different. These shots remind those watching that practitioners are always putting pen to paper; they are still exploring the directions of their paint cans. Such embodiment practices beckon toward continual newness, highlighting what Nadine George-Graves calls "performativity in flux."[54]

THE DIASPORIC THUG

Kenyan artists cite U.S. Black themes in the music, but they do not use one of the most popular global figures in rap, the gangsta or thug. Hip hop is both a magnet and a filter for global racial politics, pulling in and sorting out ideas of blackness and Africanity that fit into the music and respond to Kenyan societal beliefs. As such, many grapple with the gangsta or thug idiom and how it confers blackness, primarily by calling it into question and ultimately rejecting it as unusable for projects of diaspora, political love, and seriousness. Evaredi's music video "Ukweli" (Truth) in this section illustrates that the reference to the thug must be fed through notions of political seriousness for it to be viable. For most artists social consciousness is a driving force for their music, and incorporating what is largely seen as a gangsta or thug aesthetic into their art would mean straying from their mission. Kenyan, and indeed many African, artists disassociate from the figure of the thug or gangsta to mark their music as socially useful and valuable.[55]

In the U.S., the thug concept has been substantively reclaimed in hip hop and is a continuation of the bad man and bad nigga aesthetic long present in Black popular culture.[56] The figure eschews formal economies for high-risk quick money and has open heterosexual exploits that often border on or fully embrace misogynoir and sexism.[57] The U.S. thug is usually cast as the venerated antihero outlaw in music and film.

In Kenya, the thug has accumulated a somewhat different meaning, and the figure is generally despised. The idea of the thug emerged during colonialism, when white authorities used the term to describe young African men in a fast-developing urban Nairobi who supposedly did not want to work in formal economies but would rather steal and cause havoc to the colonial social order. During the Emergency, it quickly became a word to describe the fictitiously inherent barbarous nature of the forest fighters.[58] For example, S. M. Shamsul Alam cites a 1954 state-run *Voice of Kenya* pamphlet, "The Kikuyu Tribe and Mau Mau: Some Factors Causing the Rise of Mau Mau," describing why people would feel compelled to join the fighters. One reason was "Little of family or clan authority and no change for the young male to prove his manhood except in chivalry, thuggery, and reversion to primitive savagery."[59] During colonialism and independence transitions, it was a racialized term to mark out the nonconforming African, and it then entered the mainstream Kenyan lexicon as a class-based description conferred on men who are apparently invested in crime instead of legitimate work. Though most Kenyans might not view the Mau Mau as thugs, the term itself has remained, as well as a societal willingness to enter people into that category. In the current Kenyan news, broadcasters speak of men who rob violently or extort money from businesses as being thugs, and it is common to hear broadcasters make statements such as "police killed two thugs."[60] These are often extrajudicial murders and are seen as easy solutions to the rife problem of gang or cartel violence in informal settlement areas in Nairobi. Such executions are meant to send messages to gangs, who community members often despise for the power they hold over residents as a result of their violence. Unlike in the U.S., there are typically no widespread romanticized notions of the gangster in Kenya; the term is mostly only used to describe people who rob with violence and occasionally kill people in the process. Rappers are, therefore, hesitant to identify themselves as gangstas or thugs in such an arena.

For example, in our conversations, Judge differentiated much of U.S. hip hop from African styles and argued that the subject of a song matters: a Kenyan rapper cannot discuss things that fall outside of cultural norms. Judge noted how in American songs, a rapper can "diss their mother," but in Africa, one's music will not sell with lyrics about parental criticism. In Kenya, there is a consistent desire for artists to create music that is deemed "positive." Judge lamented that gangsta rap lies far from his creative purview:

> There's some people who will rap about violence and people will rap about killing each other, you know. And music, I normally believe that it has a very big inspiration whereby if you say something, you don't know it, but someone will be listening to that music, and he or she is in that situation whereby you can react or whatever. He or she is listening to—because I normally believe . . . music . . . touches some other parts of the brain.[61]

Judge's comments notably tell how artists parse through U.S. hip hop as they engage in their citational practices. As mentioned, he participated in "Amandla." Throughout his music, he has drawn on notions of blackness, naming his group Black Duo, and in chapter 2, I analyze the song "Rap kwa Mic," which samples from U.S. artists Talib Kweli and Bahamadia. He, like others, is hyperaware that society views the music through the lens of the gangsta or thug, which many argue does not capture the full diversity of rap culture. I asked many rappers about the general reception of hip hop in Kenya, and Nafsi Huru immediately discussed how the cultural othering of the music comes from people's perceptions of gangsta rap. He disagreed with this association, explaining that he does not see himself as a gangsta rapper and has grown frustrated at the constant association between hip hop and gangsta rap.

> *RP:* How does Kenyan society view hip hop?
>
> *Nafsi Huru:* There are some people, like parents, who don't really love hip hop. They think it's like for gangsters or for people who do drugs or something like that. They don't see the positive side of it. But I think with time, they are going to understand what we are doing, and they will get to follow us.
>
> *RP:* And where do they get that perception from?
>
> *Nafsi Huru:* I think it's just a conception because people who do hip hop are energetic, and we have swag and things like that. So, they, society, expect you to go to school, you dress official and things like that, and you just go to work in a corporate company . . . When you are doing hip hop, when they haven't heard your lyrics, . . . they stereotype you to being someone who doesn't understand what he is doing.[62]

Nafsi asserted that perceptions of the music originate from how rappers perform the culture, such as through swag and clothing styles, which signifies the thug or gangsta for nondevotees. Nafsi stated that people who dislike rap do so without listening to the lyrics, meaning that the assumptions nonlisteners make are based on a disengagement with the music. Social norms, including how to act, how to dress, and where to work, propose that there are certain behaviors deemed suitable, and rap is continually measured against these actions. Artists rebel against social norms, which often manifests as generational and class-based resistance. His mention of parental dislike of rap exemplifies how age differences are influenced by how people navigate American influences. When hip hop first started, it was a youth music, and globally, it has still retained this notion, even though its fifty-year permanence now means that many popular artists across the globe who pioneered the genre are well beyond middle age. In Kenya, parents disapprove of their children becoming rappers because of specific cultural expectations around what it means to become an adult. Many ethnic communities in Kenya have circumcision rites for boys, specifically for young teenagers, after which they become men and assume certain responsibilities. Due to cultural and historical factors, including how the colonial and postcolonial states have hijacked circumcision for their aims, there exists an entire discourse surrounding manhood transitions in Kenyan society.[63] While the artists I spoke to never elaborated on this as a reason for their parents' disapproval, circumcision discourse rests securely inside of the differentiations between youth and adulthood, specifically for many cismen.

Although few will admit it outright, rappers do care about how they are perceived. The sustained resistance to social norms that the culture celebrates has limits, and the goal for all artists is that some elements of the political urgency of their music resonate with larger society. Judge implied that external societal perceptions of hip hop are tied to what themes rappers avoid.

> Like here in Kenya . . . people have been thinking like hip hop is for gangsters, you know? . . . Let's say if you are doing hip hop . . . they normally expect that you to start doing and saying the "f-word." Or the "b-word." And start being hood, and start like putting some dreads on your head, and be like, ah, you're a bad boy?[64]

Judge's description exemplifies how rap carries negative signifiers: if an artist were to "be hood" and wear locks (or dreads or dreadlocks), they would be associated with gangsta rap. Of course, such meanings carry local connotations as well. Locks have long been seen as nonnormative and improper in Kenya. Only in the past fifteen or so years have large numbers of middle-class men and women in Nairobi begun to wear them. However, these styles are heavily refined and symmetrical, thus making them ideologically distant from the large and uncultivated locks historically associated with Mau Mau fighters and also with Rastafarians and Mungiki groups.[65] While these organizations have a variety of reputations, with the Mau Mau being remembered with recognition for its contribution to independence, the hairstyle still conjures up notions of useless rebellion.

The cultural location of rap in Kenya and elsewhere in Africa relates to its pejorative gangsta association. Nondevotees of the music see it as reflecting a blind western mimicry, the appropriation of a harmful pejorative lifestyle full of empty violence and meaningless consumerism. Rap music's supposed inability to generate meaning outside of its commodity status and its rebelliousness and social deviance often clash with established modes of respectability. For many artists, the figure of the gangsta does not travel well to Africa. Msia Clark's discussion of Somali-Canadian rapper K'Naan and his song "What's Hardcore" captures this complexity.[66] K'Naan's contribution to the hip hop game in Kenya should be noted as well, as he has spent much time in Nairobi, where he recorded songs such as "Soobax" (Come Out). In "What's Hardcore," he juxtaposes violence-ridden Somalia with life on the U.S. streets to highlight the artificiality of U.S. street life compared to the ongoing battles for peace in Somalia. Clark notes that K'Naan's identification with U.S. Black culture, his use of Ebonics or African American Vernacular English (AAVE), and his work with U.S. rappers means his discussion is not flimsy or appropriative. However, K'Naan's comparison, while elucidating the tragedies of Somalia, is slightly irresponsible, as he does not locate the gangsta within multilayered structural, economic, and historic antiblackness that continues to destroy Black communities in totalizing ways. Still, his larger conversation is significant. Like many Kenyan artists, K'Naan's affinity with Black culture is complex and intimate, yet he never embraces the figure of the gangsta and its relationship to violence.

Thug subjectivities fly in the face of political love in Nairobi rap. Such love does not mean that everything in hip hop is revered, just as explorations of diaspora do not translate to an open acceptance of everything that has the potential to confer blackness. Although spreading political love appears one-directional, that is, artists spread love to Kenya, they also desire to be valued by Kenyan society. Because of these yearnings, many artists trenchantly confront the criticisms that seem to be leveled at them constantly. When MC Bagol uses the *nyatiti*, he connects rap to the beauty of Kenya's other musical expressions; such exercises exemplify practitioners' love of the self through culture. Many artists also create uncountable forms of ludic corporealities and lyrical maneuvers meant to undermine structures of power and produce spaces of immersive creativities. However, utilizing the thug as a rebellious figure rarely works in maintaining underground spaces because its very construction is built on society's credulous derision. Michael Jeffries extrapolates how the U.S. thug rapper understands that onlookers (both white and respectable Black) have an endless supply of judgment and contempt at what they see as the thug's unnecessary nihilism and wanton violence. He notes, "Thug subjectivity is rooted not only in outsider and rebel status but in the fact that *existence as a thug is based on the premise and knowledge that you are hated.*"[67] In U.S. rap, these characteristics of gangsta rappers who are men and sometimes women bad bitches can both apply pressure to the contradictions of the U.S. state's excessive eagerness to author violence and resist the respectability politics that trap Black people in unwinnable scenarios. In comparison, Nairobi underground artists do not accept society's hate; instead, they aim for a recognition that their music is valuable and effective. Therefore, the image of the deviant thug does not map onto Kenyan society with the same subversive force.

Much like the tomboy, the image of the gangsta thug rapper is entangled with ideas of excess and mimicry. Women who act as men in a context where artists are already rendered copycats of the west face many difficulties. The same is true for the gangsta thug. In a setting where artists must prove their worth as creative producers, such a label is not something that most can afford. The gangsta, like the tomboy, embodies too much excess, too much masculinity where there should not be, too much toughness, and too much blackness. If artists are to cite blackness from the U.S., it must be the kind that is supposedly generative, useful, and politically salient. The undercurrent of respectability is found within discussions of the gangsta thug, just as it is present in discussions of the tomboy. Artists want their bodies to be read as defiant and forceful, but only to a point. Women can be rappers, but only if their presence does not destabilize the entrenched notions of masculinity that mark and constitute hip hop culture. Furthermore, formations of the thug are simply not profitable in the underground scene. It is doubtful that any NGO, and indeed no church, would host a gangsta rap event. It is also unlikely that artists would want to draw any potential associations with gang organizations or street cartels that widely and often violently operate in Nairobi, especially given the police's readiness to inflict violence on these groups.

Evaredi's song "Ukweli" is fascinating in that he incorporates the thug into the song's general themes of Pan-Africanism and working-class consciousness. Evaredi and much of his crew wear T-shirts with the wording "T.H.U.G. Familia [family]" on them. Thug Familia is his former rap group, which he was a part of before going solo in the late 2010s, and here, T.H.U.G. is an acronym for True Heroes Under God. The term is redefined as a part of political seriousness and articulated as something purposeful for hip hop culture, which is one of the only ways it could be used in the underground. However, for this video analysis, it is quite difficult to see the wording *familia* on the T-shirts. Also, Thug Familia was not as well known as other groups, meaning that what viewers mostly visually encounter in "Ukweli" is the word THUG. Nonetheless, Evaredi's reconception of the term aligns with the earnest premise of fortitude and social consciousness found throughout the song. At the beginning of the song, he raps, "Hey Bana, I'm a Blackstar ka Ghana, Bafana Bafana, Mwafrika kwa sana."[68] In this line, Evaredi captures the Africanist thrust of much of the Nairobi underground. The line translates to "Hey man, I'm a Blackstar like Ghana, Bafana Bafana, a true African." Evaredi asserts a Pan-African subjectivity when he raps that he is "a Blackstar like Ghana" and a "Mwafrika kwa sana." He uses "Blackstar," which is the name of Ghana's football (soccer) team, while also contending that he is a "Black star." His references to Ghana's Blackstar and South Africa's Bafana Bafana, both football (soccer) teams, espouse his Pan-African subjectivity vis-à-vis sports. Not a player for either team, he uses these references to develop his politics as an African rapper. In this single line, Evaredi reaches across several borders to usher forth notions of African resilience and strength, as Ghana was the first sub-Saharan country to obtain its independence, and South Africa is often cited for its uprisings and defeat of apartheid. He calls forth African struggles by drawing lines from one country to the next, positioning himself as a true African or *Mwafrika kwa sana*.

Evaredi also goes by MC Snarl and is from the working-class area of Embakasi. As already mentioned, EMBA 33 is the basis for his small-scale clothing line, with "33" as a reference to Embakasi's *matatu* route. Additionally, the settings of his music videos often create a presentation of wealth. In my interview with him, he argued that hip hop has the power to stop conflict and gave the example of when the government commissioned artists to hold concerts after the 2007–8 postelection violence. Evaredi acknowledged that these concerts featured other types of popular music, but upheld that hip hop works best to carry a message: "The main thing is the message. What you are telling the people. Like I can say, hip hop is the best tool for peace. For people to stop war. Hip hop is true." When I asked him what "war" he referred to, he responded:

> Artists are capable of getting down to the common *mwananchi*,[69] the slums, yeah, the second-class houses. That's hip hop; that's where hip hop is. Basically for me, I know that for me you can't hip hop in a big estate . . . that guy won't be talking, won't be talking of peace, but he don't know what war is. You can't talk of peace when you don't know what war is.[70]

Here what Evaredi describes is a class war, where the poor suffer. These references to poverty also align with the themes in "Ukweli." Krunkid's chorus is: "Ukweli wa mambo (The truth about problems) / Nakupa ukweli wa mambo (I give you the truth about problems) / Twakupa ukweli wa mambo (We give you the truth about problems) / Cuz it's the way this world is unfair to me/ I gotta keep it real for real, it's true to me."[71]

Furthermore, Evaredi's lyrics, just like Ran-D's lines about social confinement, position him in a place of knowing in opposition to what he perceives as social ills. He raps about his sense of hustle, which has supposedly brought him upward mobility, and relatedly briefly performs the "making it rain" gesture. His bodily movements and stances in "Ukweli," which exude confidence and self-assurance, communicate additional knowledge about how to confront society's difficulties. Evaredi raps in front of his crew, which is composed of all men except for Krunkid and a small child. Some of the men look into the camera and bob their heads as Evaredi raps, while others look away or down as they listen. This common performance communicates that Evaredi can speak or rap on behalf of their experiences, which he does with self-assuredness. Evaredi enacts what Miles White describes as "street swagger," which "indexes not only rhythm and style in one's performance of physical self and personal carriage, but a high degree of self-confidence, the knowledge that one can handle himself in any situation with cool and sophistication."[72] Evaredi performs repetitive gestures throughout the video. When he is sitting, his hands move toward and away from his body in sharp and clear movements to the beat of the song and the flow of his lyrics. At times, he puts his head down in contemplation while putting his hands up as he finishes a lyric.

This video shows bright and contrasting colors and a shiny and crisp background. Evaredi wears a backward hat, a Converse jacket, designer jeans, and sunglasses. His protégé, Krunkid, dresses in expensive clothes and wears flashy jewelry and sunglasses studded with rhinestones. The venue is Le Vans, a moderately priced club on Uhuru Highway on a perhaps symbolic precipice of east and west Nairobi. Though it is a modest location, the framing of the video creates the illusion that it is a high-end establishment.

The term thug has a double meaning in this video. Not only is it reconceptualized as something useful for political seriousness, but it also easily joins with the song's portrayal of the working-class grind and hypermasculinities. In "Ukweli," the lyrics do not present such economic activities within the perhaps conventional thug rhetoric of illicitness and violence, but rather Evaredi's hood success is crafted as both vague and benign. In most rap music, just like in this song, all we know is that the hustle is possible, but outside of selling music, we do not know exactly what the occupation is. This shifty refusal to say what work rappers do outside of making and selling music is part of the defiance of being unsurveillable. Moreover, both versions of the thug are masculinized and globally recognizable

FIGURE 14. "Ukweli" music video, featuring Evaredi and Krunkid. Screenshot by author. Source: #id33ke musiq, "Snarl Evaredi Ft Krunkid—Ukweli Official Video," YouTube, October 15, 2012, https://www.youtube.com/watch?v=EDrAH3BwXco.

and, therefore, become pliable toward the different aims of this particular video. Evaredi's most enthralling intervention is how he plays with the word, emptying out its historic definition in Kenya as a socially hated figure and then concurrently surrounding it with the well-worn markers of the term. This simultaneous resistance and compliance to conventions is at the core of the effectiveness of a hip hop politics of subversion. Further, his wordplay, alongside the song's other themes of rap culture's street hustle, invites a critical question about whether the figure of the thug, partly pulled from Black U.S. rap, can fit into Nairobi hip hop's paraphernalia of customary citations. Artists dedicate themselves to disruption as a theoretical practice of making good music and disturbing the social norms often deemed pernicious and unusable for many lower-class African youths. "Ukweli" both conforms and departs from the common underground text, with the help of the figure of the thug on both fronts.

THE TIME FOR DIASPORA

Michael Wanguhu and Russell Kenya's 2010 documentary, *Ni Wakati* (It's Time), holds contemporary discussions about hip hop diaspora in Kenya and about themes of African and Black revolution, commercialization, and hip hop homelands.[73] The film is centered around two noncommercial African American rappers, M1 from Dead Prez and Umi from P.O.W., and follows the duo as they take a trip to Kenya and Tanzania. It highlights some of the historical connections between East Africans and African Americans. As *Ni Wakati* unfolds, the audience witnesses how the rappers mostly work with a version of diaspora that locates rap traditions in Africa and how they see themselves as making a return to a distant cultural homeland. They speak with various actors in the Tanzanian and Kenyan industry about blackness as an imposed subjecthood due to historic trafficking and enslavement in the U.S. and describe themselves as Africans who have been estranged from their native land. Umi and M1 spend the film traveling to hip hop events, namely WAPI Nairobi and WAPI Tanzania, performing, talking to artists, fielding interview questions at radio stations, spending time in the studio, and reporting on their numerous excursions.

Although the film seeks to see hip hop as indigenous to Africa, in the end, it confirms that the music is rooted firmly in U.S. blackness. In so doing, *Ni Wakati* works with two interrelated conceptions of diaspora found throughout the music. First, it directly mirrors the Afro-Atlantic diaspora, whereby the characteristics of hip hop are considered to have begun among African griots and drumming tradi-tions, after which it moved to the New World, eventually emerging in the South Bronx via the urban and Black descendants of kidnapped Africans, and finally returned to Africa amidst its spread around the globe.[74] It should be noted that Kenyan rappers are often dissatisfied with their exclusion from this diaspora and make claims about the existence of East African oral historians and musical prac-tices, thereby including themselves in the continental contributions of the origins of rap culture. The second type of diaspora stresses that the autochthonous set-ting of hip hop was in the U.S. before it moved outward to various sites in Africa and around the globe.[75] The film seeks to communicate that the second form is widely known in rap circles and needs reconsideration, which is the core theme of Umi and M1's journey to East Africa. As they move to different sites throughout Tanzania and Kenya, these rappers aim to highlight that the first type of diaspora, beginning in Africa and moving outward, is less known and underappreciated.

Ni Wakati includes interviews with an impressive array of people, all providing insight into their understanding of the general theme of hip hop across borders. In the beginning, as Umi and M1 pack up and head to the airport, the film introduces Davy D (also written as Davey D) and Toni Blackman. Davy D is a U.S. journalist, historian, radio host, college professor, and longtime activist whose work in hip hop and Black politics spans several decades. A member of the old-school group Orange Krush, he is also known for working with artists such as Run DMC and Kurtis Blow in the 1980s and has played bass for Public Enemy. In the early 1990s, Toni Blackman formed the workshop Freestyle Union. She is also the founder of Rhyme Like a Girl (RLAG) collective, where she continued to focus on the impor-tance of the cypher. Blackman has also served as the U.S. Hip Hop Ambassador with the State Department, for which she has traveled internationally to give lec-tures and facilitate workshops. Like Davy D, she has also taught college courses. Her presence in the documentary is apropos, as she has collaborated with African artists throughout the diaspora.[76] Soon after Davy D and Blackman appear, so too does Binyavanga Wainaina, the late Kenyan author and journalist. Wainaina wrote several essays, including "How to Write about Africa" and the book *One Day I Will Write about This Place: A Memoir*.[77] The late Geronimo Ji-Jaga Pratt, the famous U.S. Black Panther, also speaks about the types of hip hop that come into Africa. Graffiti images of his godson, Tupac Shakur, from either Tanzania or Kenya, are interspersed throughout his dialogue. Pratt discusses his apprehension about hip hop surfacing on the African continent, given what he sees as the "negativity" of U.S. styles. However, recognizing the work of Kalamashaka and UFMM, he concedes the beneficial contributions that the music makes to societies. In the film, Pratt speaks from Tanzania, where he lived for the latter part of his life until he passed in 2011.[78]

Charlotte Hill O'Neal, better known as Mama C, and her husband, Mzee Pete O'Neal, who reside in Arusha, are also featured. The couple runs a community organization, the United African Alliance Community Center (UAACC). In the 1960s, Mzee Pete was the chairman of the Kansas City Chapter of the Black Panthers. He fled into exile in the 1970s after being arrested for a gun charge and then spent time in Algeria before settling in Tanzania with Mama C.[79] The film captures a fireside discussion about Pan-Africanism among M1, Umi, Mama C, Mzee Pete, and other unnamed artists. Notably, Mama C appeared in the collaborative 2017 album of the Afrikan Hip Hop Caravan alongside Mic Crenshaw, Khusta, and others (discussed earlier in this chapter). She is a long-standing spoken word practitioner, adept in the *nyatiti* and other African instruments, and frequently creates music with African rappers. In the 2017 Caravan album, she raps in "Soul Power" and "Zimbabwe." In the film, the couple speaks to rappers as elders, counseling young people and performing ceremonial libations and Africanist elder and ancestral acknowledgment that are both indigenous to Africa and practiced throughout the diaspora.

Through their travels, M1 and Umi position Africanity as a foundational element in hip hop. After arriving in Kenya, both announce their Africanness and discuss the failure of the U.S., a country that they argue is not their factual homeland. Viewers see M1 rapping his signature, "I'm a African / I'm a African, uhh / And I know what's happenin'" from Dead Prez's well-known song "I'm a African." To compare, in the song "Amandla" and its music video, Mic Crenshaw brings blackness and Africanity into one conceptual space. Mic Crenshaw's avowal that he is "Black American" occurs in the same sonic space as the expression "Amandla," the *nyatiti*, Nairobi hoods, and the *matatu*. In *Ni Wakati*, Umi and M1 do not name blackness as a primary current and instead do something entirely different. For them, blackness falls out of their self-definition, seeing it as representative of how the U.S. has disarticulated African peoples from their original homelands through forced displacement and enslavement. Throughout the documentary, the artists speak to audiences about the need for African hip hop to avoid the many snares of American styles, such as corporate takeovers and the bodily celebration of wealth through items such as jewelry and clothing, often detested in conscious rap communities. M1 and Umi proclaim that they have witnessed how consumer culture has eliminated the music's political force, or to cite S. Craig Watkins, "[dulled] the oppositional edges" of U.S. hip hop, and that their goals are to avoid the same trend in Africa.[80] Their solution is frequently espoused by Black nationalist artists and concerns the need to seize creative and economic control over the production and circulation of the genre. These artists seek to paint Africa as a hip hop homeland and a place of purity and relative incorruptibility compared to the fraught U.S. music industries.

M1 and Umi's understandings of Africa and Africanity are framed through the lens of U.S. Afrocentricity. While they remove blackness from their self-definitions, what they miss is how their views are deeply embedded in a Black and Afrocentric idea of Africa. M1 and Umi desire to ground their work in Africanness, but the politics of diasporic liberatory movements force to the surface just how much U.S. blackness is embedded in their version of hip hop's Pan-Africanism. At one point and in front of an audience, they proclaim "RBG!" (or Red, Black, and Green), which is an ode to Dead Prez's musical themes and the flag of Black Nationalism and Pan-Africanism. While many in Kenya are familiar with the flag and Garveyism, the declaration "RBG!" is uncommon.[81] It is not that Kenyans or other Africana peoples would not understand the intentions behind RBG; it is more that the term has a particular resonance in politically conscious hip hop communities in the U.S. In another moment in the film, M1 begins a speech by greeting people with a shout of "uhuru!," Swahili for "freedom." However, this is no longer the rallying cry it once was during independence in East Africa, nor is it a greeting in the region. Hence, the audience does not respond to his call. His speech about his return to Africa does receive enthusiastic applause for the weight of his words, but at the end, when he calls out "Ashe!/Àṣẹ!" the crowd does not respond again, as the word has little cultural relevance in East Africa.[82] This borrowing from Yoruba philosophies is a long-standing practice in the U.S. among those who point their cultural orientations toward Africa.[83] M1's speech-acts are a few of the many ways Black people in the U.S. form understandings of African contexts and cultures through rap.[84] Paul Gilroy describes in his oft-cited magnum opus *Black Atlantic* that Afrocentricism is often "heavily mythologised Africanity that is itself stamped by its origins not in Africa but in a variety of pan-African ideology produced most recently by black America."[85] Hence, even though M1 and Umi proclaim Africanity, it is cultivated through U.S. reference points.

M1 and Umi present themselves as willing to learn about the particularities of Kenya's ethnic landscape beyond a facile and tourist encounter. During one scene, then-Kenyan radio DJ Albert Josiah asks them questions about their time in the country. Umi answers that he has been hanging out in the hood and recently ate Mukimo. The dish, consisting of mashed potatoes, greens, and corn, among other vegetables, is eaten by many in Kenya and is popular in the central provinces and the Kikuyu, Embu, and Meru communities. They both wish to make a point that they are not tourists in the conventional sense, coming into the country and bouncing from airport to coast with little interaction with Kenyans outside of the service sector. To eat Mukimo, they had to visit someone's house or go to a restaurant specializing in more traditional dishes. While it is not difficult to locate such eating spots in Nairobi, in the city's commercial districts, which many foreigners frequent, it is much easier to find fast food and *nyama choma* (roasted meat) restaurants. As Umi proclaims his recent consumption of the food, M1 grins and bobs back and forth alongside his traveling partner. He then shouts, "We Kikuyu boys now!," eliciting chuckles from Josiah and the others in the studio.[86] While proud of his knowledge of Kikuyu foods, M1 appears to know little about the etiquette surrounding ethnicity and the historical ways in which it can confer divisiveness, power, and privilege in Kenya. M1's tossing of the term Kikuyu into radio space was perhaps uninformed. Kenya and Wanguhu's decision to include this moment in the film is odd, especially given the tense atmosphere surrounding ethnic identities. Nonetheless, these are the rappers' attempts to recognize the unique social landscape of Kenya.

The film highlights the methods of artists' indigenization processes. Binyavanga Wainaina contributes to the conversation, stating that Kenyan hip hop is a literary movement that cannot be contained by the written word alone. According to him, the music has fundamentally altered how people see themselves and the world, and he scoffs at older people who lament about artists' apparent deep desires to be western or American. Wainaina criticizes these ill-advised people for spending too much time listening to Luther Vandross or Congolese Lingala music and then discusses how rappers have built an industry of production, recording, and performance that is uniquely Kenyan. His comparisons between rappers and older devotees of non-Kenyan sounds are stark and poignant. For Wainaina, rappers have created a system of cultural production that is far more indigenized and embedded in Kenyan social life than the older Kenyans who criticize them for copying the U.S.

A moving moment occurs when Kamah from Kalamashaka speaks to M1 and Umi in a car as they transition between destinations, testifying, "You guys inspire us like crazy, we get it from you, you know? You know, it's our culture, we're in Africa. We were supposed to know our culture, but you guys made us look for our cultures."[87] Here Kamah emphasizes that hip hop originates in African culture but that it is not recognizable to Africa until it is seen from afar (the U.S.) and then reimported into the continent. Kamah's comment articulates a fundamental difference between African Americans and Africans as demarcated by borders and power. Here, I believe that both notions of diaspora are at work in Kamah's statement. While he solidifies that the music's elements are rooted in the cultures of Africa, he also understands that U.S. artists created the music and made it legible for African rappers to use as a cultural system. In this statement, the U.S. is both a starting point and a part of the diaspora responsible for birthing the music.

The film is also a reminder that the practice of cisgender masculinity helps to make hip hop diasporic and politically conscious, whether in the U.S. or East Africa. After arriving in Tanzania to do a WAPI performance and visit Mama C and Mzee Pete, Umi and M1 visit Coco Beach in Dar es Salaam. M1 appears on the beach, playful and cheerful. He bobs and dances, creating his own rhythm, and raps, "I wanna go, I wanna go, I wanna, I wanna, I wanna, I wanna, I wanna, I wanna go, I wanna go, I wanna, I wanna go to Africa / Not being pimped like a ho in America / Not being pimped like a ho in America."[88] According to M1, being in America or dealing with the U.S. hip hop grind is similar to being held in the inescapable feminized position of "ho," wherein he is exploited and abused sexually. Likewise, his desire to be in Africa is equated to a desire not to be "hoed out" and therefore to be able to exercise full cisgender masculine autonomy over his gifts. This inflection of masculinity reveals an important part of M1's diasporic articulations; his desire to be in Africa is rooted in his affirmation of his cisgender masculinity. Together, his dance, bob, and lighthearted freestyle elucidate a common practice in underground and politically conscious circles: the alliance of the ludic and masculine within hip hop creativity. Artists are considered inventive, sharp, and witty when they can insert ideas about what it means to reaffirm the genre's masculinity in new ways. M1's beachside orature presents the playful and seemingly innocuous assertion of the disavowal of a femininity that is read as deprecatingly sexually promiscuous.

There are only a few brief appearances by women rappers in the film, although the elision appears unintentional. At one point, UFMM rapper Empress Vicky is filmed at a WAPI voicing an ode to the culture using a Malcolm X quote. Other than this, the interviews with Toni Blackman mainly fill the space of what should be a hearty contribution of African women and other rappers of marginalized genders. One specific scene in the film captures the paternalizing silence that women rappers continue to endure. The traveling duo are in Tanzania, speaking about the lack of women within East African hip hop while fielding questions during an interview. M1 frames the absence of women artists as a problem that East African hip hop must undoubtedly confront. As he speaks about an artist he met named Anna, the film cuts to her recent WAPI performance. Anna is shown rapping on the stage and commanding the respect of those who watch her, yet the voice of M1 discussing the absence of women is placed over the footage of Anna and her performance. Rather than showing her rapping with full sound, the film only displays Anna's body and her performance, and her raps are muted for the sake of M1's voice, which discusses the lack of women artists. Anna is only partially embodied; her body is present, but her voice is not. M1 interprets the embodiment of Anna's mic-rocking, and the film's viewers, therefore, know little about her embodied flow. The prioritization of M1's diagnoses over and literally on top of Anna is an appropriate allegory for how men artists perform a gendered knowability that is often at the expense of women. The film does include Toni Blackman's lengthy and significant discussion about the place of women in hip hop, but her statements do not recuperate the film's gendered arc that results from instances like the silencing of Anna and M1's beach pimp and ho performative.

Ni Wakati affirms two details: that U.S. hip hop blackness serves as a consistent mention and that the music is a globally masculinized culture. Even when M1 and Umi insist on making a return to what they see as a hip hop homeland to identify the real and authentic origins of the music, they tell their story through the lenses of African Americanness, using the historically masculinized theoretical practices of Afrocentricity and U.S. Black nationalism, further affirming that U.S. hip hop blackness is a constant reference point. They frame their trip as a *going back* and, in brief instances, paint African hip hop as an ungarnished music not touched by the dirtiness of American commercialism, mirroring the notions of a static African past unsullied by attempts at modernity. The undercurrent thematic elements of going back and an African past draw away from the intensely fruitful conversations present throughout the film that highlight the historical and contemporary connections between U.S. Black people and East Africans, including how hip hop enhances those narratives. Moreover, the film's most persuasive point is that Nairobi rappers and other practitioners in East Africa insist on their place in the music's diaspora. *Ni Wakati*, in many ways, does not lend itself to Marc Perry's notion that artists work from a diaspora composed of multiple elements of Afro-Atlantic blackness. Yet Perry also writes about "nationally transcendent modes of black diasporic identification," where thinking beyond the way nations construct categories of racial difference is imperative.[89] Similarly, the rappers, figures like Mama C and Mzee Pete, and the numerous commentators work from a fundamental principle of Pan-Africanist solidarity. All participants in the film grasp that Pan-Africanism often runs against the dominant ways that Kenyan and Tanzanian societies present racial categories, especially given the complicated representations of U.S. Black Americans. M1, Umi, and other rappers put forth the idea that viewers of the film must understand hip hop's African origins to posit its complexity. By the end, what is most evident is that despite the goal of constructing the music culture as beginning in Africa, the film mostly confirms that it works from a U.S.-inspired masculinized diasporic blackness, which operates as a continual fulcrum for other forms of the global music.

This diasporic blackness is malleable and, in Kenya, fitted to mostly express a lower-class cultural sentiment of resistance to forces like commercialism and imperialism that practitioners see as impeding on their lives. There are several moments where the film achieves Paul Zeleza's point that we ought to move beyond a search for Africa's roots in the New World, and instead look to understand how Africa contributes to the back-and-forth musical flows and cultural practices that make Africana musics so rich. For one, the film introduces Dead Prez's groundbreaking

2000 album *Let's Get Free*, reiterating its then popularity across the continent and Kalamashaka's foundations in making Kenyan hip hop possible. These artists are presented alongside each other as having the same missions of economic and social autonomy for Africana peoples. Throughout the film, we hear Kenyan artists drawing influence from U.S. rappers, as well as a specific point when M1 affirms that his cultural inspiration is Africa, after which the film moves into a beautifully compelling guitar-accompanied freestyle that includes Nairobi artists MC Kah, Kamah, Zakah, Labala, Agano, Swaley, as well as M1 and Umi. Moreover, after discussing the largely unappreciated labor and conscious messaging that Kalamashaka put into the music, Albert Josiah concludes that "[Kalamashaka] are our Mau Mau." After showing the famous images of the detained Dedan Kimathi, the film cuts to a Malcolm X image and excerpt from the 1963 speech "Message to the Grassroots," where he states, "There's been a revolution—A Black revolution going on in Africa, in Kenya. The Mau Mau were revolutionaries."[90]

Ni Wakati, thus, succeeds in helping to recount a story, not of a rigid and static Africa as a needy recipient of the west's tools but as an active participant in conceptualizing Black music and its imperative themes of political consciousness. Zeleza writes that Black musics of the past have been constituted through "returns, both permanent and periodic, physical and psychic, through migrations and increasingly the mass media[, which have] created loops of musical influences."[91] *Ni Wakati* represents hip hop in the same manner. From M1 and Umi's return, lyrical cyphers occurred, and practitioners and activists alike had conversations about attaining Pan-Africanist visions and resisting corporate control in music. Among this, viewers were reminded that U.S. hip hop has sculpted influence from Kenyan movements and themes for social revolution and, additionally, that Kenyan music engages in an assiduous citational exercise that pulls from U.S. Black music while creating something new and sustaining.

Ni Wakati provides critical instances of how artists construct ideas of global blackness to constitute the culture of music communities. In her seminal article "Defining Diaspora, Refining a Discourse," Kim Butler theorizes how to conduct the imperative work of ascertaining distinguishable elements of diaspora, writing that diaspora can, in fact, be a "framework for the study of a specific process of community formation."[92] Butler elaborates on the careful work of identifying diasporan groups, their dispersal, the places that host them, and their relationships to their respective homelands. She asserts that diasporas are self-defining by people whose identities, while unstable, are central to understanding their lives concerning dispersals and homelands. Inspired by Butler's work, I determine that Kenyan artists make decisions about how to exercise creative agency in producing diasporic blackness. Rappers use it malleably to explore Kenyan social and political life, to assert ideas about Pan-Africanism, and to affirm their participation in a global hip hop community.

4

The Sounds of Imperfect Resistance

Just as bodies bestow meanings in hip hop, so too does sound. Rappers use sonic qualities to distinguish between underground and mainstream music. To any ear, the music can sound "underground," "mainstream," "commercial," "real," "sold out," or any combination of these ambiguous and often fraught categories. According to many Kenyan underground rappers, hip hop music is intended to grind away at the barriers that keep the poor disenfranchised. They state that upper-class rappers can afford to sing about their leisurely lives because these privileged artists do not face poverty and the hustle and grind of the industry. Such conversations often deduce that music that sounds too commercial conveys little social value and betrays the diasporic missions of the culture. Melodious, danceable, and leisured tracks, including commercial gospel that more easily makes its way onto radio and television, are considered too compliant with the status quo. These songs contain supposed unwillingness to work against the state to affect real social change. Yet, underground rappers do not completely renunciate the mainstream. Many often incorporate what elements of music work. They discard what does not. This delicate dance that artists do with mainstream music politics and broader social ideologies reveals their position as cultural laborers who strategize about their careers and make the music they love.

In this chapter, I explore how sound is a significant device to distinguish underground artists from commerciality. The ludic and the sonic often interact to produce the music's potency. The sonic qualities in hip hop confer with economics, access, and music standards to create meaning about the world that artists navigate. These rappers have a complicated relationship with capitalism. They seek to earn money through selling their music, do not want to be sellouts, and mostly refuse to use the palatable sounds of commercial music to make theirs more commodifiable. They believe they are the major drivers of the culture but also criticize each other's failures to earn monetary success from music. On one side, they regard capitalism as a solution to the state's inability to provide for Kenyan people. On the other, these same rappers reject industry standards in part fueled by capitalist practices, seeing the aurally pleasurable sentiments of mainstream sounds as a major problematic that waters down the force of the music. These practitioners use harder sonic qualities to interface with their corporeal interventions, producing sustained conversations about Kenyan society, the state, and the commercialism of music.

Sound serves as an indicator of access to mainstream channels. Underground artists understand that radio and television are going to give airtime to the catchy, synthesized, and danceable pop tunes that convey an African urban wealthy cosmopolitanism and carefree sense of leisure. Mainstream rap that takes on Afropop elements and has easier access to commercial spaces, for them, is not loyal to lower-class urban culture. These rappers seek to alter a dynamic wherein society's values are flawed and skewed in favor of easy listening. In the underground, artists use untranslatability in lyrics, sound, and performances, which results in a political imperative around listening. Hard and disruptive sounds reflect the insistence that music induces social change when it jars and unsettles, not softens or anesthetizes.

I rely on the constructed boundaries around the mainstream and the commercial while recognizing that these categories are messy, blurry, and reductive. Caroline Mose interrogates this binary in "Jua Cali Justice: Navigating the 'Mainstream-Underground' Dichotomy in Kenyan Hip-Hop Culture."[1] Mose contends that hip hop studies has mapped U.S. categories onto the Kenyan scene and that this process has become an unsustainable description of what occurs on the ground. She exemplifies how mainstream artists write socially conscious music and that those in noncommercial scenes also rhyme about topics widely taken up in commercial music, such as women, partying, and sex. Her point is that the "dichotomy [has boxed] artists in categories that do not reflect the fluidity that is characteristic of hip hop culture."[2] Mose's argument helps me consider the songs I analyze, which also do not fit into neat confines. The underground artists I highlight ally with neoliberal principles and some commercial artists rap about political subject matter. Given this, there are two ways I depart from Mose's discussion. First, the categories of mainstream and underground in Kenya are not only academic imports from the U.S. While there are artists in Kenya who defy these muddled borders, many others are invested in and create meaning using these two descriptions. For better or worse, rappers rely on this dichotomy to locate themselves within the culture. The definitions of these groupings are not precise, and artists still use the terms mainstream and underground to indicate one's access to the industry. Many of their observations are accurate; the more a song conforms to standard aural elements, the more likely it

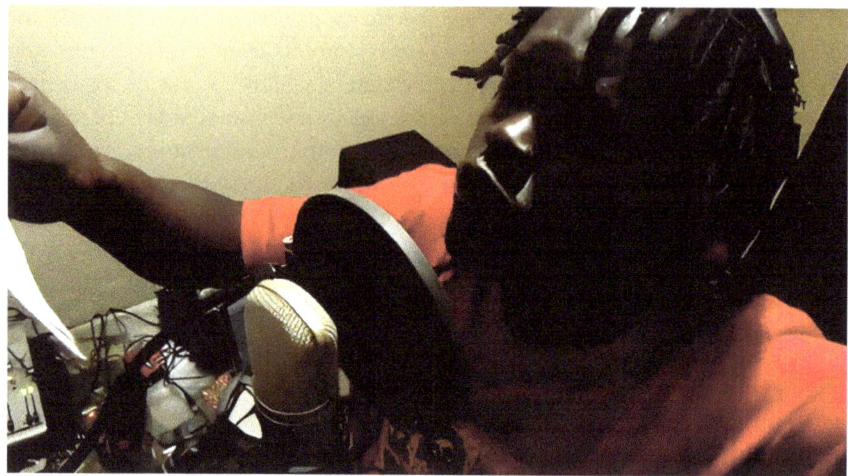

FIGURE 15. "Amandla" music video, featuring Judge. Screenshot by author. Source: Nomadik Studio, "'Amandla' Ft. Khusta, Mic Crenshaw, Ran-D, Judge and MC Bagol," YouTube, December 14, 2015, https://www.youtube.com/watch?v=usamqjWxtyk.

is to receive slots on television and radio. Second, Mose's argument relies almost solely on lyrical content to determine a song's categories. Sound, and how sound fuses with embodiment, often signifies whether a song is considered mainstream or underground. Many underground artists use aurality and corporeal embodiments as methods of defiance and believe that music that appeals to mainstream criteria at the sonic level compromises political commitments because the messages either will not be heard in the same way or will not be comprehensible as a method of resistance.

I argue several points in this chapter. First, practitioners use aurality to help determine whether a song is underground or mainstream. Many reject mainstream sonic formulas because such standards are signs of selling out, which inevitably undercuts political seriousness. For them, their positions are not empty stances; rappers who imagine themselves as activists hold a commitment to making music that intervenes in society. There are unresolvable contradictions that emerge from the need and desire to make money within an industry with specific criteria. Artists often find themselves in a bind because they want to make money and have fans, but ideally, to do so, they must make music that appeals to a broad audience. Songs profiled in this chapter include Sue Timon and Flamez's "Ulimi" and Judge and Washamba Wenza's "Shupavu." These examples underscore practitioners' choices to make grittier beats and exude hip hop's core elements of ludic embodiment, sonic resistance, and political seriousness.

Second, gospel rap fits into this politics of underground sound tied to modes of resistance and ethics of economic self-discipline. Those artists who incorporate Christian-referenced lyrics still believe the objective is to make music that remains true to underground culture. Christianity holds authoritative weight in popular discourse and is posited as a solution to the problems of the nation. Some underground artists identifying as Christians have explicitly religious themes in their songs, while others slip biblical references into lyrics. They often advance precepts of hard work and personal responsibility, both of which are neoliberal ideals and additionally fundamental to political seriousness. These characteristics, however, do not mean that the sound changes, and in fact, these gospel songs hold similar sonic qualities to other underground songs. Using "Ulimi" I explore Christianity-infused lyrics and how the song reflects neoliberal ideas of self-regulation, hard work, and good deeds.

I determine that performance practices join the seemingly contradictory themes of self-discipline and sonic dissidence. This fusion appears when artists perform armored gender, combining the figure of the rapper as a hard worker with the trope of the "warrior" borrowed from the Mau Mau. Both "Shupavu" and "Ulimi" display these corporeal gender politics, which not only fit into global trends but mark the music as distinctly Kenyan. Relying on masculinities from the past tropes of the warrior, in other words, helps to solidify hip hop as Kenyan, and through this, underground rap confirms its local cultural relevance and its status as a Kenyan music genre. After the sections on song analysis, I contextualize hip hop's relationship to capitalism, both its propensity to adhere to neoliberal ideals and its rejection of an industry that sets standards and gives a platform to specific music. The capitalist-based hard work ethic artists purport as a solution to state corruption and greed is not a sentiment particular to the underground but found throughout Kenya. In this sense, practitioners' perspectives on capitalism, including how they criticize each other's failures to be apt businesspeople within the industry, add to how the music reflects its location as profoundly embedded in Kenyan contexts.

Lastly, I include artists and songs regarded as mainstream and commercial to illustrate that sound determines access. The mainstream songs Jaguar's "Matapeli," Juliani's "Utawala," and King Kaka's "Wajinga Nyinyi" contain messaging that calls people to be politically minded and to challenge the state and the inequalities it exacerbates, defying notions that only underground artists produce such music. These songs exemplify how a certain type of mainstream sonority is privileged in the industry, which I contend limits commercial music's capacity to blur, obscure, trick, and disrupt as compared to the work that underground music does. I discuss Bamboo, an artist born in Kenya who grew up in the U.S. and has returned to the country. His music, privilege, proximity to U.S. blackness, and the way his voice and music "sound" have garnered much conversation in the music world.

I use rappers' opinions of Bamboo, which are that he does not stay true to the underground, to highlight how sound often dictates the boundaries that the noncommercial world draws and reflects the realities of the larger music culture in Kenya.

SOUNDING LIKE A WARRIOR

The song and video "Shupavu" by rapper Judge and rap duo Washamba Wenza demonstrate how masculinities, a reliance on capitalism, and a disavowal of the Kenyan state cohere in an underground text. Judge and Washamba Wenza filmed the video in Ngara, a lower-class area near the Central Business District (CBD), and where Judge grew up in Ziwani. Washamba Wenza includes Kev Mamba, Flamez, and Smallz Lethal.[3] Smallz is from Kisii and moved to Nairobi after high school, Flamez is from Dandora, and Kev Mamba is from Jericho, a lower-middle-class neighborhood in the east Nairobi area.

The song's sonic resonances confirm the themes of underclass masculinity within a bleak socioscape. The audience is encouraged to drop their heads, bob to the music, and listen intently and purposefully. Helpful to this analysis is Julian Henriques, who discusses sounding in *Sonic Bodies: Reggae Sound Systems, Performance Techniques, and Ways of Knowing*. Henriques states that sounding occurs when "sonic bodies produce, experience, and make sense of sound."[4] Sounding embodies practitioners' interactions with sound systems and audience members' movements to the music; it is the sonic affect felt through all registers and how these practices produce theories about arrays of power, such as class, gender, and race. To use this concept as a framework to understand "Shupavu" and other Kenyan music is to consider how artists produce and interact with sound and how these collections of sounds acquire social signification in a Kenyan context. Henriques describes Jamaican dancehall as both *bass* culture with low frequencies and high volumes and *base* culture, or the sounds that emerge out of the economic base of society. The same is true of the Kenyan underground, which often uses heavy bass sounds from "the street, often the unpaved ghetto street."[5] The term *underground* captures much of the textures of Nairobi base or bass music: low frequencies, the use of bass sounds, industry and societal marginalization, music that represents lower-class people and *jua kali* workers of the economic base, and even references to the Land and Freedom Army fighters who took to the forest and fought in stealth.[6] Purposeful hiding and social invisibility are the foundations of this type of hip hop sound.

"Shupavu," meaning "brave" or "warrior," I argue, heavily draws on a Mau Mau–inspired underground theme. The practitioners I follow have long imagined themselves existing within a trajectory of anticolonial fighters in Kenya and throughout Africa. Evan Mwangi asserts that "the dominant Kenyan imaginary presents Mau Mau as the ultimate symbol of ordinary people's bravery and resolve to wrest power from colonialists toward ultimate political self-determination."[7] In his larger argument, Mwangi explores how, in postindependence, activists and political rivals developed the Mau Mau as an antigovernment trope deployed against the first two administrations, which became a normative and populist stance, as he notes, "a dominant opposition."[8] The way the Mau Mau was fed into popular culture often produced conflicting and gendered narratives of the army. After the peak of Ukoo Flani Mau Mau rap in the mid-2000s, many songs have continued to draw on the prevalent resistance in Kenyan social imaginaries. Incorporating struggle and warriorship have appeared in their songs even as more explicit references to the Land and Freedom Army have diminished. In the music, Mau Mau warrior tropes produce a gendered armor of masculinity, merging with the figure of the artist as a capable economic actor. The figure continues the legacies of freedom fighting while demonstrating artists' unwavering economic and social survivability in a contemporary landscape.

"Shupavu" illustrates how the performances of African, Black, and Kenyan subjectivities are sonically defined. Along with the rappers' vocal contributions, the song utilizes a single-pluck guitar strum, violin, the kick drum, and synthesized hand claps. There is no excess of sound, only utilitarian sonic unfolding. One of the most noteworthy aspects of the song is where most of the bass sounds come from: not from the synthesizer but from the rappers' vocalities. The chorus starts with "Wamezubaa," with the rappers drawing out the last syllable: "Wamezubaaaaaa . . ."[9] This short "a" sound, the "aaaaaaa," rhymes with the second line of the chorus, "Shupavu," and the extended "Shupaaaaaaa(vu)." The pronounced "aaaaaaaa" in both words serves as the bass presence in the absence of heavy computerization and is affectively felt as being bodily and raw. Although monosyllabically produced, this moment resembles how beatboxers construct creative imageries that mimic the percussive drum machine. Shanté Paradigm Smalls contends that artists interface with societal categories such as race, gender, sexuality, and class in beatboxing, and the characteristics of bass sounds, like beatbox rhythms, are often rendered masculine.[10] The gendered diasporic bass that the artists in "Shupavu" lean into and contribute to fuses with the meaning of "Shupaaaaaaavu," the masculinized brave warrior. Again, masculinity is fed through class positions. The heavy computerization of sounds and vocal synthesizing found in Afropop has acquired connotations such as smooth, refined, and finished, thus creating a sound often associated with wealth and privilege. In "Shupavu," the unrefined voice, especially the rasp that Judge's voice offers, furnishes a lower-class masculinity. The rappers affirm masculinity within the culture by disrupting an elitist standard of sound in popular music. These aural elements might be described as crude and unsophisticated by outside listeners, but the rappers cultivate the technologies of rawness as an artistic form and, in some small way, intervene in industry standards that determine which sounds are appropriate.

The processes of sounding, both in live, mediated presentations of "Shupavu" and the recording of the song, indicate that sonic subjectivity is a performed practice. Henriques describes the dancehall floor as consisting of heartbeats, breathing, and movements, which make up the "corporeal vibrations" of the scene.[11] Judge and Washamba's corporeal vibrations are integral to the song and create a sensorily haptic feeling; in other words, the listener perceives the bodily vibrations of their voices as they produce the familiar traits of peripherality and masculinity. The artists become the bass sounds, and listeners can experience their representations of hip hop's low culture through them.

Their live performance of the song captures how their subjectivities as rappers are about the visuality of the performance and their aural presence merging and informing each other. In chapter 2, I discuss Sue Timon's ludic orature in the live stage performance of "Shupavu" at Sarakasi Dome as one that works to disrupt a masculine culture and affirm her presence. While she was grooving to the beat, the bass coming out of the speakers at Sarakasi was almost deafening. Every time the audience sang along, and the mics absorbed the rappers' vocalizations of "Shupaaaaaaaavu" or "Wamezubaaaaaaaa," the "aaaaaaaa's" shook the large auditorium, and the acoustics swallowed the subsequent lyrics to the point of incomprehensibility. I imagine that this is similar to Henriques's descriptions of the dancehall floor; both consist of euphoric bodies, the distinct aroma of pungent perspiration, and the movement of a collection of people in sync with each other who share in and contribute to the ephemeral sonic embodiments of the moment.[12] There is only a slight difference in that Washamba Wenza and Judge insert their sounding bodies into the recording of "Shupavu"—they produce the bass—so that even without the audience, the inexpensive sound system, and the ill-fitting hall, the corporeal vibrations of their "aaaaaaaa's" remain a part of the text.

The rappers in "Shupavu," Judge and Washamba Wenza, bring together the tropes of the rational economic actor and the tough and impassable masculine fighter to demonstrate their competence. The song is a boast rap that sets out to argue for their *ipso facto* authority in the hip hop game. They do this by reminding the audience that they are confined by the imbalance that shapes the unfairness of their lives. Despite the barriers of poverty, they exist at the hip hop zenith, which only serves as testimony to their sheer survivability: "Tunawaramba na mabavu, Shupavu! Tunakusanya ka viabu" (We finish / crush them with force, [We are] brave / warriors! We make money).[13] Being a warrior means not just fighting physically; it also means using one's armored gender to survive and thrive economically. Although subtle in this particular song, the references to warriorship are part of a wider practice within the culture of drawing on Mau Mau tropes. The affirmation of masculinity through the warrior trope draws directly from how the anticolonial struggle is remembered, and in that way, "Shupavu" uses masculinity to articulate a music that is Kenyan. In the video, the rappers affirm their ability to survive in hip hop and life itself, delivering their message to their witnesses, who appear to be only cismen. The absence of other genders reiterates how much of underground culture writes texts that affirm and rely on cishet masculinity. In the videos that Evan Mwangi analyzes, "Angalia Saa" and "Mashairi," rappers compose women as static objects of nationalism, and "the oppression of women [occurs] in glib summaries, which invoke the idealized figure of mother Africa."[14] Here, women and gender-expansive people are simply nonexistent, implying a setting where cismen are the ones to survive and fight when society breaks down into predictable chaos. Hence, the armor of gender is a performance of a subject position that draws on the global circulatory components of hip hop blackness while also being deeply entrenched in the ways that a specific Kenyan history has shaped gender politics. In short, the armor of gender and its reliance on masculinity makes the music more Kenyan.

"Shupavu"'s trace of Mau Mau themes in the gendered armor is not the only marker of Kenyanness in the song; stringed instruments are included. Guitar strums and violin chords, both synthesized, remind listeners of the Kenyanness of "Shupavu," which is exemplary of hip hop's location in Kenyan music's traditions of chordophones. "Shupavu" has a slow tempo, and this, combined with Washamba and Judge's quick rapping, makes intent focus necessary if one is to hear and understand the words. The song's sonic qualities produce inconspicuousness, and the rappers' desire to fit all their verbosely packed verses into the song outweighs their need for listeners to comprehend the words masterfully or even memorize the verses easily. The slow tempo, the quick delivery of lyrics, and the vocal bass elements make it difficult to obtain a surface-level understanding on a first listen.

Linguistic characteristics contribute to the deliberate and limited legibility of "Shupavu." The artists utilize a localized Sheng from Ngara and the surrounding areas in some parts of the song, and one that not everyone can easily understand.[15] For example, the end of the chorus is "Tunakusanya ka viabu," which means "we gather money" or "we make paper/money." This phrase is spoken in a Sheng that is specific to Ngara. While Sheng is said to have originated in Eastlands, relatively near Ngara, there are neighborhood, regional, urban, peri-urban, and rural language variations.[16] Furthermore, the variation of Sheng that emerged twenty or thirty years ago is still spoken by many people (especially older people) in Kenya. Younger Kenyans, in turn, actively create new words, phrases, and sentence constructions, making Sheng (or perhaps the different *Shengs*) a vibrant and dynamic set of languages rather than merely a diminutive of the putatively more formal Swahili. As the rappers draw viewers into the video through unsettling images of strife, the viewer or listener can still appreciate the flow even if they do not know the type of Sheng used and therefore cannot understand every word.

The lyrical constructions of songs such as "Shupavu" say something specific about the neighborhoods of their artists. The densely filled verses of these songs, often created by rappers' swift deliveries, correlate to everyday living conditions in high-density areas. Ngara has 100 people per hectare (one hectare is about 2.4 acres) and is not as densely populated as informal settlement neighborhoods. In Dandora, where Judge is from, there were about 403 people per hectare in 2010, and in 2020, figures reflect an increase to 585 residents per hectare. The numbers are worse in Kibera, where "Looking Up" was filmed. Approximately 672 people resided in 2010 for every hectare, increasing to about 986 people a decade later.[17] It seems that artists' lyrical commentary, often fast and full of content, is symmetrical to places such as Ngara, Dandora, and Kibera. Just as there is a relative lack of space in these settings, so too is there a lack of spatiality in the songs.

"Shupavu" is a video that portrays urbanity's obscene undersurface as a place where the awful and the beautiful clash. A lack of daylight suggests dystopian features. Throughout the video, the camera points upward toward the rappers, presenting them as authoritative actors within a harsh and pitiless landscape. The sounds that narrate the video are likewise hard, repetitive, and jarring. There is a solid and unflinching air of competitiveness, as the first proclamation in the video is "Wamezubaa!" (They are confused!), meaning that Judge and Washamba's rivals are unknowing or dazed by the knowledge that the artists deliver. If competitiveness is constructed along masculine lines in the song, so too are social isolation and disempowerment. The video shows several scenes where men gather outside with the rappers. Some young men huddle around fires, purportedly to keep warm, while others walk around and sit together. An image of an angry and barking dog appears during Kev Mamba's verse. These scenes evoke strong images of disenfranchisement and despair. Widespread poverty is portrayed as being collective and tragically unjust. At one point, Judge shakes both fists, pointing upward, and looks to the sky while proclaiming, "Shupavu!" This gesture indicates weariness with his current situation and a plea for a reprieve from something above him (perhaps a God). Judge sings the chorus several times and looks bothered, rolling his eyes and shaking his head in frustration, never offering so much as a grin. His stances are serious, affirmative, and steadfast. While rapping, his arms move tightly and confidently around his body. These performances indicate that although Judge has no power to change the present, he can marshal his own will to get through it.

Profound structural restraints inhibit the rappers in "Shupavu" and produce an insufferable vulnerability. In Flamez's scene, he raps while sitting in a stairwell between two walls, where the concrete is crumbling and stained by water and dirt. His motions are aligned with the song's beats, moving his hands toward and away from his body as he raps. The structure around him seemingly determines Flamez's gestures and words, and his bodily presence occupies the space while defying its attempts to restrict him. Eloquently boasting, he raps, "Tara sina taratibu, wamezubaa, ninawatibu (I am in no hurry, I go slowly, they are dazed and I am [lyrically] healing them) / Nawatoboa tu kama kichungi, na ukipenda unikashifu (I go through them like a sieve, and you can come against me if you like)."[18] The video cuts to shots of him interacting with his peers, standing around, talking, and walking through the neighborhood. However, he only raps from the concrete stairwell. These moments symbolically indicate the significance of corporeality—while structural limitations confine his voice, he exercises some freeness through bodily movement.

The video portrays the music industry and the Kenyan state as obstacles to freedom. Judge raps, "Tunachukiana badala ya kuinuana, wasanii ndani ya game, muziki laana" (We hate each other instead of lifting one another; to be a musician in the game, music is a curse).[19] Though this is a braggadocio rap, Judge recognizes that the music industry creates a harsh environment where he is left to compete with fellow rappers. He calls out the industry for its promotion of antagonism rather than unity. Likewise, the representations of the state solidify the idea that the rappers are not only bound by the struggles of making it in the rap game but also face the ongoing threat of state violence. During Flamez's verse, the state is denoted through the police figure. The camera shifts to one group of young men sitting outside, with only their silhouettes visible against the building and the obsidian setting. Suddenly, they stand up and run as the shadow of a police officer appears to walk toward them. This officer slowly approaches the group in this shot and throughout the video, with the shadow of his semi-automatic weapon swinging lightly at his side. This unhurried perpetual saunter terrifies the men, who quickly dart from the scene and toward the camera. Like someone watching a horror movie where the vulnerable run and the pursuant struts assuredly in their direction, the viewer is left rooting for the fleeing men.

Accompanying the sonic and linguistic dodginess in "Shupavu" are the visualities in the music video, as the graphics exude an incomprehensibility that adds to the futuristic-yet-tragically-present-day aura. The hood, in this case, Ngara, is located at the margins of society, but it is also the place that capital relies on the most—the place where poor, working-class, and expendable laborers are housed. The entire music video is shot at night, and viewers never see the assumed clarity of daylight but rather darkness and the various forms of light that only the nighttime can value. The light from multiple fires and streetlights combined with caliginosity produces two dominant colors: a subdued yellow against a beautiful blackness. These hues create a surreal setting that is not readily identifiable, a neighborhood widely found throughout Nairobi yet indistinguishable from the next hood.

What devotees hear and see when they watch videos such as "Shupavu" is a map, one that is visual, linguistic, sonic, and performative. Artists use both language and imagery from their hoods: the sounds reflect desperation and strength, and the gendered armor serves as a remedy to these artists' difficulties. The messaging in "Shupavu," similar to that in the song "Looking Up," is not a call for destroying global capitalist enterprises. Instead, it tells the story of what exists on the margins of society in places where people are simultaneously socially invisible and highly noticeable, as almost 60 percent of Kenya's population lives in informal settlement neighborhoods.[20] The music's loudness and underground quality reflect this contradiction, indicating that a sound can make a mark on society while that same society writes the music off as being too hood, a copy of the west, or simply bad music. An important conversation exists in a text such as "Shupavu." The performance of Judge balling his fists and shaking them as he looks past the sky and to the heavens while proclaiming his warriorship is a commentary on the basic facts of hood living: that space is a faraway luxury and basic amenities are often in short supply. Those with their ear to economic discourse might see this as part of a larger conversation about capitalism as an unremittingly failed project. However, Judge and Washamba Wenza want listeners to understand their sheer fortitude in encountering the disasters of this system and encourage listeners to see the state, symbolized in the video as the armed officer with the methodical gait, as the orchestrator of their misery and a barrier to a righteous and self-determining life.

THE TONGUE IS A WEAPON

Artists make Christian music as a way to move through the industry with limited resources. Several of the practitioners with whom I spoke identify as Christians or have, at one point, produced gospel songs; this included L-Ness, Sue Timon, Demaine Jabez, and Sheria. I spoke with artists who stated explicitly that they have used churches to record music and have made gospel songs because of the genre's popularity and widespread acceptance. Such moves exist within a much larger and more difficult setting that causes musicians to turn to alternative venues such as gospel. Given the tight constrictions of today's industry, it is not surprising that many artists would create gospel music to increase their likelihood of success.

Underground hip hop enters a context in which Christianity has a complicated presence in Kenya that ties into the politics of postcolonialism and privilege.[21] After 1963, Christianity helped form the nation and larger ideals such as citizenship and belonging.[22] The Moi era saw a bolstering of gospel music as both an unintentional by-product of the elimination of dissent and a direct result of Moi's attempts to legitimize his reign. Gospel earned a position in Kenya as a politically neutral and thus acceptable genre in the face of growing dissent.[23] Because many musicians were censored at this time, artists from outside Kenya found opportunities in the country, as they were less likely to produce anti-Moi music. Kenyans who avoided censorship or sought to appeal to a wide audience composed songs in Swahili or Lingala fit with Christian references.[24] The religion's rise and popularity in the Kenyan music industry has also resulted from industry factors. Churches began to fill voids in the music industry during the 1980s as multinational recording companies in Nairobi started to decline. For instance, Baptist Communications and Nairobi Pentecostal Church-Valley Road had begun to host recording sessions for a number of artists by the mid-1980s.[25] Additionally, the Nairobi Pentecostal Church owns and runs the radio station Hope FM.[26] Currently, several

Pentecostal churches continue to sponsor musicians and host concerts, providing the artists with readymade audiences and potential customers. Many of these religious institutions are also large businesses. They fund artists' production costs, host rap concerts, and open avenues for artists to appear on radio and television. Gospel music, in part due to the position of these churches, is now so influential that "musicians [reinvent] themselves as the recording industry's market has turned to the lucrative wave of commercial, Pentecostal-Charismatic Christianity."[27] It is within this context that some underground artists attempt to tap a market that is relatively easier to access compared to radio and television.

Pentecostal-Charismatic Christianity has a long history in Kenya and has influenced hip hop culture. Pentecostalism reached Africa in the early 1900s, and by the 1970s, it had become widely popular in Kenya.[28] Although it occupies a dominant place in Kenyan society, it breaks from mainline denominations, such as Anglicanism, Catholicism, and Methodism. In Pentecostal-Charismatic denominations, worship services focus on energetic dancing, lively performances, the giving of testimonies, glossolalia, and engaging sermons. Most have a youth wing that aggressively attempts to draw in members by espousing ideals of individual spiritual transformation, cosmopolitanism, modernity, and economic prosperity. Concerts can include hip hop, dancehall, and reggae music, all of which contain Christian messages. Rather than recoiling from worldly issues, these churches address societal problems, occasionally critiquing the state and interfacing with formal politics.[29] They often provide economic assistance along with a hefty dose of prosperity gospel, which dictates that God wants the faithful to be successful financially and that the more one gives to the institution and believes in the will of God, the more one will receive economic rewards. This philosophy appeals to many because it provides methods of spiritual fortitude: as people build up their belief systems while waiting for monetary benefits, they are afforded a type of resilience that enables them to make it through tough times. For those who live in precarious realities and those seeking to grow their wealth, Charismatic-Pentecostalism gives people hope and allows them to exercise a faith-based capitalist outlook. Just like corporations—and insofar as megachurches can be corporate entities—people view these institutions as viable sources of support when the state fails.

Today, gospel music receives much airplay on television and radio. Pastors and ministers of megachurches appear on television programs during the week and far outside of Sunday hours, and gospel music regularly plays during music slots on television. These realities emphasize Damaris Parsitau's argument that Kenyan "gospel music is popular culture."[30] Parsitau notes that in the 1990s, the Kenyan media ushered gospel music into commercial spaces, taking advantage of radio and television liberalization. For Parsitau, people angry and confused about rampant political corruption, poverty, and the HIV/AIDS crisis readily received such programming and music to make it through adversity.[31]

Not surprisingly, artists recognize the central place that Christianity, especially Charismatic-Pentecostalism, has come to occupy in Kenya and noted that they have sought out and performed at venues such as Deliverance Church and Nairobi Pentecostal Church. These artists have tapped into gospel's normative cultural location to make the types of rap music vital to them, a point emphasized by Jean Kidula.[32] She notes that all kinds of Kenyan gospel music have dynamic elements that incorporate African styles from around the continent, Black and white American aspects, and older Kenyan traditions. Artists' decisions to integrate components into gospel are often because of taste and faith but are also strategic, as "gospel musicians intentionally explore, exploit, and manipulate arenas . . . for commercial and religious expediency."[33]

Given that Pentecostal Christianity seeks to attract youth and position itself within popular culture spaces, it makes sense that rappers would seek out these institutions. Before Sue Timon joined *I Am*, she made music with Christian references. She stated at the time, "I'm able to rap about real-life issues. I write about the government. I can write about, ah, God. I can relate to people. And that is what makes it powerful. Because it affects someone, and someone can feel what I am saying."[34] Her sentiments echo another artist, Decence, who asserted that being a gospel artist does not mean that one must only discuss Christianity: "I wouldn't say that I talk just about the Bible *kabisa*,[35] because there is so much going on . . . . You know people need to wake up. Actually, there is so much to talk about. Politicians and stuff, yeah."[36] These statements reveal artists' needs to lean on the openings offered by gospel and redefine their music on their terms as much as possible. Their decisions not to rap about the Bible *kabisa* also exemplify how they take advantage of Christianity's social position to make the music they want. This sentiment differs from that of other artists who explicitly identify as Christians, such as Juliani, discussed in a later section in this chapter. Their decisions to make gospel are smart and deliberate in many ways because they recognize that gospel messages make rap more palatable to a broader audience.

"Ulimi" (Tongue) by Sue Timon and Flamez from Washamba Wenza warns its listeners concerning the obligations devotees have to their communities. The song, released around 2011, folds Christian values into a strict underground ethic. "Ulimi" is about the power of one's voice, and according to Sue Timon and Flamez, the tongue is a weapon, "ulimi ni silaha," and rappers have a moral duty to use their words to spread encouragement, hope, and positivity rather than triviality and pessimism.[37] The song elicits the corporeal and fleshy just like "Shupavu," and does so through its explicit reference to the tongue as voice. It contains a typical underground sound that captures the political seriousness of the culture with its solemn and overly heavy beats. The sonic energies of "Ulimi" mirror its lyrics and materialize as a warning call to those who influence others. There is little carefreeness in the song, as listeners are asked to inventory their lives and make appropriate changes for the good of society. The religiousness of "Ulimi" uses noncommercial sound and lyrically heavy quality typical of underground music.

FIGURE 16. "Ulimi" music video, featuring Sue Timon in front of other rappers. Screenshot by author. Source: Flamez Mshamba Mwenza, "Ulimi Sue Timon & Flamez (Washamba Wenza) Official Video," YouTube, January 28, 2013, https://www.youtube.com/watch?v=zkwx RjBpoLs.

"Ulimi" adheres to the same Pentecostal-Charismatic notions found in many churches, mainly through the individualist notion of religious self-policing. In "Ulimi," Sue Timon raps, "Ulimi ni silaha, unafa ukatekate maovu, kungine ni dawa unaposhwa poshwa, wacha maovu" (The tongue is a weapon, you are supposed to eliminate bad deeds, elsewhere it is medicine, it relieves pain, [delivered as a directive] stop bad deeds!).[38] The idea of the "tongue as a weapon" alludes to Christian notions about policing one's actions in the service of faith. Using the biblical idea of "tame the tongue," Timon and Flamez construct their voices as weapons. The message is the same: be careful about what you say. Timon and Flamez specifically construct themselves as agents who take on social responsibility. "Ulimi" has many characteristics that typify the Nairobi underground, such as encouraging listeners to discipline themselves to live a better life and expressing the notion that the voice can be used as a weapon to fight injustice. Following the traditions of both Pentecostal-Charismatic and underground ideals, it focuses outward on society. In the lyrics, Timon and Flamez refer to the evils of the music industry, postelection violence, and colonialism. Whereas the song's overarching theme is that one must control what one says and use their voice for good, the call to do better is situated within harsh historical and contemporary realities. What emerges is a text that sounds obstinate and almost merciless, counseling people within the context of a broad concern for the welfare of Kenyans.

"Ulimi" was produced at Audio Kusini studio, where I met and interviewed several artists in the beginning part of my fieldwork, including Nafsi Huru, Agano,

FIGURE 17. Sue Timon in the "Ulimi" music video trailer. Screenshot by author. Source: Flamez Mshamba Mwenza, "Ulimi Sue Timon & Flamez (Washamba Wenza) Video Trailer," YouTube, January 11, 2013, https://www.youtube.com/watch?v=ShuCJ2992yo.

and Funzo Kuu. Nafsi's "Still Strong," the song I examined in the previous chapter, was produced at Audio Kusini. Soon after this visit, artists reported that the studio leadership had decided to restructure its focus and gear its music toward Christian gospel. Audio Kusini had "kicked everyone out," according to rappers, when I returned in 2012 and only hosted "gospel artists." Years later, artists told me that people regularly joked that someone performed witchcraft on the studio because of its unexpected turn, which resulted in chaos and frustration.

Audio Kusini's website now boasts an assortment of gospel songs, primarily ones that fall within a mainstream commercial sound. There are several hip hop songs, including ones by Kaktus Kusini, the named founder and CEO of the studio. In an interview on WemaTV, a Christian Kenyan online television station, Kaktus spoke of rapping in his childhood, starting the studio with help from his family, eventually drinking, straying from his Christian faith, and ultimately returning to a more religious life.[39] Kaktus never mentioned what happened with the former rappers at the studio, so it is difficult to glean where they fit into his timeline of struggle and transformation. The studio shifted from a very specific underground sound to more industry-compatible music. There is also a difference in the finishing quality of the two types of videos. "Still Strong" and "Ulimi" appear less polished than Audio Kusini's current catalogs, implying that there may have been modifications or upgrades in studio technologies. Kaktus continues to make rap songs and produce other artists, but the music does not carry the same underground spirit as "Ulimi." Critically, one underground artist explained of the current Audio Kusini tracks that "you can't hear the soul of hip hop in the music anymore."[40]

Despite the studio's shifts, it must not be forgotten that "Ulimi" is a gospel song. There is not much difference in lyrical messaging between "Ulimi" and the songs that Audio Kusini now produces, and although "Ulimi" draws on biblical themes, the song and video are not included on Audio Kusini's website. It is difficult to conclude why this is the case, and Kaktus Kusini certainly has the freedom to build and implement his studio and company in whatever way he sees fit. The prominent difference between a song such as "Ulimi" and the current music at Audio Kusini lies in the sound. In "Ulimi," Sue Timon and Flamez rap over a stark and resolute beat, and the bass is heavy and occupies much of the song's sonic space. The lyrics are delivered quickly and without much pause, and the sentiment is cautionary and exasperated. Much of Audio Kusini's current music carries an uplifting tone set to commercially synthesized sounds and a marked lack of the sonic heaviness of underground bass; that is, it is no longer underground but aboveground, matching much of the popular music that circulates in media spaces.

CAPITALISM IS THE "SOLUTION"

In late 2017, commercial artist Juliani reported that he would host a large-scale tribute concert for Kalamashaka and would be inviting sponsors through his Dandora Hip Hop City project. He mentioned Ukoo Flani Mau Mau, Wenyeji, and Mashifta as some of the artists on the concert bill. While the concert did not materialize as indicated, the headlines stood out as important. Juliani stated in a related interview, "Kalamashaka did so much for the industry, but look at them now. Look at them now: they are neglected; nobody cares about them."[41] He is kinder than other artists, who have expressed frustration and ridicule over Kalamashaka's inability to establish a veritable career in the rap game. These criticisms reveal the tensions and angst artists often feel about themselves as economic subjects in a late capitalist system. Kalamashaka and UFMM have developed a dual reputation as the cultural founders of the music and as individuals who have failed to whip their profits into something sustainable, which is at the heart of a much larger discourse in Kenya about artists from the hood.

During a discussion I had with a man practitioner, I queried him about the difficulties that artists face when attempting to profit from selling music. I told him about a previous interaction in a music stall in the Central Business District. I had asked the vendor for underground music, but they had responded with confusion and mild shock before stating that they did not sell "that type" of music. I asked for the artist's thoughts on the interaction, and their response is worth quoting at length:

> You know, like, I'm not even looking at it like an artist or whatever. I'm looking at it like from a business point of view, business perspective. Most of these guys are usually not serious. Okay, like yeah, they might, like, shoot me if they hear me talking like this, but it's true. Most of these guys are not serious. So, they are not aggressive; they don't push their product that much. Plus, . . . most of the hip hop artists in Kenya don't even have managers and all that. So, the business element of hip hop in Kenya is very poor compared to like Uganda, Tanzania, so like, *if you're talking like let's say, Ukoo Flani or Mau Mau or whatever, . . . by now they should be riding hummers and shit . . . cuz they started way back in 1996.* They used to actually do world tours. You know like, if they go to Europe, do some tours there, South Africa, but mismanagement is what actually brought them down. So, they are good lyrically, but businesswise, no, most of them are poor.[42] (emphasis mine)

The scenario I laid out prompted the artist to discuss the ineptitude of UFMM rather than any structural reasons that could explain rap's absence in the stalls, such as the negative associations of underground sounds or even the vendor's personal decision not to sell rap because of a perceived notion of what the music entails. This practitioner saw the dearth of rap music in the stalls as the artist's responsibility to correct. The inability of artists to cope within the industry is seen as their failure to make suitable and rational choices rather than as a misdeed of the institutions and individuals that gatekeep and maintain the industry. These assessments of other rappers, thus, enforce a disciplinary logic where an artist is always judged for their economic actions. To be a capable rapper is to know one's field and to act accordingly; in short, it is to govern one's actions in the face of or in accordance with structures of power.

There do exist hardy critiques of capitalism when discussing UFMM. To return to the documentary profiled in chapter 3, *Ni Wakati*, Albert Josiah, a former radio presenter at KISS FM, edges close to a condemning assessment of capitalism in his discussion of the rich and poor. Josiah accurately dismantles the claims about Kalamashaka that they could not secure economic benefit because of their shortcomings. Josiah also frames the argument within a broader historical setting. He identifies how Kalamashaka's story is similar to that of the Mau Mau fighters: "If you think about it honestly, [Kalamashaka] bore none of the fruits of that struggle. Does that sound like a familiar story?"[43] As soon as he asks this, *Ni Wakati* transitions to a scene from the 1952–59 State of Emergency in Kenya, wherein the colonial state exerted catastrophic violence on Africans in an attempt to hold on to the colony. Josiah then states the following:

> They are the guys that are fighting for your rights for the belief that, you know, there is something more to do, that Kenya shouldn't be on its knees begging the World Bank, "Nisaide, nisaide, za zote" (Help me, help me, all the time). That we shouldn't be yoked with that elusive, invisible hand meddling in our business, and stealing our souls, and taking our babies, and destroying our future. We shouldn't just sit back and look at it happen; we need to say something. And that, you know, a lot of the part of you being poor and unhappy, some of it has to do with people who are rich because they took what was supposed to be yours.[44]

Josiah's statement is one of the most impactful interventions in the film, and it offers several points. He asserts that the Mau Mau fighters who survived the conflict still sacrificed enormously, as many who managed to survive were still landless and poor after independence. Thirty years later, landless and poor artists paved the way for well-off artists and other industry players to turn hip hop into a profit-generating genre. Josiah's point is that the rich are rich because they stole from the poor, not because they worked hard, and Kenyans should not beg for money from entities that represent a larger global system that has turned Africa's valuable commodities into incredible wealth for the global north. Josiah's comment directed at the greedy shifts us toward a welcome indictment of the inherently unfair economic system. Though rappers do not necessarily move toward a wholesale critique of capitalism, many agree with Josiah's point that politicians and well-connected businesspeople who monopolize industries and hoard wealth stand in the way of the freedoms of working-class people.

Most rappers do not put pressure on the economic system but on individual actors, like politicians and themselves. They reflect wider societal values of hard work within capitalist contexts and tie these beliefs into the culture of hip hop, upholding the ideas that one should work hard for their success and that difficult obstacles are not a reason to stop making music.[45] This emphasis on labor in Kenyan society is connected to how people earn and exercise self-determination in a context structured around global capitalism. Hence, it is of little surprise that the genre is often defined through its use-value. Consider the following statement from underground rapper Demaine Jabez:

> Hip hop is a way of expression. And hip hop music is powerful. Music changes societies. Music shapes cultures, and music brings up generations, you know? So I find hip hop, huh, as a tool where one can stand out and do music and cause his plea to be heard. It's like a CV; you have to bring your CV before the guy you want a job from. So hip hop is like a CV.[46]

I have heard many similar sentiments: that the music is a resource that leads to greater opportunities. Other rappers with whom I talked discussed the need to approach hip hop as a small business, reiterating the idea that if artists are to succeed, they must build their brands. Many argued that rappers who have failed and left the game have either not worked hard enough or neglected to craft them-selves as a marketable product. Such views reflect the economic circumstances and are reasonably understandable given that most underground rappers are from working-class backgrounds, and even those who have managed to form a career out of their music do not have inheritable wealth and thus find themselves in an ongoing hustle.

L-Ness fully acknowledged the difficulties of developing a music career while also viewing the process as being full of necessary and inevitable hard work and personal sacrifice:

> *L-Ness:* Most artists, some people actually stop, they give up the game cuz they're like, I've done a song, I've paid a video, a good video, I've paid a good studio—a very good song. And then they put all their hope into it. All their money into it. Then they take it to the stations, it runs only one week. Then it doesn't play. You don't get shows; you don't get your money back. Some people are just like "fuck it." You know [laughs]. So many artists . . .
>
> *RP:* So, I mean, is that understandable? Or do you . . . not agree with it?
>
> *L-Ness:* I don't agree with it because here are so many ways, so many things hap-pening in scene. We also have cartels that are controlling the game. But that shouldn't make anybody give up. Cuz you can, you don't focus on Kenya. When you make your music, you focus on outside Kenya. So if Kenyan sta-tions don't play, Tanzanian stations will play. Ugandan stations will play; South Africa will play. But it's hard; it shouldn't be like that. It shouldn't be like that.[47]

Immediately before this explanation, she had objected to the music industry's informal payola system. Additionally, she discussed elsewhere in the conversa-tion how women artists encounter hardship in maintaining a rap career because of familial duties and pressures. L-Ness knows that people face industry hardship; despite that, she believes one should persevere under any circumstances. She is not alone in this belief; the notion that one must be a fit and rational economic actor is a widespread ideal among underground musicians. Such ideals can be regarded as bolstering and placing one's faith in the same capitalism that marginalizes artists in the industry. However, rappers have melded compliant economic subjecthood into a practice of defiance and subversion, which simultaneously emerges through gendered armor subjectivities. What appears is a rugged work ethic dictating that rappers should be capable businesspeople within an oppressive reality, easily fit-ting with masculine ideas of toughness and survivability. Thus, L-Ness's comment that artists should persevere despite familial pressures on women and industry limitations for many lower-class musicians also points to a more endemic set of codes about how subtle masculinities operate.

For rappers, capitalism, or their marginal position within it, is not the problem in their lives; instead, it is the available solution to the obstacles they face. Much of the pressure rappers put on themselves and others to be capable and able to survive the rap hustle surfaces from their class positions and their views of the state. Most see capitalism as a way to obtain greater opportunities, while the kleptocratic state is seen as impeding their journey toward economic self-actualization. Many practitioners think the government misuses capitalism, which could be beneficial. If only politicians would not be so greedy, artists—and people in general—could exercise personal potential within capitalist practices. Rappers argue that the state does not allow them opportunities to work, make money, and acquire wealth and that the government impedes economic freedom. Furthermore, underground artists believe they can be wealthy, but that wealth must be garnered through selling products that do not conform to mainstream standards. Most assume that rappers who make it do so by compromising. These rappers explicitly understood that those who remain pure to hip hop are bad businesspeople and never able to earn money consistently, and those who become affluent sell out. There is an inherent and unresolved paradox because those who hustle must succeed, and wealthy rappers who started as poor are almost always considered as having sold out.

The idea that capitalism is a solution to how the state impedes people's path toward economic security is not something that exists only in hip hop spaces; it is a widespread societal belief in Kenya. I encountered this notion early in my fieldwork. In 2010–11, a famine hit Turkana, the northeastern part of Kenya. After the then-government spokesperson Alfred Mutua denied that people were suffering and dying, many Kenyans were outraged. Corporations, including Safaricom, Kenya Commercial Bank, Media Owners Association, and the Kenya Red Cross, led a campaign called "Kenyans for Kenya," which raised food and resources for the region.[48] I attended one of the campaign's fundraising events, where businesses competed to see who could raise the most money. Kenyans across the country and those abroad donated funds, and people regularly discussed how they could confidently donate because they knew their money would not be swallowed into mismanaged and corrupt government initiatives. The idea that Kenyans could and should help each other independent of state assistance proliferated during this time, and the able and generous helped raise billions of Kenyan shillings after the campaign appeared on television and radio. "Kenyans for Kenya" served as a nation-building exercise. For many, it proved that Kenyans could come together in a crisis just a few years after the tragedies of the 2007–8 postelection violence. The unanimous discourse at the time was that people did not need the state to remedy the crises afflicting the country and that with the assistance of corporations, Kenyans could help themselves.

According to media reports and press releases during this time, the people in Turkana lacked food because the area was semi-arid and prone to drought. However, larger structural analyses of how famines are avoidable and often the result of global racial capitalism were left out of these conversations. For example, people's livelihoods and the ability to exercise pastoralism, a long-held and thriving practice in Turkana, have been made difficult by a drying climate and the extractive oil industry's presence there. Land has long been seized for oil exploration, and in 2012, production began. Charis Enns and Brock Bersaglio discuss how civil society in the region organized for rights from the very oil companies inducing the economic and social shifts.[49] They describe the Turkana oil camps as another example of resource enclaves, for them "spaces of corporate control," where workers—usually not from Turkana—live in protected gated compounds and have access to excess food and amenities. In contrast, in the surrounding areas, many people live in poverty and subsistence.[50] Rarely is there a hearty analysis of how racial capitalism enables government violence and instability and thus creates and exacerbates other societal problems, such as the arrivals of dispossessed Sudanese to the Kakuma refugee camp and the Kalobeyei Integrated Settlement or the cattle rustling and economic conflicts between Pokot and Turkana communities.[51] Ignoring how capitalism creates and is dependent on inequities positions corporations as the solution to, in this case, the ill-suited barren environment and the inept state.

Of course, "Kenyans for Kenya" only built on and hardened the already-in-place notion that capitalist Kenya is a solution to these social problems. Upon independence, Jomo Kenyatta sought to sell capitalism to the populace as inherently African and socialism and communism as an anathema.[52] He aligned the country with the U.S. and the west during early independence, both economically and militarily, a strategic Cold War–driven set of moves.[53] By the time Daniel arap Moi began privatizing government parastatals, liberalizing the media, and permitting multinational corporations into the country in the late 1990s, capitalism was positioned as a remedy to his authoritarianism. Institutions such as the World Bank claim that the growth of capitalism is a goal for "developing" countries, but these beliefs have also been absorbed and pursued by Kenyans of all classes. Corporations are seen as "cleaning up" Kenya, bringing infrastructure and employment to people. Additionally, as China's investment in Kenya and its close relationship with the country's presidents have intensified over the past few decades, the skepticism Kenyans have had with this form of investment has been directed at China itself rather than at corporate practices at large. The conditions of capitalism are regarded as inevitable, and the origins of inequalities are misidentified as accidents or the result of human failure, including of the greedy rich and the poor and lazy.

SYNTHESIZING RESISTANCE

In the underground world, mainstream music standards are a thorn in the sides of artists who believe their music is worthy of occupying ample amounts of space on radio and television. Artists regard those who make mainstream music or incorporate hip hop elements such as rapping into Afropop songs as sellouts. Many see adhering to neoliberal values, such as disciplined hard work, as acceptable, while artists who adhere to capitalism by being overly commercial are seen as disloyal to the culture of hip hop. Judge argued that commercial rap, which typically incorporates dancehall and Afropop elements, delivers watered-down lyrics, which he calls "ABCD rhymes," "nursery rhymes," and "cartoon rhymes."[54] This comment refers to simplistic lyrics that are basic in their structure and those that do not take up strong critiques of society, both of which are largely derided in the underground.

I spoke with some artists who fuse their music with Afropop instrumentations, either for diversity, taste, or marketing purposes. Rapper Baby T, who appears in the song and video "Looking Up," stated that Afropop and dancehall both carry weight in the music industry. She argued that rap is more "cumbersome" due to its often heavy lyrics and that "hip hop goes underground because many people don't want to take the time to listen to it."[55] For her, these are all reasons why someone may want to make more mainstream music:

> Most people love dancehall more than hip hop. . . . I'd say that hip hop artists are working hard to make, to bring hip hop back alive. When it comes up, you just have to mix it with other things to get people to listen. So, if you do a fusion of maybe hip hop and dancehall, people listen to it because there's a bit of dancehall, so, yeah. I think there will be a fusion, and maybe sometimes you even might overlap some dancehall.[56]

The cumbersome nature of underground music, as Baby T noted, has everything to do with the sonorous elements: the bulky sounds, the closely packed lyrics, and the overall heavy tonalities. Her argument presents questions about when listening feels laborious and demanding and relates to an industry-wide sentiment: that the music should be set to accompaniment that aids listeners and consumers in easily appreciating the music and taking in the lyrics. It is important to note that the dancehall that Henriques describes in *Sonic Bodies* does not retain its low or othered signification as it travels across the Atlantic to the African continent. Dancehall in Kenya materializes as part of commercial music that middle- and upper-class youth listen to. Although it is recognized as a relative of low-cultured reggae, which is also historically popular in Kenya, it preserves an alternative connotation as being attached to an affluent ethos. Dancehall music's sound systems, computerized vocoders, and synthesizers are machines of access and excess. Artists who have the resources to produce a finished product can make use of computer technologies, which thus come to signify an upper-class sound. Of all the artists I spoke with, Baby T was the most dedicated to making mainstream music and once aspired to collaborate with U.S. rapper Meek Mill. Much of Baby T's music has made it to Kenya's evening music video slots on television. She exemplifies the straddling that Caroline Mose writes about in "Jua Cali Justice," as the artists Mose writes about, like Jua Cali, Madd Traxx, and Wenyeji, are similar to Baby T. These artists produce music that has a range of subject matter from political oppression to partying and sexual relationships and therefore do not fit into neat categories of either mainstream or underground boxes that, for Mose, are "unreliable" and "non-specific."[57]

Several mainstream songs take on socially salient topics or contain subversive messaging, but this does not dissuade underground artists from writing off the music as commercial and mainstream and thus inauthentic to the culture.

In hip hop, aesthetic and sonic characteristics and political commitments are closely intertwined. When mainstream artists create conscious music with sonic appeal, the earnestness of their songs can easily appear thin or hollow because the sound does not align with the content. Unlike the heavier sounds and thick lyrics in songs such as "Ulimi" and "Shupavu," in many commercial songs the words can be clearly heard and are matched with a buoyant and easily singable chorus. There are three songs I examine here: Jaguar's "Matapeli" (Conmen/Con people), Juliani's "Utawala" (Leadership/Rulership), and King Kaka's "Wajinga Nyinyi" (Y'all Stupid).

Jaguar's 2012 catchy and then-popular song "Matapeli" decries government corruption and the blatant and gross profiting off the multiple episodes of disaster capitalism in Kenya. The first few lines are as follows: "Ona tuliowachagua, wanatuchezea kama marioneti, hakuna anayetujali, wamekuwa watu wa pesa (Look at the ones we elected, they are playing us like marionettes, no one cares about us, they have become money people) / Bei ya unga inapanda wakati mahindi inaoza kwa shamba. Eeh! Maziwa inaganda wakati kwa duka bei inapanda (Price of flour is going up while maize is rotting on the farm. Eeh! Milk is getting sour while the price at the store goes up)."[58]

Here, Jaguar, also known as Charles Njagua Kanyi, references the claims that politicians created and benefited from one of the many maize scandals that have become relatively commonplace in Kenya. Politicians and businesspeople create intentional maize shortages to profit from them. The National Cereals and Produce Board (NCPB) is the institution that buys maize from farmers, and they keep stockpiles of it to account for demand and in case of drought or hardship. The scandal occurs when the farmers attempt to sell the maize to the NCPB, and the board inaccurately tells the farmers that the product is worth less than market value, insisting they need to buy it at a drastically low price. The farmers will, in turn, not sell the maize and hold off for better prices because they cannot break even, causing the silos to run low. The NCPB then states they must import maize because of this manufactured shortage, and the board then buys maize from colluding government officials who oversee the importation of new product. When this imported maize is, in turn, sold at a higher price, this ultimately yields billions of Kenya shillings in profit for all involved. In addition, sometimes the maize is sold to shell companies or "briefcase millers," who then sell the product outside the country and make an incredible profit.[59]

Upon first listen, it is easy to be swept up in the progressive reach of this popular artist and his willingness to engage with public art that articulates everyday people's concerns and the gross corruptive practices of the government. For instance, the video shows several images from the folk hero art of Pawa 254's 2012 Mavultures graffiti project that appeared on buildings along streets such as Moi Ave and Koinange Street throughout Nairobi and portrayed politicians as vultures who devour the citizenry and the country's resources.[60] However, a cursory look into the song and video reveals its collaboration with the normative parameters that arrange the music industry and state power. For instance, Jaguar includes politician Mike Sonko in his video, demonstrating his closeness to the government. Sonko is a long-embattled former MP, former senator, and Nairobi governor. He appears in the video as a *jua kali* shoeshiner. As an MP, he acquired a reputation for being closely connected to youth and hip hop culture by wearing urban streetwear in public settings and donning earring studs on the Parliament floor, much to the dismay of other MPs who called for decorum and respectability.[61] At the time of the video, Sonko was a senator for Nairobi and had crafted himself as a controversial, outspoken ally of poor youth. However, he has had a turbulent career, facing accusations of drug trafficking, being arrested for corruption, and being impeached and removed from governorship in 2020.[62] Sonko's controversies aside, his presence as a state figure in a music video about the greed of political elites is contradictory at best.

The sonic qualities of "Matapeli" also align with industry criteria. Like many other pop songs, it includes computerized vocal instrumentalizations, a quick tempo, and a danceable beat. Jaguar's delivery of the lyrics is somewhere between rapping and singing. His vocals are certainly not the fast and cutting delivery of rap bars in hip hop traditions but rather a smoother sing-song rhyming style. Unlike the jolting tonalities often found in much of rap music, especially noncommercial forms, Jaguar sings with smoothed-out vocals that cushion his indictment of social issues.

Throughout the song, "Eh eeh eh eeh eeh, Eh eeh eh eeh" can be heard in chorus-like echoes.[63] While this utterance can be easily overlooked, it deserves an explication. The "Eh!" is a Kenyan (and African) exclamation of disgust meant to convey a harsh rebuke. People smack their lips or suck their teeth and shout "Eh!" when they are maddened and repulsed at a given situation. In the context of the subject matter of "Matapeli," which details how well-paid and resourced politicians sought to turn food shortages into profit, this expression could be apprehended in a musical context to Africanize dissent and to encourage the contempt that many Kenyans felt during this time. However, this speech-act materializes through the synthesizer and occurs within the rest of Jaguar's machinic vocals. The thrust of defiance and revulsion that might otherwise convey opposition is lost. What listeners hear is a profoundly distinct buffered and veiled "Eh!" and what is meant to proffer indignation floats out in the aural space as pacifying and harmonic scatting.

"Matapeli" foretells Jaguar's subsequent political career. Jaguar regularly performed for then-presidential hopeful Uhuru Kenyatta's campaign, which began circa 2013. When Uhuru came into power, he tapped Jaguar to lead a youth wing before appointing him as director of a semigovernmental body, the National Authority for the Campaign against Alcohol and Drug Abuse (NACADA). In 2017, Jaguar was voted in as an MP for the working-class area of Starehe in Nairobi.[64]

If his sentiment of dissent meant to press against the monopolistic state power structure was questionable in "Matapeli," his participation in the gears of the state solidifies his inability to intervene in rap's traditions of sustained resistance.

King Kaka's 2019 song "Wajinga Nyinyi" does not follow the same musical blueprint as "Matapeli" and "Utawala," the latter of which is discussed below. "Wajinga Nyinyi" is formatted like a poem and prayer that calls out Kenyans' numbness to the scandals of political elites. King Kaka, who initially went by the name Kaka Sungura, established himself as an Eastlands-born rapper, as detailed in songs such as "Eastlando." Over the years, Kaka has started several businesses, such as the bottled water company he established in 2015, Kaka Empire's Majik Water.[65]

"Wajinga Nyinyi" is the most sonically effective of the three songs. "Wajinga" avoids a catchy sonic structure, and King Kaka sets his prose to a solemn piano sound. The song addressed yet another maize scandal in 2018, the joblessness of college graduates, a corruption controversy involving former minister and Kirinyaga governor Anne Waiguru, a failed government-funded laptop project, and the troubling exile of government critic Miguna Miguna.[66] As the song progresses, one may anticipate a predictable beat to drop and a rap flow to form, but neither ever comes. Instead, King Kaka delivers his intense lyrical montage alongside a piano sound that seems almost off-beat to his words. Listeners are left slightly uncomfortable, wondering if a predictable song formula will develop. This deviation from the expectations of sound causes listeners to pause slightly, hesitate, anticipate, and wonder, all predicated upon sonic uneasiness. Kaka does not use the synthesizer's predictable Afropop formula to numb his words as Jaguar does in "Matapeli." Instead, fans are forced to speculate on the sonic divergences and, in the process, absorb the lyrical content.

The song lyrics match the sonic themes of popular opposition but also undercut pleas for resistance through ableist tropes. Kaka contends that Kenyans have become indifferent to corruption. To be sure, it is difficult to be outraged by every news headline that reports on an official siphoning funds into their personal bank accounts, which is an exhausting, if not impossible, response. Kaka's song urges listeners who are stupid, or *wajinga*, to continue applying pressure to the state. Indicting people as stupid is attention-grabbing and surely meant to be a rallying call for action. However, it also works to judge inaction through foolishness, a fallacious opinion that ultimately concludes people's unintelligence should be blamed for state greed. Additionally, for him, "sisi ni vipofu na viziwi" (we are blind and deaf), and people must avoid the impassiveness that leads to apathy and the tacit allowance of Kenya's kleptocracy.[67] Kaka's line leaves the listener with the difficult question of whether a mass uprising against politicians *eating* money, as it is phrased in Kenya, would lead to systemic change or a heavy-handed state response of force and bloodshed. However, he curtails his argument by implying that sightlessness and hearing loss parallel political unconcern. Kaka's encouragement for people to fight through corruption fatigue may be reasonable, but not when people's dissent is measured through the register of a normate body.

"Wajinga Nyinyi" stirred much attention in the media and with governmental officials, probably and partly because of its shock value ableism. After its release, Governor Waiguru filed a lawsuit and later dropped it against King Kaka, stating that he had defamed her.[68] Kaka also said that he feared for his life and reported that he had received calls from President Kenyatta, among other leaders. In December 2019, with media cameras rolling and legal representation and other musicians at his side, he reported to the Directorate of Criminal Investigations (DCI) for questioning after taking to social media, stating that the office had called him in. However, the DCI released a formal statement saying that the office had, in fact, not summoned him there and retorted that Kaka's arrival was a media publicity stunt.[69] If Kaka's goal was to whip up attention to magnify the iniquitous state attention on him or to produce headlines, it worked well. Artists Juliani, Wahu, and Eric Wainaina, along with Boniface Mwangi (the activist discussed in chapter 2), among others, appeared in front of the DCI and spoke in news interviews about the inherent right to create art to protest in a democratic country and to be protected under the constitution. Eric Wainaina famously faced government censorship with his 2001 song "Nchi ya Kitu Kidogo" (A Country of Bribes), which commented on the culture of corruption under President Moi's administration.[70] "Kitu kidogo" (something small, as in *give me something small*) is the commonplace saying and practice of bribes; to escape police harassment or to complete a transaction at a government or private office could involve handing over extra money. In his interview outside the DCI, Wainaina discussed his past censorship and stated that Kaka's outspokenness reflected a general sentiment of Kenyans' outrage that should not be ignored.[71]

The third song of this discussion is Juliani's "Utawala." As Kaka walked to the parking lot from the DCI, Boniface Mwangi, Kaka, Juliani, and others began to sing the chorus to "Utawala" as cameras surrounded them.[72] "Utawala" is a 2014 upbeat anthemic track that ties governmental corruption and ethnic-based nepotism in Kenya to the country's lack of job opportunities, inadequate sanitation in poor areas, and police violence against protestors. As they sang, "Sitasimama maovu yakitawala" (I will not stand while evil rules) and pumped their fists to the beat, there was a cheerful energy among the people singing.[73] Perhaps these activists understood that the cameras provided some safety against the government officials who seemed to have their eyes on Kaka and that this was a small victory in the fight against the censorship of musicians.

Juliani, who composed "Utawala," is a gospel hip hop artist who once hailed from the UFMM camp and who has managed to acquire success and popularity.[74] He boasts a large social media following and has matched his music-making with a variety of spearheaded initiatives. The Dandora Hip Hop City project, to name one, hosts many events and community projects, including collaborations with organizations and businesses. In his writing, he reflects on his dissatisfaction with the gross levels of inequality in Kenya and attempts to maintain a solid perspective about the poor.[75] The artists I spoke with had mixed sentiments about him. While most saw him as an authentic rapper dedicated to helping the community, others regarded him as too tied to commercialism. Juliani raps with crisp vocals, and the content is similar to underground songs. However, conforming to mainstream standards, many of his songs lack the hefty bass sounds that typically interact with his rap bars. "Utawala," like "Matapeli," seems to produce and demonstrate the formula for commercial songs that are politically conscious, as both songs set their denouncements of the government to sanguine tunes. The seemingly spontaneous performance of "Utawala" in support of King Kaka's "Wajinga Nyinyi" exemplifies how Kenyan protest songs are tied together through similar critiques of government mismanagement and corruption. "Utawala," furthermore, exists in the archives of significant protest music in Kenya.

In what ways might popular music contribute to the political listlessness that King Kaka refers to? For Jaguar, musician-turned-politician, his attachment to the state apparatus severely decreases the possibility that "Matapeli" will enter Kenya's protest song history, which does include songs such as "Nchi ya Kitu Kidogo," "Utawala," and "Wajinga Nyinyi." His political status aside, Jaguar's catchy tunes in "Matapeli" have succeeded more in anesthetizing people's outrage at the state's lootocracy than bolstering it. The song's lack of opacity demonstrates what Glissant would call uncreative transparency or a "lukewarm humanism, both colorless and reassuring."[76] It transforms people's indignation toward corruption into a feel-good tune, and it contains none of the hip hop aesthetics of untranslatability, including intentional shiftiness through embodiments, music, lyrics, and sound. Often, a song's afterlife can acquire new significations of resurgent political possibilities; it can be sampled or referenced, thus pumping new energies into its initial force, as in the case of "Utawala" in the DCI parking lot.

Juliani's "Utawala" exists in a murky area between political agitation and industry compliance. The continued circulation of "Utawala" and its reemergence in places such as outside of the DCI means that it intervenes in cultural and political discourse surrounding corruption. Yet, a part of the song's popularity is due to its affectively pleasing sonic qualities, upbeat tonalities, and chantlike structure. The song is subversive enough to materialize in the unprompted yet perhaps media-encouraged performance outside the DCI. Yet "Utawala" is also subdued enough to be co-opted by the state. In November 2020, President Kenyatta's Jubilee political party used the song without permission in their Building Bridges Initiative (BBI) promotional video. Under the banner of government efficacy and unity, BBI has sought to make changes to Kenya's constitution, most notably expanding the powers of the executive branch, including both prime minister and president, the latter of which would be given the power to select two deputy premiers.[77] Many people have been critical of these moves. Disturbed by the video, Juliani responded by issuing a letter through legal counsel stating in part that Jubilee must cease using the song and "admit liability for infringement of intellectual property rights."[78] The fact that Jubilee would find the song rousing yet tepid enough to use in their initiative is evidence of the pacificatory aural similarity between "Utawala" and "Matapeli." To compare, the dark and dystopic "Shupavu" and the gripping "Ulimi" would never make it into a Jubilee promotional video. While the interventions that "Utawala" makes in public discourse should be acknowledged as profoundly more effective than those of "Matapeli," the two songs lack the shifting, defiant aesthetics that have come to signify hip hop.

This analysis of "Wajinga Nyinyi," "Matapeli," and "Utawala" should not be the only applicable formula of critique for Kenyan commercial music at large. The type of sound preferred by radio, television, and other venues matters, and yet, we should consider how mainstream music mediates Kenya's social discourse. A catchy and danceable song does not necessarily mean it fails to accomplish cultural work. Instead, we must consider other factors in determining the relevance of commercial music. Imani Sanga, for instance, writes how Tanzanian popular music expresses a "postcolonial cosmopolitanism," which adheres to a worldbeat music system. For Sanga, artists facilitate unique indigenization processes and nation-building exercises, while maintaining their regional or international recognizability.[79] Most importantly, popular music presents what Sanga terms as "postcolonial consciousness," a loaded sensibility that both departs from the colonial condition and inescapably adopts notions of otherness into the music.[80] We should see Kenya's mainstream music similarly—as style that affirms Kenya not as a destitute nonentity but one that stands alongside other African music in its ability to make sounds that celebrate a familiar hip and urban sophistication. Afropop, for instance, is a genre that has encroached upon the central position that western music holds in Kenyan radio stations. American music still occupies a large portion of the diet of Kenyan radio, but Afropop continues to carve a substantial niche in this market. The making of a continental genre that Kenyans, Ugandans, Tanzanians, Congolese, and others collectively listen to and consume should not be disregarded, even with its ability to set standards in the industry. Afropop likely engenders social collectivities through listening, dancing, and critiquing.

One of the most enduring qualities of Afropop and Afrobeats has been the continual emergence of dance styles accompanying this music. Within Kenya alone, there have been dances like Lipala, Odi, Obe, and Bazokizo, in which practitioners perform boast-style footwork and hip movements that convey urbanism and Afrodiasporic commonality. These dances join a vast African continental repertoire of movement made possible through the circulatory registers of Instagram, Facebook, and Twitter. Ghana's Azonto and Pilolo, South Africa's Gwara Gwara and Vosho, the Shaku Shaku and Zanku from Nigeria, and Botswana's Gweta are among a vast library of performances. The dances are often made popular by musicians and their accompanying songs and then go viral and take on new and exciting reinventions, meaning that these embodied practices travel, transform, and produce continually unfolding ideas about movement.[81] The styles additionally open inquiries about Afrodiasporic corporealities that explore joy, pleasure, urban life, digital competition, and the circulation of African popular cultures.

SWAG AND THE LIMITS OF LUDICITY

Artists often respond to commercial pressure by guarding the underground. There is no broad acceptance or anything-goes ethic when artists define "real" hip hop. Just as Kenyan cultural critics police what Kenyan music is and should be, underground rappers determine what the music is. This patrolling regularly occurs through considerations of how a piece of music sounds and how artists perform it. By positioning the genre's audibility and corporeality in conversation with the values of the underground, artists decide what counts as hip hop and what sounds are merely imitative. Practitioners typically reject a complete alliance with the music's more mainstream qualities, such as conspicuous consumption, materialism, and commercialism. Songs of the underground may link with capitalism's insistence that bodies labor away exploitatively despite offering no real economic promises. Still, the sonically subversive and performatively ludic are a respite from the governance that late capitalism forces upon bodies. To preserve the politics of the body as a sacred enactment of freedom, artists cast off mainstream music and its accompanying bodily presentations by asserting that it waters down and robs the authentic soul of hip hop. These are the limits of ludicity, occurring when artists theorize their unwillingness to suture their bodies to consumerism and mainstream music standards.

To make these arguments, artists identify others who do not live up to hip hop's standards. One rapper who has continued to surface in these conversations is Bamboo, who also goes by Simon Kimani and Abraham Kimani. Bamboo is a former member of the mainstream group K-South. He was born in Kenya, grew up in Inglewood, California, moved back to Nairobi as a teenager, and has made music for American and Kenyan markets.[82] He has traveled back and forth between the U.S. and Kenya and once did a remake of Akon's "Mama Africa," though it did not gain widespread recognition in the U.S. market. His diasporic positioning as someone who does not just cite blackness but who has also lived in the U.S. and returned to Kenya makes him a complicated figure. Bamboo is the embodiment of the Kenyan hip hop diaspora. He is the figure who has roots in Kenya, has resided in the Black U.S., and has returned home. Much like the genre's return to a continent to which it is said to have begun, his homecoming has been no easy landing. Bamboo represents the deep internal conflict about Kenyan music, as his wealth and success have been tied to his "Americanness," mainly because he has rapped in English with an African American accent. He rests at the very core of what it means when people demand that Kenyans do not appreciate Kenyan music, as practitioners have long spoken of notions of his derivativeness.

In the early 2000s, K-South released two albums, *Nairobbery* and *Nairobism*. Unlike most underground artists, Bamboo has had endorsement success, including with Coca-Cola Africa, Kenya Brewery, and Chandaria Industries. In 2013, Bamboo performed for and publicly endorsed Uhuru Kenyatta's presidential campaign.[83] Around 2016, he converted to Christianity, made gospel music, and became an outspoken critic of African spiritualities, voudon, and "witchcraft." In the past few years, he has claimed that much of his early career was spent fighting the forces of others "bewitching" him.[84]

In 2013, Bamboo released a track and music video appropriately entitled "2-5-Flow," yet another appearance this phrase makes in rap culture. The song is about his return to Kenya's rap game after spending some time in the U.S. Bamboo's video captures much of the intricacies and politics of Kenyan music, including how his embodied performance and sound come together to signify notions of commercialism. In the video, Sugar, who also appears in "Looking Up," sings the chorus in repetition: "2-5-Flow! / Get your damn hands up!" Bamboo and his supporting crowd of followers, including children, use their fingers to put up the numbers two and then five, and when Sugar sings "Flow!" everyone moves their arms in unison in a wave-like motion.[85] Their arms "flow" across the screen, creating the visuality of mobile togetherness. The sentiment is fun, leisurely, and cool, with camera shots bouncing to the beat of the song and alternating between black-and-white and color scenes.

Many artists I spoke with have critiqued Bamboo as being too American, which also means too wealthy, imitative, and disconnected from Kenyan realities. The accusations surrounding Bamboo tended to lie in the corporeal and the sonic; he acts and sounds too American. Their concerns over his work have reflected the idea that practitioners are deeply invested in maintaining a nonderivative hip hop aesthetic that demonstrates Kenyanness. Bamboo's corporeality and sound in music videos engender claims of imitation, which underground artists are all too familiar with. Regina Bradley writes about a U.S. mainstream *hip hop sonic cool pose*, in which performances of masculinity materialize through "sonic signifiers of black manhood, experiences, and coolness."[86] For Bradley, the sonic and performative masculine blackness can be contained both within and outside of music and are furthermore bound up in the complicated politics of blackness as historically propertied and currently commodified. Bradley's analysis encourages a consideration of how Bamboo's sonic iterations of blackness and masculinity land in Kenya. The discussions circulating around Bamboo reveal how aural and embodied performativities become coded and racialized. Bamboo has personified an excessive and disproportionate commodifiability of African Americanness, meaning that how he produces a hip hop diaspora is constantly read as faulty.

Many discussed Bamboo and stated that while he has rap skills, he is dismissed because of his supposedly imitative American swag. In the U.S., now that white Americans and the mainstream media have long adopted the term "swag," American Black people have abandoned its usage, and it is now considered obsolete or used in other ways. In Kenya, the term "swag" has continued to carry important meanings and serves as a discourse about agency, economics, globality, and cultural imperialism. During my fieldwork, I asked directed questions about bodily performances, and from these, swag emerged as an important signpost for the Kenyan music style. The term has its origins in hip hop aesthetics, typically connoting styles of dress and how one carries oneself. Mecca Jamilah Sullivan mainly ties swag to masculinity, and Bettina Love connects it to resistance, writing that it challenges societal disenfranchisement.[87] Caroline Mose offers that swag is "made up of braggadocio, lyrical and performance skill [giving] an artist a unique 'street' identity and . . . a symbolic capital . . . representative of a marginalized periphery."[88] Mwenda Ntarangwi, writing about East Africa, notes that swag is an invented way of performing wealth: "[Rappers] get caught up in a life of 'swag,' doing things so that others can see how successful they are even when such success is often a façade."[89] Therefore, combining these approaches, I observe that swag is a corporeal compilation of masculinist energies and boast styles that have deep roots in both a defiance of social norms and an embrace of capitalist sensibilities by celebrating oneself along materialistic or consumerist lines. Swag draws from lower-class urgencies to protect oneself from being poor, as Mose contends, and one of its practices in accomplishing that is materialist consumption. Although femme rappers can and do adopt embodiments and ideals of swag through clothing, style, and wealth, the standards and origins of swag are still rooted in masculinity.

Many underground rappers see Bamboo's sonic speech qualities of sounding African American as inauthentic, even though Bamboo may have picked up Black English from spending his formative years in California. One graffiti artist made this common quip: "Like it's so simple. If I sent [Bamboo] to a country like India for ten good years, he wouldn't get that accent [an Indian accent]. You know what I mean?"[90] Bamboo, in turn, has wholly repudiated that his sound is mimetic. The following is taken from an interview with Bamboo:

> *Jamati:* You have been criticised for sounding too 'American'. How do you balance the American and African sides so that both are happy, or do you? Do you think that it works against you to sound too African?
>
> *[Bamboo:]* Well I do Swahilli [*sic*] music for Kenyans, and English music for my western fanbase. If it's not in [S]wahilli [*sic*] they should understand that its [*sic*] not really for them its [*sic*] for an audience which only understands [E]nglish..I don't have an [A]frican accent so if I tried it would be fake and sound funny as hell! Lol.[91]

Bamboo's way of speaking is what Regina Bradley calls "sonic scripting of the black male body," which can be read as either real or derived and can occur both inside music and in everyday encounters.[92] In the eyes of many artists, Bamboo should not and need not imitate American artists because Kenyan styles are valuable enough. In Bamboo's opinion, his voice belongs to himself. Many rappers believe that Bamboo does not see himself as African American and think instead that his intentional usage of a U.S. Black accent is done so his music will sell and he will gain or sustain fame. It is also possible that his accent could have resulted from having grown up in the U.S. with the pressure to assimilate, especially given that in recent public appearances, his speech now mirrors that of other Kenyans. Practitioners' opinions of Bamboo reveal that just as there are acceptable ways in which Kenyan practitioners can draw from U.S. Black styles, such as through naming, sampling, citations, and collaborations, there are also practices that are considered improper. Having or co-opting an African American accent when one is Kenyan, for many, exists too explicitly within the framework of imitativeness and commercialism, and Bamboo is thus seen as putatively turning himself into a commodity without agency.

Swag performances in Kenyan hip hop elicit automatic debates about westernization, Americanization, cultural imperialism, and consumerism. Just like with the figures of the thug and tomboy, the swag rapper embodies superfluousness; in this case, the excess of material things that mark wealth. Many nondevotees dismiss Kenyan rappers who incorporate what they see as swag because of their bodily performances, clothing, and rapping. Just as Bamboo has been scorned for his accent, other commercial artists such as Kaligraph Jones are derided for their English-dominant lyrics, which are seen as marketing to a phantom U.S. audience or to upper-class Kenyans who might not know Swahili or Sheng well. Either way, working-class artists often feel excluded from an art form meant to represent them, and coupled with ongoing industry marginalization, this can feel like an entire system of actors working against them. For the underground Nairobi rappers with whom I spoke, the question is whether swag can be a legitimate personal expression or whether it is only a defective allegiance to the United States. I talked to a gospel artist who asserted that Bamboo's pose is "copied swag."[93] Another artist said that the way Bamboo performs his body indicates his lack of loyalty to the Kenyan scene and that when one sees Bamboo, he does not look like an African. When I pressed about what it means to look African, they responded, "Africans, we are simple people," and stated that even rappers should present themselves in humble ways.[94] This comment reveals that bodily dress, performance, and aural characteristics converge and are intertwined. When concluding that Bamboo betrays Kenyan culture, those in the underground consider how Bamboo presents himself, especially in his pre-gospel days, with his thick chains, expensive clothing, and, in music videos, his stance in front of pricey vehicles. Although a well-established, upper-class consumer culture exists in Kenya, such practices are automatically attached to the U.S. for many rap artists.

Bamboo's "2-5-Flow" does share significant similarities with underground songs and cannot be seen as a complete outlier. Like his noncommercial counterparts, Bamboo creates diaspora by rapping from inside a Kenyan context while indicating outward to a larger imagined global rap culture. For Bamboo, it seems that "2-5-Flow" is a journey beyond the borders of Kenya and a call back to home. Moreover, underground rappers posit neoliberal hard work as a solution to poverty in the same way that Bamboo constructs celebrations of wealth to express his version of Kenyanness. Both sentiments reveal an adherence to the idea that the codes of racial capitalism will result in upward mobility in a system that, in reality, offers little assurance. In other ways, the song stands in strong contrast to underground sounds. The logic of "2-5-Flow" articulates an upper-class ethic unbound by the structures of poverty and the characteristic callousness of the state that is so often found in noncommercial rap. It has no representations of the state found in many underground songs. "2-5-Flow" contains leisured performativities and slowed rhyming that are not the same as the content-filled lyrics and ludic performances that buck state power and eschew a society that pushes the poor into invisibility.

Bamboo exemplifies nearly every characteristic of what it means to make Kenyan music. He is an uneasy performance of hip hop diasporic blackness. He is the Kenyan diaspora that has left and come back to the country and been culturally unrecognizable. His persona is seen as being rooted in his excessive mimicry of African Americanness. Though Bamboo is labeled as an imitator, he has made music that is rooted in Kenyan life. The rappers with whom I spoke do not like his work, and his political alliances and allegiance with state actors, namely Uhuru Kenyatta, have further eroded his credibility.

The Kenyan music industry's appetite for Bamboo-style rap songs and Afropop's catchiness leaves the brazen underground tunes largely invisible and unheard. Mainstream music works to smooth out the supposed jagged fringes of Kenya. Rather than portraying images of state violence and poverty, its music videos often show dance routines, vacations, parties, and clubs. Much of the music itself is full of mellifluousness and easily memorized choruses. The industry and its actors create popular musical tastes that are designed in line with Kenya's social order. However, underground artists do not take these social and sonic preferences as a given and believe there is a need and desire for a particular type of sonic quality in their gripping, truth-telling music.

I take Caroline Mose's provocation about the blurriness between music categories seriously, as many artists and songs fall through the gaps of the underground-commercial duality. Simultaneously, artists pump meaning back into the same binary that appears to misconstrue their work. The ways artists discuss this binary help to tell a story about their experiences in the hip hop game and how society fails to hear and see them properly. These practitioners continue to invest energy in and create an understanding of their music through these categories. Access to resources, class, and opportunity overwhelmingly can structure how their music sounds and, therefore, where it is played, in addition to informing how underground and commercial rappers and devotees determine musical value. There is a correct way to embrace capitalist ideals: through the push of hard work and the maintenance of discipline. Where mainstream music strays, according to noncommercial artists, is through a problematic endorsement of materialism and commercial sound.

Conclusion

Hip Hop Flow as Kenyan, as Black

This book uses corporeality to understand not just hip hop but Kenya and its history, the celebrations of its diaspora, and the everyday stories people tell about their lives. Performance is a method, a device to approach and study the world that accounts for the numerous ways people can be creative agents within their respective settings. Underground rap performances allow us to witness and experience what articulations of freedom look like in a musical community where its members are always on the move, seeking new and old venues, navigating laws and policies, and attempting to earn enough to continue making music. The circulatory globality of U.S. blackness is brought about as a product, a commodity, and a performance, and how it is bound in the formations of antiblackness helps to create meaning in places like Kenya. Performances, thus, become ways that artists move through, resist, and make pacts with power. Ludic embodiments in the music are similar to José Muñoz's notion of disidentification, which "neither opts to assimilate within [the dominant ideological] structure nor strictly opposes it; rather, disidentification is a strategy that works on and against dominant ideology."[1] Disidentificatory performances, for Muñoz, refer to how queers of color create complicated self-making through modes like camp and drag and how those processes turn away from a basic, straightforward narrative of identity formation. The artists I followed use practices like disidentification to divest from elements like commercialism and state-sponsored ethnicity and create hip hop genders to live through power structures while still operating as creative makers and innovators. Muñoz emphasizes, "There would be no theory . . . without the cultural work of the people"; and then, "The making of theory only transpires after the artists' performance of counterpublicity is realized with my own disidentificatory eyes."[2] I depart from this latter point because I understand embodiments as the site of theoretical interventions by themselves, including those that fall under disidenti-fication. Embodied performances can be the building blocks of theory, helping to contribute to how we think about hip hop as a holistic music culture. Additionally, orature is theory in and of itself. For the body must be understood as a site of phil-osophical interventions on its own terms to understand how artists' musical, per-formative, and lyrical work says something profound about the world they inhabit.

Years after the bulk of my fieldwork, artists are still in the studio, producing and releasing singles and sometimes music videos and relying more than ever on digital circulation. Many obstacles have remained unchanged: the difficulties of airplay, the lack of royalty collection for those who do appear on the airwaves, the transient nature of underground events, and the lack of venues willing to host. I first met many artists in 2012 when NGO events were more regular and consistent. Nafsi Huru, L-Ness, and Judge disagreed on why the events have waned over the years. Judge blamed the organizers for mismanagement, and L-Ness, who has had many gatherings at Goethe-Institut, stated that NGOs need to acquire revenue and that many underground fans do not want to pay entrance fees.[3] Nafsi Huru adamantly disagreed with any assertions that economic woes prevent events, argu-ing that Sarakasi's Hip Hop Hookup was funded and supported and drew crowds. Instead, he asserted that over the years, NGOs have looked unpropitiously at any-thing hip hop and have rejected event proposals by rappers. During a conversa-tion in the fall of 2021, Nafsi told me he is preparing to launch another attempt at rehabilitating Sarakasi events, in which he will most likely be successful, at least for a time.[4] Most accept the idea that events at venues will come and go, and it is artists who need to be pliable, prepared, and resolute in chasing down any opportunity. They continue this work because they can make some money, but also because they are concerned with the welfare of Kenyan society, even when that same soci-ety often does not love them back.

There are always rappers who have long hiatuses from making music or tire of the hustle and decide there is insufficient return in ripping tracks and recording music videos. As I wrapped up my research in 2018, Baby T was beginning a sus-tained break from the studio to reevaluate her music career. While Baby T enjoyed her projects with ATL Entertainment, she expressed a need to experiment with her music differently and take more creative control over her songs and videos. The producers at ATL listened to her input and feedback and largely shaped the direc-tion of her work. When she first started, she was grateful for the guidance. After spending about a decade making music, she wants to bring more of her creativities into production directly. Baby T's experience is generally unlike the other rappers I spoke with, who, due to their limited funds and "your best friend with a camera helping you with your video," as Nafsi Huru put it, must give much input into their work out of necessity.[5] Even though she has more resources than other artists, Baby T's next moves indicate a general desire for rappers to use music to express their autonomy. She plans to create songs that incorporate *gengetone* and *kapuka* with hip hop and aims to perform at bigger concerts rather than rap gigs in clubs. It is not enough that Baby T's music appears on television and radio—perhaps more than the other rappers I followed in this book—she must be a director of her own craft. She explained, "I think I wanna be more aggressive in the videos. I wanna be more like Missy Elliott in videos. If people are dancing, she's there dancing with them. She just becomes the center of the videos, so I think I wanna be more active."[6] Unsurprisingly, this brief statement suitably touches the core topics in this book of the performance of gendered armor (aggressiveness), diasporic citations (Missy Elliott), and creative agency.

Furthermore, comments like Baby T's provoke me to think about the multiple roles many Kenyan producers play in making underground music, like staging bodies and props in videos, helping to make and choose beats, and marketing the finished product. My research does not address the roles of producers and studios in depth, which would undoubtedly add to the analysis of corporeality, as well as to the music at large. Future research would include a robust investigation of this topic.

Many artists I follow who rap about inequality also do work to fight injustice in their communities. Their devotedness to those economically stymied reveals the sustained desire to undo structures of power that disallow people to enact choices in their lives. Judge, who has not been in the studio since 2019, is unsure when he will return. He has started a program, Rhymes Behind Bars, with other rappers, such as Roba from Kalamashaka and Agano from Wakamba Wawili, where they run workshops in Kenyan prisons about spoken word and the skill of rhyming.[7] Judge detailed the struggles to solidify funding for this project but stated that he has secured some sponsorship from the Kenyan Commercial Bank and affirmed his commitment to continue the initiative. Nafsi Huru has continued to make music and found other rappers and musicians with whom to collaborate. At the time of our follow-up interview, he was working on a song titled "Simba Wa Magongo" (Lions of Magongo), and he aimed to work with artists, activists, and athletes from his neighborhood, Magongo, Mombasa. He stated that the song is his way of highlighting the people he considers the powerful lions of his hood who do not usually receive admiration for who they are as leaders and activists.[8] The love of his hometown does not stop there; at the time of our last interview, he was organizing a crew of other artists to bring funds and supplies to a children's home in Magongo.

L-Ness, who still makes music, has been working on a theater project with the Nairobi Musical Theatre Initiative (NBOMTI). The project is called "Escape" and will be a hip hop musical composed and performed in Sheng. L-Ness also raises funds for the Korogocho Transforming Development and Self-Help Group (KTDG), and during the COVID-19 pandemic, she collected and distributed personal protection supplies, foodstuffs, and other needed items to poor areas in Nairobi such as Korogocho, Embakasi, Kahawa West, and Githurai. Additionally, since 2018, she has been an interviewer and ethnographer in working-class neigh-borhoods for the African Population and Health Research Center (APHRC). I asked L-Ness to describe if being a rapper assisted her in her career outside of music. L-Ness responded by explaining how when out collecting data for APHRC, she encountered people serving as gatekeepers who did not want outsiders in their communities and who made entering and extracting information difficult:

> You find the boys seated there, and you need to penetrate an area, and I would have to tell them, "Look, you know I am UFMM [Ukoo Flani Mau Mau], you know, don't play with me! You know I'm a rapper!" . . . If they do not want you to access an area, you will not, you see, but *my hip hop demeanor* has helped me in how I approach them.[9] (emphasis mine)

L-Ness's description of the ways she uses rap culture to move through cer-tain spaces exemplifies the everydayness of rap corporeality, the reliance on an armored gender, and the ways the music is deeply concerned with Nairobi's work-ing-class urbanity. L-Ness confirmed that hip hop provides an embodied method to interact with others and do the community initiatives she finds necessary. She described what Aimee Meredith Cox terms as "staying in the body," which is the "place of intuitive knowing that allows movement to both feel and look organic."[10] L-Ness's testimony of "staying in the body" makes plain the centrality of perfor-mance and how rap embodiment appears in everyday life. Such corporeality is deeply enmeshed in Kenyan postcolonial anxieties over what it means to exercise freedoms in the context of limitations. Moreover, L-Ness's embodiment practices are the individual choices that reflect and contribute to a Kenyanness connected to the global politics of the culture.

This study of Nairobi hip hop belongs within Kenyan cultural and hip hop stud-ies and firmly within U.S. Black studies. P. Khalil Saucier and Tryon P. Woods published a piece in 2014 proffering a compelling and necessary declaration for hip hop studies to disentangle itself from the (neo)liberal university and become Black studies. By that, they mean that hip hop studies desperately needs to shift away from the ways universities and many scholars have hijacked it to advance a multicultural approach that waters down, if not obliterates, hip hop's radical Black origins and continued political interventions.[11] As Saucier and Woods note, we must not forget how the music, and its sonorous elements and its performative aesthetic, bears an entangled relationship to and emerges out of "state violence against black communities and their concomitant structural dispossession."[12] To respond, it seems that that even in the face of corporate takeovers, scholars have walked the field back into Black studies, pronouncedly in the wake of the diverse and global movements for justice for Black lives that intensified circa 2015. How-ever, one way to solidify hip hop's unquestionable place in Black studies is to rec-ognize the diasporic elements of the music's blackness as it reconfigures during its movements throughout the globe. Identifying diasporic blackness in places like

Kenyan rap does not elide or displace how the music has been indigenized in Nairobi; rather, it illuminates the projects that artists are doing on the ground. *Nairobi Hip Hop Flow* proves that performance provides a gripping contribution to the argument that hip hop studies must be Black studies. In Kenya, the music draws from the urgency of the Black radical tradition, and as it has indigenized, narrativizes how cultural production in Nairobi is a part of the story of the formations of early governments, the postcolonial state, the dictatorship years, politicized ethnic conflicts, the failures of neoliberalization, and ongoing state ineffectiveness. In this way, a practitioner becomes an archivist of Kenyan history, a theorist of political and economic thought, and an expert on the machinery of a greedy state. Rappers have continued and created anew the monumental and surviving work of those before them, igniting their devotees, making pathways to give resources to their communities, and creating an enduring musical culture. Kenyan hip hop studies is greatly enhanced through in-depth considerations of transnational dialogues between the U.S. and Kenya. The tensions and connections that the Mau Mau struggle induced, the ways the fighters have been remembered, however imperfect and incomplete, and the emergent culture in Kenya provide potentially endless and fruitful conversations about diaspora. The connectivities between the Black U.S. and East Africa deserve attention. The stories of Mic Crenshaw, Umi, M1, Mama C, Mzee Pete, and Toni Blackman are all examples of how, if we delve into the particularities of the Black experience in the U.S., we might arrive in Nairobi or Arusha. Moreover, there is a continued opportunity to explore and learn how the underground music in other places thrashes out ideas of the diasporic details of blackness and Black culture.

Acknowledging L-Ness and Baby T's accounts in totality and the ones outlined throughout the book, there is something crucial about centering performances in the study of underground music. My research approach has been heavily informed by ethnography. The embodiedness of rappers has been the first and most significant element I encountered in the hip hop field, and it guided and framed the research. Dwight Conquergood writes that ethnography "privileges the body as a site of knowing," both for the ethnographer's experiences and for their study of cultural performance, which "functions as a special form of public address [and] rhetorical agency."[13] Embodied performances were always the primary aspect of the music I experienced visually and felt auditorily and affectively. Centering these performances allowed for a framework whereby I could analyze the fine detail and intricacies of not just performances but also the statements rappers made and the music videos they created. Thus, Baby T's aspirations to be a protagonist in her videos and to be more "aggressive" on the mic, as well as L-Ness's "hip hop demeanor," would perhaps not have been given the depth deserved had I not centered corporeality.

We stand to understand better the textures of hip hop's blackness and how it provokes antiblackness by centering performance. Both blackness and antiblackness are globally flung about and come to rest in places like Nairobi. For every artist that rejects the gangsta because such a figure impedes the project of political seriousness's respectability, other artists reference, draw on, cite, and mention Missy Elliott, Drake, Kendrick Lamar, Nicki Minaj, and many others. The rejection of one figure and embracing something different are about how U.S. blackness travels and how it is consumed and reconfigured. Artists make music suitable for their own aims, and as this book has shown, we must be willing to sit with how and why the music's blackness continues to serve as a utilitarian and referential goalpost as rappers explore power, ethnicity, inequality, and liberation in their own contexts. Moreover, through the lens of orature, which is a comprehensive Africanist method of regarding the projects of these practitioners, we understand the multiple layers they draw on and add to in their quest to make embodiments, sounds, and visualities. This book allows us to understand that conceptualizing the culture's Black diasporic tendencies and how the music is profoundly rooted in Kenya's history of violence, subjection, and ideas of self-determination often overlap and are not necessarily in opposition or tension. We must continue to offer up new analyses about how the spinnerets of racial capitalism produce the qualities and practices of antiblackness found throughout the globe and, in turn, are absorbed in cultural spaces like hip hop.

This study of orature has initiated questions about ethnicity that I could not fully answer. I was not able to access how ethnicities are performed and how they are differentiated from each other. For instance, questions remain about how performances of Kikuyuness, Luoness, and Luhyaness intersect and stand in tension and cohesion with blackness and artists' larger musical projects. What was most available for analysis was the sustaining and sinewy projects of hip hop love and political seriousness that joined people across lines of division, which, for me, ultimately impeded a probe into ethnicity. The powerful characteristics of love and seriousness within the music stood as barriers to uncovering how ethnic subjectivities materialized in the interstitiality of the music. The manners in which the postcolonial states of Jomo Kenyatta, Daniel arap Moi, Mwai Kibaki, and Uhuru Kenyatta have all used ethnicity to frame political power and enflame tensions, what Bruce Berman calls "uncivil nationalism," have had dramatic effects on people's everyday lives.[14] We must think through what it would mean for Kikuyu rappers to take on an embodiedness that reckons with their working-class realities even with membership in a larger, even disconnected, group that continues to hold state power. Likewise, we are called to think about how an embodied Luoness calls on a history of attacks on Luo cultural masculinities even though elites from this community have enjoyed political positions. The public conversations about the assumed inherent capabilities of Kikuyu men, who are traditionally circumcised, and Luo men, who may not be, ride just below the surface and emerge around moments of political divisiveness, like most tragically during the 2008 chaos, when Kikuyu groups reportedly attacked Luo men.[15] We must think through how, as artists formulate their genders of armor, they use these historical and public conversations about Kenyan masculinities, what Grace Musila aptly calls the "phallocratic aesthetic."[16] Moreover, how rappers of all ethnicities, particularly those named, have sorted through these traumatic moments and the continued aftereffects has been a hard question to address in the research. Lastly, we would be wise to consider how long-standing cultural traditions within rappers' respective ethnic communities inform, and perhaps even amplify, embodied performance practices, even when these artists work with political love as an ethic of commonality.

This book brings together the fields of performance, feminism, and gender studies in the U.S. and Kenya. Much overlap exists between U.S. hip hop studies and the Kenyan and East African scholars who examine power and difference in the music. U.S. Black and African scholars, however, sit on no even plane. I heed the call of Tanya Saunders, who contends that a hip hop feminism needs to "[de-center] the . . . hegemony of the United States" and "give[ ] space to a . . . praxis that challenges the discreetness of geo-political and linguistic boundaries."[17] Decentering the U.S. and giving space to African scholars, in particular, are gestures toward the comradeship that should exist among scholars of the African diaspora. Such nods can acknowledge the inherent power relations operating in global academia and encourage us to recognize that many of our colleagues in African countries face barriers in the circulation of their research, securing funding for international conferences, and publishing full-length single-authored book manuscripts. Here, I add to Saunders's shift by pressing the field of global hip hop studies to attend to how scholars of non-U.S. hip hop continue to overlook U.S. Black feminist hip hop scholars who are gender-expansive people and women. These academics have shaped our understanding of the ways misogynoir, anti-blackness, and queer antagonism converge in the music culture and detail how people, including those of marginalized genders, manufacture transformative and complicated spaces to create music. Black feminists' work deserves recognition. Building from this idea, we must ensure that we cite women and gender-expansive scholars in Africa and throughout the diaspora, as such moves assist in avoiding the hierarchies that plague academia.[18]

I have spent much of this book discussing hip hop performance's theatrical, thaumaturgic, and piercing qualities. It is possible that my mission to delve into and describe what is better left seen, felt, and embodied has been culturally blasphemous to the music's ethic of obscurity and ineffability, which is a burden I accept. I hope what these conversations make poignantly clear is that ascribing words and descriptions to rap's corporeality is not a simple mission. Quite possibly, analysis robs the music of its core elusive beauty. After all, Jeff Chang warns, "Interpretation should never be the place where art goes to die."[19] For better or worse, this book spends much time describing the mechanics of play and the boundless fissures opened by the workings of the ludic and the serious. The ludic only appears to have no endgame or real purpose within capitalism; it just plays inside a context that favors a system of production and labor. In reality, play is deeply intertwined and dependent on the political for its emergence, allowing artists to create self-making, even when such commencements are ephemeral and loaded. We must remind ourselves that the ludic will never be understood fully, as performances are not legible enough for any neat conclusion. The music's ludic opacity and its refusal of strict assignment mean that at least some of its magic has been missed in this discussion. Hip hop is an intensely visual music, but this is not tantamount to conspicuousness because artists intentionally duck legibility in the exercise of play. In my research, there must have been countless features of rap minutiae that I surely overlooked. I hope this book merely scratches the vinyl surface of the music's work. Rappers manufacture nodes of freedom in many places in Nairobi where play can exist even in the context of a postcoloniality structured by intricacies of global antiblackness and racial capitalism. And inside these meeting points, one can find the embodied flow of Nairobi hip hop.

NOTES

INTRODUCTION: *2-5-FLOW!*

1. Tavia Nyong'o, "Afro-philo-sonic Fictions: Black Sound Studies after the Millennium," *Small Axe* 18, no. 2 (2014): 175.

2. Mbũgua wa Mũngai, "'Made in Riverwood': (Dis)locating Identities and Power through Kenyan Pop Music," *Journal of African Cultural Studies* 20, no. 1 (2008): 57.

3. Caroline Mose, "'Swag' and 'Cred': Representing Hip-Hop in the African City," *Journal of Pan African Studies* 6, no. 3 (2013): 106–32.

4. Anthony Kwame Harrison, *Hip Hop Underground: The Integrity and Ethics of Racial Identification* (Philadelphia: Temple University Press, 2009), 11.

5. Mwenda Ntarangwi, *East African Hip Hop: Youth Culture and Globalization* (Urbana: University of Illinois Press, 2009), 130.

6. Ntarangwi, *East African Hip Hop*, 129.

7. See Halifu Osumare, "Motherland Hip-Hop: Connective Marginality and African American Youth Culture in Senegal and Kenya," in *Rhythms of the Afro-Atlantic World: Rituals and Remembrances*, ed. Ifeoma C. K. Nwankwo and Mamadou Diouf (Ann Arbor: University of Michigan Press, 2010), 171.

8. See H. Samy Alim, Awad Ibrahim, and Alastair Pennycook, eds., *Global Linguistic Flows: Hip Hop Cultures, Youth Identities, and the Politics of Language* (New York: Routledge, 2009); Jannis Androutsopoulos and Arno Scholz, "Spaghetti Funk: Appropriations of Hip-Hop Culture and Rap Music in Europe," *Popular Music and Society* 26, no. 4 (2003): 463–79; Marina Terkourafi, ed., *The Languages of Global Hip Hop* (London: Continuum International, 2010); Elaine Richardson and Gwendolyn Pough, "Hiphop Literacies and the Globalization of Black Popular Culture," *Social Identities* 22, no. 2 (2016): 129–32; Quentin Williams, "Youth Multilingualism in South Africa's Hip-Hop Culture: A Metapragmatic Analysis," *Sociolinguistic Studies* 10, no. 1/2 (2016): 109–33; Awad Ibrahim, "Remixing Culture, Language, and the Politics of Boundaries in Education: Toward Critical Hip-Hop

Ill-Literacies," in *Handbook of Cultural Studies and Education*, ed. Peter Pericles Trifonas and Susan Jagger (New York: Routledge, 2018), 224–35.

9. Ngũgĩ wa Thiong'o, *Penpoints, Gunpoints, and Dreams: Towards a Critical Theory of the Arts and the State in Africa* (Oxford: Oxford University Press, 1998), 105.

10. Mĩcere Githae Mũgo, "The Woman Artist in Africa Today: A Critical Commentary," *Africa Development / Afrique et Développement* 19, no. 1 (1994): 57.

11. Ngũgĩ wa Thiong'o, *Decolonising the Mind: The Politics of Language in African Literature* (Nairobi: East African, 1992), 23.

12. Mũgo, "The Woman Artist," 59.

13. Thomas DeFrantz, "The Black Beat Made Visible: Hip Hop Dance and Body Power," in *Of the Presence of the Body: Essays on Dance and Performance Theory*, ed. André Lepecki (Middletown, CT: Wesleyan University Press, 2004), 64–81.

14. Robert F. Thompson, "An Aesthetic of the Cool," *African Arts* 7, no. 1 (1973): 41; Katrina Hazzard-Donald, "Dance in Hip-Hop Culture," in *That's the Joint! The Hip-Hop Studies Reader*, ed. Murray Forman and Mark Anthony Neal (New York: Routledge, 2012), 513.

15. Katrina Hazzard-Donald, "What Hip Hop Dance Says," in *Droppin' Science: Critical Essays on Rap Music and Hip Hop Culture*, ed. William Eric Perkins (Philadelphia: Temple University Press, 1996), 229.

16. Julian Henriques, *Sonic Bodies: Reggae Sound Systems, Performance Techniques, and Ways of Knowing* (New York: Continuum, 2011).

17. See Regina Bradley, "Contextualizing Hip Hop Sonic Cool Pose in Late Twentieth- and Twenty-First-Century Rap Music," *Current Musicology* 93 (2012): 55–70; Shanté Paradigm Smalls, "'Make the Music with Your Mouth': Sonic Subjectivity and Post-Modern Identity Formations in Beatboxing," *Lateral* 3 (2014): 1–15.

18. Jeremy F. Lane, *Jazz and Machine-Age Imperialism: Music, "Race," and Intellectuals in France, 1918–1945* (Ann Arbor: University of Michigan Press, 2013), 3–6.

19. Alexander G. Weheliye, *Phonographies: Grooves in Sonic Afro-Modernity* (Durham, NC: Duke University Press, 2005), 70–71.

20. DJ Mos, interview by RaShelle Peck, December 8, 2011.

21. Maina wa Mutonya, "The Beat Goes On: Performing Postcolonial Disillusionment in Kenya," *Humania del Sur* 5, no. 8 (2010): 48.

22. Chege Githiora, "Sheng: Peer Language, Swahili Dialect or Emerging Creole?" *Journal of African Cultural Studies* 15, no. 2 (2002): 159–81; Peter Githinji, "Ambivalent Attitudes: Perception of Sheng and Its Speakers," *Nordic Journal of African Studies* 17, no. 2 (2008): 113–36.

23. Mickie Mwanzia Koster, "The Hip Hop Revolution in Kenya: UkooFlani Mau Mau, Youth Politics and Memory, 1990–2012," *Journal of Pan African Studies* 6, no. 3 (2013): 87.

24. Mbũgua wa Mũngai, "'Is Marwa!' It's Ours': Popular Music and Identity Politics in Kenyan Youth Culture," in *Cultural Production and Change in Kenya: Building Bridges*, ed. Kimani Njogu and G. Oluoch Olunya (Nairobi: Twaweza Communications, 2007), 52, 53.

25. Victor Turner, "Body, Brain, and Culture," *Cross Currents* 36, no. 2 (1986): 171.

26. Lindon Barrett, *Blackness and Value: Seeing Double* (Cambridge: Cambridge University Press, 1999), 58–61.

27. Édouard Glissant, *Poetics of Relation* (Ann Arbor: University of Michigan Press, 1997), 18, 165, 168.

28. See Androutsopoulos and Scholz, "Spaghetti Funk"; Alastair Pennycook and Tony Mitchell, "Hip Hop as Dusty Foot Philosophy: Engaging Locality," in *Global Linguistic Flows: Hip Hop Cultures, Youth Identities, and the Politics of Language*, ed. H. Samy Alim, Awad Ibrahim, and Alastair Pennycook (New York: Routledge, 2008), 25–42; Verónica Loureiro-Rodríguez, "'If We Only Speak Our Language by the Fireside, It Won't Survive': The Cultural and Linguistic Indigenization of Hip Hop in Galicia," *Popular Music and Society* 36, no. 5 (2013): 659–76.

29. Tony Mitchell, ed., *Global Noise: Rap and Hip-Hop outside the USA* (Middleton, CT: Wesleyan University Press, 2001), 2.

30. Dipannita Basu and Sidney J. Lemelle, *The Vinyl Ain't Final: Hip-Hop and the Globalisation of Black Popular Culture* (Ann Arbor, MI: Pluto Press, 2006), 5.

31. H. Samy Alim, "Intro: Straight Outta Compton, Straight aus München: Global Linguistic Flows, Identities, and the Politics of Language in a Global Hip Hop Nation," in *Global Linguistic Flows: Hip Hop Cultures, Youth Identities, and the Politics of Language*, ed. H. Samy Alim, Awad Ibrahim, and Alastair Pennycook (New York: Routledge, 2008), 17.

32. Elaine Richardson, "Global Linguistic Flows: Hip Hop Cultures, Youth Identities, and the Politics of Language—Edited by H. Samy Alim, Awad Ibrahim and Alastair Pennycook," *Journal of Sociolinguistics* 14, no. 2 (2010): 267.

33. Richardson, "Global Linguistic Flows," 267.

34. Richardson and Pough, "Hiphop Literacies."

35. See Alex Perullo and John Fenn, "Language Ideologies, Choices, and Practices in Eastern African Hip Hop," in *Global Pop, Local Language*, ed. Harris M. Berger and Michael Thomas Carroll (Jackson: University Press of Mississippi, 2003), 19–52; Mūngai, "'Is Marwa!'"; Chris Wasike, "Jua Cali, Genge Rap Music and the Anxieties of Living in the Glocalized City of Nairobi," *Muziki* 8, no. 1 (2011): 18–33; RaShelle R. Peck, "Love, Struggle, and Compromises: The Political Seriousness of Nairobi Underground Hip Hop," *African Studies Review* 61, no. 2 (2018): 111–33; Jeong Kyung Park, James Nyachae Michira, and Seo Young Yun, "African Hip Hop as a Rhizomic Art Form Articulating Urban Youth Identity and Resistance with Reference to Kenyan Genge and Ghanaian Hiplife," *Journal of the Musical Arts in Africa* 16, no. 1/2 (2019): 99–118.

36. Eric S. Charry, ed., *Hip Hop Africa: New African Music in a Globalizing World* (Bloomington: Indiana University Press, 2012), 16.

37. Charry, *Hip Hop Africa*, 3.

38. Charry, *Hip Hop Africa*, 283–316.

39. Msia Kibona Clark and Mickie Mwanzia Koster, *Hip Hop and Social Change in Africa: Ni Wakati* (Lanham, MD: Lexington Books, 2014).

40. See Derek Pardue, *Ideologies of Marginality in Brazilian Hip Hop* (New York: Palgrave Macmillan, 2008); Jesse Weaver Shipley, "Aesthetic of the Entrepreneur: Afro-Cosmopolitan Rap and Moral Circulation in Accra, Ghana," *Anthropological Quarterly* (2009): 631–68; H. Samy Alim, "Global Ill-Literacies: Hip Hop Cultures, Youth Identities, and the Politics of Literacy," *Review of Research in Education* 35, no. 1 (2011): 120–46; Tara Jabbaar-Gyambrah, "Gender Politics of Hip-Hop and Hip-Life Music in New York and Ghana," *Afro-Americans in New York Life and History* 39, no. 1 (2015): 7–31; Tanya L. Saunders, *Cuban Underground Hip Hop: Black Thoughts, Black Revolution, Black Modernity* (Austin: University of Texas Press, 2015); Richardson and Pough, "Hiphop Literacies."

41. See Patricia Hill Collins, *From Black Power to Hip Hop: Racism, Nationalism, and Feminism* (Philadelphia: Temple University Press, 2006); Whitney A. Peoples, "'Under Construction': Identifying Foundations of Hip-Hop Feminism and Exploring Bridges between Black Second-Wave and Hip-Hop Feminisms," *Meridians* 8, no. 1 (2008): 19–52; Aisha Durham, "Using [Living Hip Hop] Feminism: Redefining an Answer (to) Rap," in *Home Girls, Make Some Noise!: Hip Hop Feminism Anthology*, ed. Gwendolyn D. Pough, Mark Anthony Neal, Joan Morgan, Rachel Raimist, Elaine B. Richardson, and Aisha S. Durham (Mira Loma, CA: Parker, 2007): 304–12; Aisha S. Durham, "Behind Beats and Rhymes: Working Class from a Hampton Roads Hip Hop Homeplace," *Policy Futures in Education* 7, no. 2 (2009): 217–29.

42. Cheryl L. Keyes, "Verbal Art Performance in Rap Music: The Conversation of the 80s," *Folklore Forum* 17, no. 2 (1984): 143–52; Cheryl L. Keyes, "At the Crossroads: Rap Music and Its African Nexus," *Ethnomusicology* 40, no. 2 (1996): 235.

43. Cheryl L. Keyes, "Empowering Self, Making Choices, Creating Spaces: Black Female Identity via Rap Music Performance," *Journal of American Folklore* 113, no. 449 (2000): 255–69.

44. Joan Morgan, *When Chickenheads Come Home to Roost: A Hip-Hop Feminist Breaks It Down* (New York: Simon and Schuster, 2017), 67, 70–71.

45. Tricia Rose, *Black Noise: Rap Music and Black Culture in Contemporary America* (Hanover, NH: University Press of New England, 1994), 147–48.

46. Gwendolyn D. Pough, *Check It while I Wreck It: Black Womanhood, Hip Hop Culture, and the Public Sphere* (Boston: Northeastern University Press, 2004).

47. Morgan, *When Chickenheads Come Home*.

48. Brittney C. Cooper, Susana M. Morris, and Robin M. Boylorn, *The Crunk Feminist Collection* (New York: Feminist Press at CUNY, 2017), 1, 170.

49. Saunders, *Cuban Underground*.

50. Soyica Diggs Colbert, *Black Movements: Performance and Cultural Politics* (New Brunswick, NJ: Rutgers University Press, 2017), 27.

51. Kyra D. Gaunt, *The Games Black Girls Play: Learning the Ropes from Double-Dutch to Hip-Hop* (New York: NYU Press, 2006).

52. Gaunt, *Games Black Girls Play*, 177.

53. Alim, "Intro," 15.

54. Catherine M. Appert, "On Hybridity in African Popular Music: The Case of Senegalese Hip Hop," *Ethnomusicology* 60, no. 2 (2016): 280.

55. Kofi Agawu, "Contesting Difference: A Critique of Ethnomusicology," in *The Cultural Study of Music: A Critical Introduction*, ed. Martin Clayton, Trevor Herbert, and Richard Middleton (New York: Routledge, 2003), 236.

56. See Aurélia Ferrari, "Hip-Hop in Nairobi: Recognition of an International Movement and the Main Means of Expression for the Urban Youth in Poor Residential Areas," in *Songs and Politics in Eastern Africa*, ed. Kimani Njogu and Hervé Maupeu (Dar es Salaam: Mkuti na Nyota, 2007), 107–28; Evan Mwangi, "The Incomplete Rebellion: Mau Mau Movement in Twenty-First-Century Kenyan Popular Culture," *Africa Today* 57, no. 2 (2010): 86–113; Koster, "Hip Hop Revolution in Kenya"; Caroline Mose, "Hip-Hop Halisi: Continuities of Heroism on the African Political Landscape," in *Hip Hop and Social Change in Africa: Ni Wakati*, ed. Msia Kibona Clark and Mickie Mwanzia Koster (New York: Lexington Books, 2014).

57. See Aurelie Marion Journo, "Hip-Hop Literature: A Case Study from the New Kenyan Literary Scene," *Postcolonial Text* 5, no. 3 (2009): 1–22; Naomi L. Shitemi, "Orality: Aesthetic and Expressive Literary Genre Exemplified by Kenyan Hip Hop Discourse," *Muziki* 7, no. 1 (2010): 1–30; Chege Githiora, "Sheng: The Expanding Domains of an Urban Youth Vernacular," *Journal of African Cultural Studies* 30, no. 2 (2018): 105–20; Esther Milu, "Translingualism, Kenyan Hip-Hop and Emergent Ethnicities: Implications for Language Theory and Pedagogy," *International Multilingual Research Journal* 12, no. 2 (2018): 96–108.

58. See Mūngai, "'Made in Riverwood.'"

59. See Jean Kidula, "Polishing the Luster of the Stars: Music Professionalism Made Workable in Kenya," *Ethnomusicology* 44, no. 3 (2000): 408–28.

60. See David A. Samper, "'Africa Is Still Our Mama': Kenyan Rappers, Youth Identity, and the Revitalization of Traditional Values," *African Identities* 2, no. 1 (2004): 37–51; Lucy Karanja, "'Homeless' at Home: Linguistic, Cultural, and Identity Hybridity and Third Space Positioning of Kenyan Urban Youth," *Comparative and International Education* 39, no. 2 (2010): 1–19; Henry Wanjala and Charles Kebaya, "Popular Music and Identity Formation among Kenyan Youth," *Muziki* 13, no. 2 (2016): 20–35; Andrew Eisenberg, "M-Commerce and the (Re)making of the Music Industry in Kenya: Preliminary Notes and Findings," report presented to the Association for Social Anthropology, April 5, 2017, https://hcommons.org/deposits/item/hc:15209.

61. See Mwenda Ntarangwi, *The Street Is My Pulpit: Hip Hop and Christianity in Kenya* (Urbana: University of Illinois Press, 2016).

62. See Wasike, "Jua Cali, Genge Rap Music"; Mose, "'Swag' and 'Cred.'"

63. See Evan Mwangi, "Masculinity and Nationalism in East African Hip-Hop Music," *Tydskrif vir Letterkunde* 41, no. 2 (2004): 5–20; Mwenda Ntarangwi, "Hip-Hop, Westernization and Gender in East Africa," in *Songs and Politics in Eastern Africa*, ed. Kimani Njogu and Hervé Maupeu (Dar es Salaam: Mkuki na Nyota, 2007), 273–302.

64. Kimani Njogu, ed., *Culture, Performance and Identity: Paths of Communication in Kenya* (Nairobi: Twaweza Communications, 2008), xvi.

65. Wasike, "Jua Cali, Genge Rap Music," 31–32.

66. Mūngai, "'Is Marwa!,'" 48, 57.

67. Milu, "Translingualism," 105.

68. See Andrew J. Eisenberg, "Hip-Hop and Cultural Citizenship on Kenya's 'Swahili Coast,'" *Africa* 82, no. 4 (2012): 556–78.

69. Joseph D. Eure and James G. Spady, *Nation Conscious Rap* (New York: PC International Press, 1991); James G. Spady, "Mapping and Re-membering Hip Hop History, Hiphopography and African Diasporic History," *Western Journal of Black Studies* 37, no. 2 (2013): 126–57; H. Samy Alim, *Roc the Mic Right: The Language of Hip Hop Culture* (New York: Routledge, 2006), 11.

70. Karla Slocum, "Negotiating Identity and Black Feminist Politics in Caribbean Research," in *Black Feminist Anthropology: Theory, Politics, Praxis, and Poetics*, ed. Irma McClaurin (New Brunswick, NJ: Rutgers University Press, 2001), 145.

71. See Emma Head, "The Ethics and Implications of Paying Participants in Qualitative Research," *International Journal of Social Research Methodology* 12, no. 4 (2009): 335–44.

72. "Home," GoDown Arts Centre—Home of Performing & Visual Arts, 2024, https://thegodown.org/.

73. "Sarakasi Dome—Sarakasi Trust," Sarakasi Dome—Sarakasi Trust, October 21, 2023, https://sarakasi.org/sarakasidome/.

74. Maurice N. Amutabi, *The NGO Factor in Africa: The Case of Arrested Development in Kenya* (London: Routledge, 2013), xxvi.

75. See S. Craig Watkins, *Hip Hop Matters: Politics, Pop Culture, and the Struggle for the Soul of a Movement* (Boston: Beacon Press, 2005), 211–15; Joel Rubin, "Hip Hop Videos and Black Identity in Virtual Space," *Journal of Hip Hop Studies* 3, no. 1 (2016): 74–85.

76. Snooker, interview by RaShelle Peck, December 10, 2011.

77. See Figaro Joseph, "Domestic Actors and Liberalization: A Case Study of Internal and External Pressures in Moi's Kenya," *Contemporary Politics* 19, no. 3 (2013): 321–38; Stephen Brown, "Authoritarian Leaders and Multiparty Elections in Africa: How Foreign Donors Help to Keep Kenya's Daniel arap Moi in Power," *Third World Quarterly* 22, no. 5 (2001): 725–39.

78. See Joyce Nyairo and James Ogude, "Popular Music, Popular Politics: Unbwogable and the Idioms of Freedom in Kenyan Popular Music," *African Affairs* 104, no. 415 (2005): 225–49.

79. Godwin R. Murunga and Shadrack W. Nasong'o, "Prospects for Democracy in Kenya," in *Kenya: The Struggle for Democracy*, ed. Godwin R. Murunga and Shadrack W. Nasong'o (New York: Zed Books, 2008), 6, 9.

80. See Kenda Mutongi, *Matatu: A History of Popular Transportation in Nairobi* (Chicago: University of Chicago Press, 2017).

81. See Alex Perullo and Andrew Eisenberg, "Musical Property Rights Regimes in Tanzania and Kenya after TRIPS," in *The SAGE Handbook of Intellectual Property*, ed. Matthew David and Debora Halbert (Los Angeles: SAGE, 2014), 148–64.

82. See Sylvester Ndubuisi Anya, Adrian Osuagwu, Emmanuel Onyeabor, Joycelin Chinwe Okubuiro, Matthew Nwankwo, Daniel Onyeonagu, and Ifeoma Pamela Enemo, "Credible Commitment or Sham Devotion to the International Criminal Court: Whither Nigeria, Kenya and Uganda?" *African Journal of Legal Studies* 15, no. 2 (April 13, 2023): 242–69.

83. P. Khalil Saucier and Tryon P. Woods, "Hip Hop Studies in Black," *Journal of Popular Music Studies* 26, no. 2/3 (2014): 268–94.

1. CULTURAL ANXIETIES, MUSIC COMMODITIES, RAPPING BODIES

1. Mũngai, "'Is Marwa!'"

2. Mose, "Hip Hop Halisi"; Wanjala and Kebaya, "Popular Music and Identity Formation."

3. Mwangi, "Masculinity and Nationalism," 103.

4. Leigh S. Brownhill and Terisa Turner, "Subsistence Trade and World Trade: Gendered Class Struggle in Kenya, 1999–2002," *Canadian Woman Studies / Les cahiers de la femme* 4 and 1, vols. 21 and 22 (2002): 169–77.

5. Besi Brillian Muhonja, "Gender, Archiving, and Recognition: Naming and Erasing in Nairobi's Cityscape," in *Kenya after 50: Reconfiguring Education, Gender, and Policy*, ed. Michael Mwenda Kithinji, Mickie Mwanzia Koster, and Jerono P. Rotich (New York: Palgrave Macmillan, 2016), 171–96.

6. *Guturamira ng'ania* is the name of the practice in Kikuyu communities; in other communities it has different names.

7. Carl Rosberg and John Nottingham, *The Myth of "Mau Mau": Nationalism in Kenya* (New York: Praeger, 1966), quoted in Audrey Wipper, *Riot and Rebellion among African Women: Three Examples of Women's Political Clout* (East Lansing: Office of WID, Michigan State University, 1986), 315. See also Mshaï S. Mwangola, "Njia Panda: Kenyan Theatre in Search of Identity," in *Getting Heard: [Re]claiming Performance Space in Kenya*, ed. Kimani Njogu (Nairobi: Twaweza Communications, 2008), 1–4.

8. Ngũgĩ wa Thiong'o, *Globalectics: Theory and the Politics of Knowing* (New York: Columbia University Press, 2014), 81–83.

9. "African Author Ngugi and Wife Njeeri wa Thiong'o Brutally Attacked on Tour in Nairobi, Kenya," *Black Scholar* 34, no. 3 (2015): 78.

10. Thiong'o, *Decolonising the Mind*, 3.

11. Roger Wallis and Krister Malm, *Big Sounds from Small Peoples: The Music Industry in Small Countries* (New York: Pendragon Press, 1984), 92.

12. See John Low, "A History of Kenyan Guitar Music: 1945—1980," *African Music* 6, no. 2 (1982): 17–18; Gregory F. Barz, "Meaning in Benga Music of Western Kenya," *British Journal of Ethnomusicology* 10, no. 1 (2001): 107–15.

13. The term "repressive state apparatus" draws from Louis Althusser. Here he argues that the RSA violently ensures the conditions of capitalist production. See Louis Althusser, *On the Reproduction of Capitalism: Ideology and Ideological State Apparatuses* (London: Verso, 2014 [1970]).

14. See Mitchel Strumpf, "Early Studies of the Music of East Africa," in *Ethnomusicology in East Africa: Perspectives from Uganda and Beyond*, ed. Sylvia A. Nannyonga-Tamusuza and Thomas Solomon (Kampala: Fountain, 2012), 37–38.

15. Strumpf, "Early Studies," 38–39.

16. Bruce Berman and John Lonsdale, *Unhappy Valley: Conflict in Kenya and Africa* (London: James Currey, 1992), 131.

17. Krister Malm, "The Music Industry," in *Ethnomusicology: An Introduction*, ed. Helen Myer (London: Macmillan, 1992), 351.

18. Bruce J. Berman and John M. Lonsdale, "Crises of Accumulation, Coercion and the Colonial State: The Development of the Labor Control System in Kenya, 1919–1929," *Canadian Journal of African Studies / La Revue canadienne des études africaines* 14, no. 1 (1980): 55–81.

19. See Chris Stapleton and Chris May, *African Rock: The Pop Music of a Continent* (New York: Dutton, 1990), 261; Kimani Gecau, "Popular Song and Social Change in Kenya," *Media, Culture & Society* 17, no. 4 (1995): 561–62; Wolfgang Bender, *Sweet Mother: Modern African Music* (Chicago: University of Chicago Press, 1991), 120.

Indians, first coming to Kenya to work on the railroads, ventured into various business opportunities and bought and sold phonograph records and played music in their shops due to a small urban market (see Bender, *Sweet Mother*, 120). After selling over twenty thousand records, Gramophone produced more music, sending it to India to be pressed onto records, then selling the music in the colony (see Strumpf, "Early Studies," 39–40).

20. Achille Mbembé, *On the Postcolony* (Berkeley: University of California Press, 2001), 31.

21. Kaskon W. Mindoti and Hellen Agak, "Political Influence on Music Performance in Kenya between 1963–2002," *Bulletin of the Council for Research in Music Education*, no. 161/162 (2004): 56.

22. Peter Muhoro Mwangi notes, "There [was not] a coherent law regarding censorship, but rather the government use[d] the GCB in an ad hoc manner to control the media whenever it produce[d] material deemed to promote antisocial behaviour, violence and breaching of the peace in the nation"; Peter Muhoro Mwangi, "Silencing Musical Expression in Colonial and Post-colonial Kenya," in *Popular Music Censorship in Africa*, ed. Michael Drewett and Martin Cloonan (Burlington, VT; Ashgate: 2016), 157–70, at 158.

23. Gecau, "Popular Song," 562.

24. See Sloan Mahone, "The Psychology of Rebellion: Colonial Medical Responses to Dissent in British East Africa," *Journal of African History* 47, no. 2 (2006): 241–58; Margaret Gathoni Gecaga, "Religious Movements and Democratisation in Kenya: Between the Sacred and the Profane," in *Kenya: The Struggle for Democracy*, ed. Godwin R. Murunga and Shadrack W. Nasong'o (New York: Zed Books, 2007): 58–89; Neil Carrier and Celia Nyamweru, "Reinventing Africa's National Heroes: The Case of Mekatilili, a Kenyan Popular Heroine," *African Affairs* 115, no. 461 (2016): 599–620; Zebulon Dingley, "The Transfiguration of Lukas Pkech: Dini ya Msambwa and the 'Kolloa Affray,'" *Journal of Religion and Violence* 8, no. 1 (2020): 5–34.

25. See Gecau, "Popular Song."

26. Ronnie Graham, *The World of African Music* (London: Pluto Press, 1992); Gecau, "Popular Song," 562.

I cautiously cite the work of Ronnie Graham, who provides extensive details on the music industries of Africa. Graham uses racist terms, i.e., describing the '80s African presidents as "barbaric," and often orients his analysis using the west or the United States as a starting point; *World of African Music*, 7, 9).

27. Gerhard Kubik, "Neo-traditional Popular Music in East Africa since 1945," *Popular Music* no. 1 (1981): 91; Bender, *Sweet Mother*, 120; Gecau, "Popular Song," 561.

28. In 1930, the German company Odéon convinced Saad to leave Gramophone and record with them (see Strumpf, "Early Studies," 39–40).

29. Ian Eagleson, "Between Uptown and River Road: The Making and Undoing of Kenya's 1960s' 'Zilizopendwa,'" *World of Music* 3, no. 1 (2014): 28.

30. P. Mwangi Mūhoro, "The Poetics of Gĩkũyũ Mwomboko: Narrative as a Technique in HIV-AIDS Awareness Campaign in Rural Kenya," in *Songs and Politics in Eastern Africa*, ed. Kimani Njogu and Hervé Maupeu (Dar es Salaam: Mkuti na Nyota, 2007), 75.

31. See Elisha S. Atieno-Odhiambo and John Lonsdale, eds., *Mau Mau and Nationhood: Arms, Authority and Narration* (Columbus: Ohio State University Press, 2003).

32. See Maina wa Kinyatti, ed., *Thunder from the Mountains: Mau Mau Patriotic Songs* (Trenton, NJ: Africa World Press, 1990).

33. In 1954, the state began Operation Anvil, which rounded up Africans into detention camps. See Bethwell Ogot, "The Decisive Years: 1956–63," in *Decolonization and Independence in Kenya, 1940–93*, ed. Bethwell A. Ogot and William R. Ochieng' (London: James Currey, 1995), 48.

34. This economic growth mostly benefited the colonial government and white farmers. The worsening exploitation of Kenyans led to increased feelings of dissent. See Elisha S. Atieno-Odhiambo, "The Formative Years: 1945–55," in *Decolonization and Independence in Kenya, 1940–93*, ed. Bethwell A. Ogot and William R. Ochieng' (London: James Currey, 1995), 27–28. For more on postwar radio and music production, see Eagleson, "Between Uptown and River Road," 31; Kubik, "Neo-traditional Popular Music," 87.

35. See Paul Vernon, "Feast of the East," www.bolingo.org, 1997, http://www.bolingo .org/audio/texts/fr145eastafrica.html; Eagleson, "Between Uptown and River Road," 28.

36. Eagleson, "Between Uptown and River Road," 29–30.

37. See "Music in Africa," Music in Africa, n.d., https://www.musicinafrica.net/.

38. During the Congo Crisis, artists left the country from 1960–65. Ultimately, musicians were among the thousands of people who fled the violence into the Republic of the Congo, Kenya, Tanzania, and Uganda, as well as to France and Belgium. See Wallis and Malm, *Big Sounds*, 32; Aaron Louis Rosenberg, "Zairo-Congolese Musicians and the Sound of Assimilation in East Africa," in *Music and Messaging in the African Political Arena*, ed. Uche T. Onyebadi, (Hershey, PA: IGI Global, 2019), 201–20. Political policies made Tanzania a more viable place for emigrating Congolese. For more, see Alex Perullo, "Rumba in the City of Peace: Migration and the Cultural Commodity of Congolese Music in Dar es Salaam, 1968–1985," *Ethnomusicology* 52, no. 2 (2008): 296–323.

39. There are structural, economic, and cultural reasons for the dissemination of Congolese music throughout the continent. It is important to note that both Brazzaville and Kinshasa had lively and always changing music scenes. Beginning in the 1930s, mining towns in the (Belgium) Congo hosted live bands that played for laborers from southern and western parts of Africa. The popularity of the music and its similarities with and borrowing from Cuban rumba made it additionally welcome in various places, especially in western Africa. See Paul Tiyambe Zeleza, "Dancing to the Beat of the Diaspora: Musical Exchanges between Africa and Its Diasporas," *African and Black Diaspora: An International Journal* 3, no. 2 (2010): 211–36.

40. Gecau, "Popular Song," 565.

41. Low, "A History," 19, 22–23; Stapleton and May, *African Rock*, 227, 229.

42. Elisha S. Atieno Odhiambo, "Kula Raha: Gendered Discourses and the Contours of Leisure in Nairobi, 1946–63," *AZANIA: Journal of the British Institute in Eastern Africa* 36, no. 1 (2001): 257.

43. Stapleton and May, *African Rock*, 230–31.

44. Traditionally, Benga originates from Luo communities. The term is also often used to describe Kenyan popular guitar music more generally. Precolonial and community-based Luo music uses a similar instrument to the guitar, a stringed lyre called a *nyatiti*. Other musical practices influenced the commercial Benga sound, such as the Luhya *litungu*-based sukuti music and Kikuyu Mwomboko genre. Musicians started by playing the acoustic (also called dry or box) guitar, and then shifted to the electric guitar by the 1960s when accessibility increased. See Low, "A History of Kenyan Guitar Music"; Stapleton and May, *African Rock*, 230–40; Stephen H. Martin, "Popular Music in Urban East Africa: From Historical Perspective to a Contemporary Hero," *Black Music Research Journal* (1991): 47. The guitar resonated for many artists because of its similarity to other stringed lyres used in different ethnic communities, like the Luo *nyatiti* and Luhya *litungu*. Still others distinguish Benga from the Kikuyu music, Mugithi. See Barz, "Meaning in Benga Music."

45. Mwangi, "Silencing Musical Expression, 160–65.

46. See Joyce Nyairo, "Kenyan Gospel Soundtracks: Crossing Boundaries, Mapping Audiences," *Journal of African Cultural Studies* 20, no. 1 (2008): 71–83; Ian Eagleson, "Between Uptown and River Road."

47. For more on Benga, see Barz, "Meaning in Benga Music." Wolfgang Bender also states: "The pan-African success of Congolese music may well be connected with the efficiency of the early broadcasting of this music. In Brazzaville, with the help of the Americans, Charles de Gaulle had set up a strong transmitter to serve 'France Libre.' There was a need to spread propaganda into African colonies as they were no longer completely 'safe'—growing dissatisfaction with the colonial regimes and resulting sympathies for the war opponent had to be countered. To motivate listeners to stay tuned to Radio Brazzaville, Afro-Cuban and newly recorded Congolese discs were played all the time in the short wave transmissions. No other African music had hitherto had an audience all over Africa"; Wolfgang Bender, "Modern African Music: An Autonomous Music," in *Sounds of Change: Social and Political Features of Music in Africa*, ed. Stig-Magnus Thorsén (Stockholm: Sida, 2004), 95.

48. Stapleton and May, *African Rock*, 229–40.

49. Zeleza, "Dancing to the Beat," 215.

50. Caleb C. Okumu, "Reclaiming Kenya's Popular Music: A Solution to a Dilemma," in *Emerging Solutions for Musical Arts Education in Africa*, ed. Anri Herbst (Cape Town: African Minds, 2005), 231–32.

51. Wallis and Malm, *Big Sounds*, 183–87.

52. There have been many versions, including by Peter Seeger, Jamaican band Boney M., Benny Anderson, and Saragossa. On one album, Makeba stated the song "came from Tanzania." William never received royalties. Others have claimed ownership and rights to royalties as well, including artists from Tanzania. Grant Charo claims he, not William, originally wrote the song and therefore should have copyright ownership to it. See *Nation*, "Malaika: Who Was the Real Composer?," June 21, 2020, https://nation.africa/kenya/life-and-style /weekend/malaika-who-was-the-real-composer—567794; Joe Ombuor, "Musician Declared to the World That Malaika Was His Original Composition," *The Standard*, 2022, https://www.standardmedia.co.ke/counties/article/2001437254/musician-declared-to-the -world-that-malaika-was-his-original-composition. In an interview with me, Mtawali also named Charo as the author.

53. Mick Jagero, interview by RaShelle Peck, November 18, 2012.

54. Mtawali, interview by RaShelle Peck, September 13, 2012.

55. Ian Eagleson, "Between Uptown and River Road," 37.

56. Ian Eagleson, "Between Uptown and River Road," 37.

57. *Waheshimiwa* translates to "those who are honored." Discussed in Mũgo, "The Woman Artist," 58. See also Maina wa Mũtonya, "Praise and Protest: Music and Contesting Patriotism in Postcolonial Kenya," *Social Dynamics* 30, no. 2 (2004): 20–35.

58. See Mwangi, "Silencing Musical Expression."

59. At first, Kamaru performed nationalistic songs, even supporting Kenyatta against a mountain of criticism when the president became unpopular. In 1975, his allegiance would shift, with his song about the slain leader Joseph Mwangi Kariuki, "J. M. Mwendwo ni Iri" (J. M., The People's Hero). This was an attack on Kenyatta's government, who most believed

was responsible for Kariuki's death, and the administration banned the song. See Maina wa Mūtonya and Catherine Bosire, *The Politics of Everyday Life in Gĩkũyũ Popular Music of Kenya (1990–2000)* (Nairobi: Twaweza Communications, 2013), 73.

60. Mūtonya and Bosire, *Politics of Everyday Life*, 73.

61. Wallis and Malm, *Big Sounds*, 257–59; Krister Malm and Roger Wallis, *Media Policy and Music Activity* (London: Routledge, 1992), 90.

62. Stapleton and May, *African Rock*, 231; Kidula, "Polishing the Luster of the Stars," 409.

63. Wallis and Malm state: "The staff were not motivated to support the efforts of the local musicians despite the hundreds of Kenyan records produced annually by Kenyan phonogram companies." They also quote a DJ on VOK: "Local Kenyan music sounds so awful you just can't think of anything to say in between numbers" (Wallis and Malm, *Big Sounds*, 258).

64. Malm and Wallis, *Media Policy*, 1.

65. Mūtonya, "Praise and Protest," 25.

66. Mūtonya and Bosire, *Politics of Everyday Life*, 57; Ruth M. Agesa, "Dynamics of Music and Political Mobilization in Post-colonial Kenya," *Journal of African Interdisciplinary Studies* 3, no. 10 (2019): 44.

Ngai is Kikuyu for God, and the song, meaning "Kenya is for God," criticizes the government for violence and corruption (Mūtonya, "The Beat Goes On," 26). Odhiambo Osumba Rateng's song "Baba Otonglo" from the album *Budget Iko High* (The Governmental Budget Is High) was an allegory about the president and his inability to keep a proper budget. The verses discuss Baba Otonglo (*Otonglo* is a Luo word for money), who cannot earn enough money to support his family. Although state officials seized copies of the song, *jua kali* vendors continued to sell it illegally. See Stevens Muendo, "How 'Budget Song' Landed Baba Otonglo Singer in Trouble," *The Standard*, 2023, https://www.standardmedia.co.ke /entertainment/news/article/2001475215/how-budget-song-landed-baba-otonglo-singer-in -trouble.

67. Fibian Kavulani Lukalo, *Extended Handshake or Wrestling Match? Youth and Urban Culture Celebrating Politics in Kenya* (Uppsala: Nordic Africa Institute, 2006).

68. See Perullo and Eisenberg, "Musical Property Rights Regimes."

69. Mūtonya, "Praise and Protest," 27.

70. Richard Joseph argues that prebendalism is marked by "patterns of political behavior which reflect as their justifying principle that the offices of the existing state may be competed for and then utilized for the personal benefit of office-holders as well as that of their reference or support group"; Richard A. Joseph, "Class, State, and Prebendal Politics in Nigeria," *Journal of Commonwealth and Comparative Politics* 21, no. 3 (1983): 30. See also Korwa G. Adar and Isaac M. Munyae, "Human Rights Abuse in Kenya under Daniel Arap Moi, 1978," *African Studies Quarterly* 5, no. 1 (2001): 1–14.

71. See Godwin Murunga, "Governance and the Politics of Structural Adjustment in Kenya," in *Kenya: The Struggle for Democracy*, ed. Godwin Murunga and Shadrack Nasong'o (Dakar: Codesria, 2007), 263–300.

72. See John Ndavula and Jackline U. Lidubwi, "Can Vernacular Radio Be Conflict Sensitive? An Analysis of Vernacular Radio Programming in Western Kenya," in *Indigenous Language for Social Change Communication in the Global South*, ed. Abiodun Salawu, Tshepang

Bright Molale, Enrique Uribe-Jongbloed, and Mohammad Sahid Ullah, 229–42 (New York: Rowman & Littlefield, 2023).

73. See Ferrari, "Hip-Hop in Nairobi."

74. Sheng for "That is tricky."

75. See David M. Anderson, "Briefing: Kenya's Elections 2002: The Dawning of a New Era?," *African Affairs* 102, no. 407 (2003): 331–42; Mai Hassan, "A State of Change: District Creation in Kenya after the Beginning of Multi-party Elections," *Political Research Quarterly* 69, no. 3 (2016): 510–21.

76. Godwin R. Murunga and Shadrack W. Nasong'o, "Bent on Self-Destruction: The Kibaki Regime in Kenya," *Journal of Contemporary African Studies* 24, no. 1 (2006): 2.

77. See Nyairo and Ogude, "Popular Music, Popular Politics."

78. See Bruce J. Berman, Jill Cottrell, and Yash Ghai, "Patrons, Clients, and Constitutions: Ethnic Politics and Political Reform in Kenya," *Canadian Journal of African Studies* 43, no. 3 (2009): 462–506; Kasarani Youth Congress, "Mobilization without Emancipation: The Case of Kazi Kwa Vijana in Kasarani Constituency" (Nairobi, 2009).

79. See Mutongi, *Matatu.*

80. See Perullo and Eisenberg, "Musical Property Rights Regimes."

81. See Macharia Kamau, "Copyright Body Destroys Pirated CDs Estimated at Sh10m," *The Standard*, 2012, https://www.standardmedia.co.ke/article/2000052183/copyright-body -destroys-pirated-cds-estimated-at-sh10m.

82. See Evelyne Musambi, "Kenyan Artistes, MCSK Lock Horns over Royalties," *Daily Nation*, October 22, 2014, https://link.gale.com/apps/doc/A387039575/GIC?u = cuny_mancc &sid = bookmark-GIC&xid = 21b7fc55.

83. Evaredi, interview by RaShelle Peck, November 22, 2012.

84. Evaredi, interview by RaShelle Peck, November 22, 2012.

85. Ndugus, interview by RaShelle Peck, November 11, 2011.

86. Funzo Kuu, interview by RaShelle Peck, November 11, 2011.

87. Giorgio Agamben, *Homo Sacer: Sovereign Power and Bare Life* (Stanford, CA: Stanford University Press, 1998), 28–29; emphasis in original.

88. Esen, interview by RaShelle Peck, July 15, 2010.

89. Mellitus Nyongesa Wanyama, "Policy and Implementation: A Case of Music Copyright Laws in Kenya," *Muziki* 4, no. 1 (2007): 28.

90. See Beth Achitsa, "Kenyan Artists Protest Foreign Music Dominance," *Music in Africa*, August 11, 2015, https://www.musicinafrica.net/magazine/kenyan-artists-protest -foreign-music-dominance.

91. Okumu, "Reclaiming Kenya's Popular Music," 229.

92. Wanyama, "Policy and Implementation," 39.

93. Judge, interview by RaShelle Peck, November 16, 2012.

94. Wanyama, "Policy and Implementation" 39.

95. An interview with Joe Murimi, an MCSK manager, confirms that since 2004 radio stations and televisions have had to pay for licenses. Murimi additionally states, "The fact that almost all broadcast stations play a lot of music from the North American pop or hip hop in their daily music rotation, MCSK ends up remitting most of the revenue collected as royalties to foreign artists." See Austine Okande and Mkala Mwangesha, "Artistes Royalties 'to Shoot Up Soon,'" *The Standard*, October 15, 2012.

96. See Ferrari, "Hip-Hop in Nairobi," 115–16.

97. Mick Jagero, interview by RaShelle Peck, November 18, 2012.

98. Judge, interview by RaShelle Peck, November 16, 2012.

99. Adrian Washika, interview by RaShelle Peck, September 15, 2012.

100. Adrian Washika, interview by RaShelle Peck, September 15, 2012.

101. Osumare, "Motherland Hip-Hop," 171.

102. Evaredi, interview by RaShelle Peck, November 22, 2012.

103. Adrian Washika, interview by RaShelle Peck, September 15, 2012.

104. Adrian Washika, interview by RaShelle Peck, September 15, 2012.

105. Ministry of Sports, Culture, and Heritage, *The National Policy on Culture and Heritage*, ed. Amina Chawahir Mohamed Jibril, 2023, https://www.tourism.go.ke/wp-content/uploads/2023/05/NATIONAL-POLICY-ON-CULTURE-AND-HERITAGE.pdf.

106. See Washington Omondi, *Report of the Presidential National Music Commission* (Nairobi: Government Printers, 1984), 162. See also Patricia Opondo, "Cultural Policies in Kenya," *Arts Education Policy Review* 101, no. 5 (2000): 18–24.

107. Government of Kenya, *National Policy on Culture and Heritage* (Nairobi: Government Printers, 2009), 3.

108. Mtawali, interview by RaShelle Peck, September 13, 2012; Judge, interview by RaShelle Peck, November 16, 2012.

109. Nafsi Huru, interview by RaShelle Peck, November 11, 2011.

110. Mtawali, interview by RaShelle Peck, September 13, 2012.

111. Esen, interview by RaShelle Peck, July 15, 2010.

112. Robin D. G. Kelley, "Forward," in *The Vinyl Ain't Final: Hip Hop and the Globalization of Black Popular Culture*, ed. Dipannita Basu and Sidney J. Lemelle (London: Pluto, 2006), xiii.

113. Zine Magubane, "Ni Wapi Tunakwenda: Hip Hop Culture and the Children of Arusha," in *The Vinyl Ain't Final: Hip Hop and the Globalization of Black Popular Culture*, ed. Dipannita Basu and Sidney J. Lemelle (London: Pluto, 2006), 216.

114. Bantu Mwaura, "Kenyan Youth and the Entropic Destruction of a Hopeful Social Order," in *Cultural Production and Social Change in Kenya: Building Bridges*, ed. Kimani Njogu (Nairobi: Twaweza Communications: 2007), 70.

115. R. A. T. Judy, "On the Question of Nigga Authenticity," in *That's the Joint!: The Hip-Hop Studies Reader*, ed. Murray Forman and Mark A. Neal (New York: Routledge, 2012), 113–14.

116. Louis Chude-Sokei, *The Sound of Culture: Diaspora and Black Technopoetics* (Middleton, CT: Wesleyan University Press, 2015).

117. Stephen H. Martin, "Brass Bands and the Beni Phenomenon in Urban East Africa," *African Music: Journal of the International Library of African Music* 7, no. 1 (1991): 72.

118. Chude-Sokei, *The Sound of Culture*, 34, 33.

119. See Carol Muller, "South Africa and American Jazz: Towards a Polyphonic Historiography," *History Compass* 5, no. 4 (2007): 1066.

120. Carolyn Martin Shaw, *Colonial Inscriptions: Race, Sex and Class in Kenya* (Minneapolis: University of Minnesota Press, 1995), 4.

121. Shaw, *Colonial Inscriptions*, 191.

122. See Mũtonya, "The Beat Goes On"; Mũngai, "'Is Marwa!'"

123. Mũngai, "'Is Marwa!,'" 50.

124. Ngũgĩ wa Thiong'o, "On the Abolition of the English Department," *Présence Africaine* 1 (2018): 104.

125. Historian E. S. Atieno-Odhiambo posits, "Kenya, as a new nation, has demanded a new postcolonial history, [one that is] arranged around the metaphor of struggle. This metaphor entails seeing our history . . . as a moral enterprise: . . . against the foreignization of the cultural ecology[, and] against the intervention of alien ideas in the indigenous discourses on nation-building"; Elisha S. Atieno-Odhiambo, "The Invention of Kenya," in *Decolonization and Independence in Kenya, 1940–93*, ed. Bethwell A. Ogot and William R. Ochieng' (London: James Currey, 1995), 2.

126. Mũngai, "'Is Marwa!,'" 50.

127. Bethwell Ogot contends: "Culture contributes to an individual's or nation's sense of identity by providing bases of social integration and offering guidelines to action during periods of uncertainty"; Bethwell Ogot, "Construction of a National Culture," in *Decolonization and Independence in Kenya, 1940–93*, ed. Bethwell A. Ogot and William R. Ochieng' (London: James Currey, 1995), 215.

128. Luis Muñoz, "Nu Nairobi: Inside Nairobi's Music Scene," *Fact Magazine*, April 9, 2018, https://www.factmag.com/2018/04/09/nu-nairobi-inside-nairobis-music-scene.

129. See Samson Kaunga Ndanyi, "Film Censorship and Identity in Kenya," *Ufahamu: A Journal of African Studies* 42, no. 2 (2021): 23–41.

130. Bethwell Ogot, "Construction of a National Culture," 229.

131. Thiong'o, *Decolonising the Mind*, 28.

132. Sylvia Washington Bâ, *The Concept of Negritude in the Poetry of Leopold Sedar Senghor* (Princeton, NJ: Princeton University Press, 2015), 212.

2. PLAY AND GENDER

1. L-Ness, interview by RaShelle Peck, November 20, 2012.

2. Ngũgĩ wa Thiong'o, "The Politics of National Theatre: The Example of Kenya," *Drama Review* 62, no. 2 (2018): 18–19.

3. This change in security seemed to coincide with adjustments in the aftermath of the Westgate Mall attack in 2013, where Al-Shabaab fighters stormed the mall, killing 71 and injuring over 200. Afterward, commercial institutions in Nairobi and around Kenya tightened security measures.

4. Philip Auslander argues that liveness and technologies are interdependent. According to him, the production of liveness in concerts, for example, often depends on technology. See Philip Auslander, *Liveness: Performance in a Mediatized Culture* (Oxford: Routledge, 2002).

5. Turner, "Body, Brain, and Culture," 168.

6. Turner, "Body, Brain, and Culture," 168.

7. Glissant, *Poetics of Relation*, 190.

8. Jayna Brown, "Buzz and Rumble," *Social Text* 28, no. 1 (2010): 129.

9. I thank Izzy Mizell for their assistance in clarifying the sonic interventions of these songs.

10. *Jua kali* is Swahili for "hot sun" and means lower-working-class people who labor under the sun or outside.

11. The 2003 Michuki laws sought to control the *matatu* industry, which until then was largely controlled by street gang organizations. Michuki compliance stated that owners had to eliminate outer graffiti decorations and loud music, install speed governors, provide uniforms to *matatu* workers, install seat belts for passengers, and paint the exterior of the *matatu* in a solid color with a horizontal yellow stripe. Prior to 2003, many vehicles regularly displayed colorful graffiti on the exterior, blasted hip hop or ragga, and drove without caution, weaving in and out of traffic. It was commonplace for the tout to cram as many people into a *matatu* as possible, termed *iko nafasi* (literally, there is always a chance; colloquially, there's always room for one more). Implementing safety belts and imposing one person to a seat meant an overall loss of money for the touts and the drivers. For more on Michuki regulations, see Mutongi, *Matatu*; Mbũgua wa Mũngai and David A. Samper, "'No Mercy, No Remorse': Personal Experience Narratives about Public Passenger Transportation in Nairobi, Kenya," *Africa Today* 52, no. 3 (2006): 51–81.

12. See Mũngai and Samper, "'No Mercy, No Remorse.'"

13. James Ogude, "The Invention of Traditional Music in the City: Exploring History and Meaning in Urban Music in Contemporary Kenya," *Research in African Literatures* 43, no. 4 (2012): 151.

14. See Samuel O. Owuor and Teresa Mbatia, "Post-Independence Development of Nairobi City, Kenya," paper presented at Workshop on African Capital Cities, Dakar, September 22–23, 2008.

15. See Paul Ocobock, *An Uncertain Age: The Politics of Manhood in Kenya* (Athens: Ohio University Press, 2017).

16. Muhonja, "Gender, Archiving, and Recognition."

17. Muhonja, "Gender, Archiving, and Recognition," 189.

18. For more on how discourses of masculinities and femininities circulate in Nairobi, see Bodil Folke Frederiksen, "Popular Culture, Gender Relations and the Democratization of Everyday Life in Kenya," *Journal of Southern African Studies* 26, no. 2 (2000): 209–22; Rachel Spronk, "Sex, Sexuality and Negotiating Africanness in Nairobi," *Africa* 79, no. 4 (2009): 500–519; Dina Ligaga, "Mapping Emerging Constructions of Good Time Girls in Kenyan Popular Media," *Journal of African Cultural Studies* 26, no. 3 (2014): 249–61; Tom Odhiambo, "Specificities: Troubled Love and Marriage as Work in Kenyan Popular Fiction," *Social Identities* 9, no. 3 (2003): 423–436.

19. Mose, "Hip-Hop Halisi," 14–15.

20. Keguro Macharia, "Unhoming Kenyan Women," *Gukira*, October 3, 2014, https://gukira.wordpress.com/2014/10/03/unhoming-kenyan-women/.

21. Godwin R. Murunga, *Spontaneous or Premeditated?: Post-election Violence in Kenya*, discussion paper (Uppsala: Nordic Africa Institute, 2011), 1–58.

22. See Craig Halliday, "Animating Political Protests through Artivism in 21st Century Nairobi, Kenya," *Law, Social Justice & Global Development*, 24, no. 24 (2019): 100–114; Melissa Tully and Brian Ekdale, "Sites of Playful Engagement: Twitter Hashtags as Spaces of Leisure and Development in Kenya," *Information Technologies & International Development* 10, no. 3 (2014): 67–82.

23. See Brenda Nyandiko Sanya and Anne Namatsi Lutomia, "Feminism Unfinished: Towards Gender Justice and Women's Rights in Kenya," in *Kenya after 50: Reconfiguring Education, Gender, and Policy*, ed. Michael Mwenda Kithinji, Mickie Mwanzia Koster, Jerono P. Rotich (London: Palgrave Macmillan, 2016), 227–52.

24. See Chi Mgbako, *To Live Freely in This World: Sex Worker Activism in Africa* (New York: NYU Press, 2016), 1–5; Sex Worker Film and Arts Festival Movies, "Mwili Wangu, Cha[g]uo Langu—My Body, My Choice | Sex Worker Fest Movies," http://www.sexworker fest.com/videos/video_type/mwili-wangu-chauo-langu-my-body-my-choice-part-1/.

25. See Edith Honan, "Outrage in Kenya: Attacks on Women in Mini-Skirts Spark Street Protest," *The Star*, November 19, 2014, https://www.thestar.com.my/lifestyle/people/2014 /11/19/outrage-in-kenya-attacks-on-women-in-miniskirts-spark-street-protest.

26. Rose, *Black Noise*, 12; also cited in Michael P. Jeffries, *Thug Life: Race, Gender, and the Meaning of Hip-Hop* (Chicago: University of Chicago Press, 2011), 56.

27. See Mwangi, "The Incomplete Rebellion"; Mose, "Hip-Hop Halisi."

28. Koster, "The Hip Hop Revolution," 84.

29. Koster, "The Hip Hop Revolution," 87.

30. Imani Kai Johnson, "From Blues Women to B-Girls: Performing Badass Femininity," *Women & Performance: A Journal of Feminist Theory* 24, no. 1 (2014): 15–28.

31. Jessica Nydia Pabón-Colón, *Graffiti Grrlz: Performing Feminism in the Hip Hop Diaspora* (New York: NYU Press, 2018), 46.

32. Pabón-Colón, *Graffiti Grrlz*, 32.

33. Pabón-Colón, *Graffiti Grrlz*, 47.

34. Sue Timon, interview by RaShelle Peck, November 20, 2012.

35. Esen, interview by RaShelle Peck, July 15, 2010.

36. Evaredi, interview by RaShelle Peck, November 22, 2012.

37. Glissant, *Poetics of Relation*, 16.

38. Judge, interview by RaShelle Peck, November 16, 2012.

39. Jeffries, *Thug Life*, 62, 61.

40. Jeffries, *Thug Life*, 67.

41. Jeffries, *Thug Life*, 94.

42. Jeffries, *Thug Life*, 62, 115–16.

43. Robin D. G. Kelley, *Race Rebels: Culture, Politics, and the Black Working Class* (New York: Free Press, 1994), 206.

44. Kelley, *Race Rebels*, 9, 7. Tricia Rose, in her seminal *Black Noise*, proclaims, "Among other things, rap music uses cloaked speech and disguised cultural codes to comment on and challenge aspects of current power inequalities" (100).

45. MzukaFlani, "MIC—Black Duo," YouTube, January 31, 2009, https://www.youtube .com/watch?v = 1LbmBvQVU3s&t = 4s.

46. MzukaFlani, "MIC—Black Duo."

47. Jeffries, *Thug Life*, 67.

48. Matthew D. Morrison, "The Sound(s) of Subjection: Constructing American Popular Music and Racial Identity through Blacksound," *Women & Performance: A Journal of Feminist Theory* 27, no. 1 (2017): 19.

49. Morrison, "The Sound(s) of Subjection," 22.

50. Ntarangwi, *East African Hip Hop*, 49.

51. Ntarangwi, *East African Hip Hop*, 49–50.

52. Ntarangwi, *East African Hip Hop*, 51.

53. Both Mark Anthony Neal and Treva Lindsay discuss a "user-friendly" patriarchy. Lindsay's discussion is found in the text *Digital Sound Studies*; see Regina Bradley, "Becoming Outkasted: Archiving Contemporary Black Southernness in a Digital Age," in *Digital*

Sound Studies, ed. Mary Caton Lingold, Darren Mueller, and Whitney Anne Trettien (Durham, NC: Duke University Press, 2018), 216. See also Mark Anthony Neal, *Soul Babies: Black Popular Culture and the Post-Soul Aesthetic* (New York: Routledge, 2002), 199.

54. Mary Njeri Kinyanjui, "Situating Fireside Knowledge in Development Feminist Academy," *Journal of Language, Technology & Entrepreneurship in Africa* 10, no. 2 (2019): 1–14.

55. Kinyanjui, "Situating Fireside Knowledge," 13.

56. L-Ness, interview by RaShelle Peck, September 24, 2021.

57. Daphne A. Brooks, "Afro-sonic Feminist Praxis: Nina Simone and Adrienne Kennedy in High Fidelity," in *Black Performance Theory*, ed. Thomas F. DeFrantz and Anita Gonzalez (Durham, NC: Duke University Press, 2014), 204–22.

58. Smalls, "'Make the Music with Your Mouth.'"

59. William Jelani Cobb, *To the Break of Dawn: A Freestyle on the Hip Hop Aesthetic* (New York: NYU Press, 2007), 90, emphasis in original.

60. DandoraMusic, "Looking Up Rmx X 254 Female Rappers (Official Music Video)," YouTube, November 6, 2014, https://www.youtube.com/watch?v = w6PoSkSuDqU&t = 2s.

61. Steven Kisuli Muendo, n.d., "Revealed: Kenyan Singer Sugar's Baby Secrets," *Pulse Magazine*.

62. Msia Kibona Clark, "Feminisms in African Hip Hop," *Meridians: Feminism, Race, Transnationalism* 17, no. 2 (2018): 397.

63. Baby T, interview by RaShelle Peck, November 20, 2012.

64. DandoraMusic, "Looking Up Rmx X 254."

65. Brooks, "Afro-sonic Feminist Praxis," 209.

66. Judge, interview by RaShelle Peck, November 16, 2012.

67. Agano, interview by RaShelle Peck, November 11, 2011.

68. L-Ness, interview by RaShelle Peck, November 20, 2012.

69. Weheliye, *Phonographies*, 28.

70. Saunders, *Cuban Underground Hip Hop*, 41.

71. Jeffries, *Thug Life*, 34–35.

72. Daniel Banks, "Hip Hop as Pedagogy: Something from Something," *Theatre Topics* 25, no. 3 (2015): 243–59.

73. Ndugus, interview by RaShelle Peck, November 11, 2011.

74. Jomo Kenyatta instituted the National Youth Service shortly after independence in order to provide opportunities for poor young men. The NYS employed and trained these men in part to appease growing postindependence discontent. See Wunyabari O. Maloba, *The Anatomy of Neo-colonialism in Kenya: British Imperialism and Kenyatta, 1963–1978* (Cham, Switz.: Springer Science and Business Media, Palgrave Macmillan, 2017).

75. See Peaceloise Mbae, n.d., "Fraudsters Stole Sh791 Million from National Youth Service, Says Devolution Cabinet Secretary Anne Waiguru," *The Standard*, https://www.stan dardmedia.co.ke/article/2000176045/fraudsters-stole-sh791-million-from-national-youth -service-says-devolution-cabinet-secretary-anne-waiguru; BBC News, "Head of Kenya Youth Agency Arrested in $78m Corruption Scandal," May 28, 2018, https://www.bbc.com /news/world-africa-44280453.

76. *Daily Nation*, "World Bank Cancels Funding for Kazi Kwa Vijana over Graft," July 3, 2020, https://nation.africa/kenya/news/world-bank-cancels-funding-for-kazi-kwa-vijana -over-graft—787724.

77. DandoraMusic, "Looking Up Rmx X 254."

78. See John M. Wambui, "A Cosmopolitan Ghetto: The Shifting Image of Kibera Slum from 'Flying Toilets' to a Centre for Metropolitan Innovation," *The Thinker* 85, no. 3 (2020): 19–35.

79. In Kenya, most schools adhere to a British educational system. Here, primary six is the sixth year of school for children.

80. Amora, interview by RaShelle Peck, November 20, 2012.

81. Marcyliena Morgan, *The Real Hiphop: Battling for Knowledge, Power, and Respect in the LA Underground* (Durham, NC: Duke University Press, 2009), 159. Anthony Kwame Harrison makes a similar observation in his ethnography of U.S. Bay Area hip hop: "[U]nderground hip hop's racial and class inclusivity does not extend across gender lines. In this regard, there is a stark contradiction between the subgenre's liberationist ideal—the belief that all people should be able to take part in hip hop regardless of race, ethnicity, class, gender or any other category of collective identification—and the existing structures for participation which significantly privilege men over women"; Harrison, *Hip Hop Underground*, 33.

82. Kinyanjui, "Situating Fireside Knowledge," 3.

83. Brown, "Buzz and Rumble," 129.

84. Brown, "Buzz and Rumble," 130.

85. Marcyliena Morgan notes something similar in her ethnographic accounts: "In the case of Project Blowed, the audience members affirm the MC by bobbing their heads, moving their shoulders in quick succession, throwing their hands up with their fingers in the shape of the letter W, or even forcing the MC off the mic by yelling repeatedly 'please pass the mic'"; Morgan, *The Real Hiphop*, 60.

86. Harrison, *Hip Hop Underground*, 39.

87. Brown, "Buzz and Rumble," 129.

3. DIASPORA, LOVE, AND LIMITS

1. Sue Timon, interview by RaShelle Peck, November 20, 2012.

2. Mose, "'Swag' and 'Cred,'" 115.

3. Marc D. Perry, "Global Black Self-Fashionings: Hip Hop as Diasporic Space," *Identities: Global Studies in Culture and Power* 15, no. 6 (2008): 639.

4. Perry, "Global Black Self-Fashionings," 641.

5. Colbert, *Black Movements*, 6.

6. See Imani Perry, *Prophets of the Hood: Politics and Poetics in Hip Hop* (Durham, NC: Duke University Press, 2004); Jeffries, *Thug Life*.

7. See Tom Lloyd, "Liminal 'Criminals': Re-thinking Historiographies of, and through, the 'Thuggee' Phenomenon," *History Compass* 5, no. 2 (2007): 362–74.

8. Perry, "Global Black Self-Fashionings," 658.

9. Keguro Macharia, "Love," *Critical Ethnic Studies* 1, no. 1 (2015): 73.

10. Koster, "The Hip Hop Revolution," 92.

11. Amora, interview by RaShelle Peck, November 20, 2012.

12. Derek Pardue describes something similar among Brazilian hip hop artists with the term *salvação* or salvation, which is "the process of becoming a hip hopper" and "a force and set of beliefs that [help] reorient their lives"; Pardue, *Ideologies of Marginality*, 5.

13. Flamez Mshamba Mwenza, "Ulimi Sue Timon & Flamez (Washamba Wenza) Official Video," YouTube, January 28, 2013, https://www.youtube.com/watch?v = zkwxRjBpoLs.

14. Evaredi, interview by RaShelle Peck, November 22, 2012.

15. Peter Kagwanja states that the immediacy of the violence suggests that it was planned. He notes that Kalenjin youths were being trained, and took oaths in the months leading up to the election; Peter Kagwanja, "Courting Genocide: Populism, Ethno-nationalism and the Informalisation of Violence in Kenya's 2008 Post-election Crisis," *Journal of Contemporary African Studies* 27, no. 3 (2009): 365–87, at 378–79.

16. See Susanne D. Mueller, "Kenya and the International Criminal Court (ICC): Politics, the Election and the Law," *Journal of Eastern African Studies* 8, no. 1 (2014): 25–42.

17. See Westen K. Shilaho, *Political Power and Tribalism in Kenya* (Cham, Switz.: Springer International, 2018).

18. Charity Marsh and Sheila Petty, "Globalization, Identity, and Youth Resistance: Kenya's Hip Hop Parliament," *MUSICultures* 38, no. 1 (2011): 132–43.

19. Marsh and Petty, "Globalization, Identity," 133.

20. Eric Kioko, "Regional Varieties and 'Ethnic' Registers of Sheng," in *Youth Language Practices in Africa and Beyond*, ed. Nico Nassenstein and Andrea Hollington (University of Cologne: De Gruyter Mouton, 2015), 119–48.

21. Esther Milu, "'Hatucheki Na Watu': Kenyan Hip-Hop Artists' Theories of Multilingualism, Identity and Decoloniality" (PhD diss., Michigan State University, 2016), 54–78.

22. Esther Milu, "Translingualism, Kenyan Hip-Hop and Emergent Ethnicities: Implications for Language Theory and Pedagogy," *International Multilingual Research Journal* 12, no. 2 (2018): 96–108.

23. See Nenpomingyi Sarah Gowon-Adelabu, Susan Mwangi Owino, and Washington Ndiiri, "The Dynamics of Political Corruption and Neo-patrimonialism in Kenya," *Dynamics* 8, no. 14 (2018): 160–69.

24. See Jeni Klugman, "Kenya: Economic Decline and Ethnic Politics," in *War, Hunger, and Displacement: The Origins of Humanitarian Emergencies*, vol. 2, *Case Studies*, ed. E. Wayne Nafziger, Frances Stewart, and Raimo Väyrynen (New York: Oxford University Press, 2000), 300; Joshia Osamba, "The Dynamics of Ethnopolitical Conflict and Violence in the Rift Valley Province of Kenya," *Nationalism and Ethnic Politics* 7, no. 4 (2001): 87–112.

25. See Joel D. Barkan, "Will the Kenyan Settlement Hold?" *Current History* 107, no. 708 (2008): 147–53.

26. See David Ndii, "Crony Capitalism and State Capture: The Kenyatta Family Story," *The Elephant: African Analysis, Opinion and Investigation*, July 7, 2018, https://www.theelephant.info/opinion/2018/07/07/crony-capitalism-and-state-capture-the-kenyatta-family-story/.

27. See Patrick Mutahi and Mutuma Ruteere "Violence, Security and the Policing of Kenya's 2017 Elections," *Journal of Eastern African Studies* 13, no. 2 (2019): 253–71.

28. Jennifer C. Nash, "Practicing Love: Black Feminism, Love-Politics, and Post-intersectionality," *Meridians* 11, no. 2 (2013): 3.

29. Paul Tiyambe Zeleza, "Diaspora Dialogues: Engagements between Africa and Its Diasporas," in *The New African Diaspora*, ed. Isidore Okpewho and Nkiru Nzegwu (Bloomington: Indiana University Press, 2009), 31–58.

30. Colbert, *Black Movements*.

31. Nafsi Huru, interview by RaShelle Peck, October 15, 2021.

32. Kevlexicon, "Still Strong [Official Video]—Kevlexicon, Nafsi Huru & NJE—Ufuoni/ Audio Kusini," YouTube, April 3, 2012, https://www.youtube.com/watch?v = eXcaXLldKQo.

33. Jean Ngoya Kidula, "The Local and Global in Kenyan Rap and Hip Hop Culture," in *Hip Hop Africa: New African Music in a Globalizing World*, ed. by Eric Charry (Bloomington: Indiana University Press, 2012), 179.

34. Kevlexicon, "Still Strong."

35. Mtemi is Swahili for "spitter." Most Swahili words are pronounced emphasizing the second to the last syllable.

36. Celia Britton, *Introduction to a Poetics of Diversity: by Édouard Glissant* (Liverpool: Liverpool University Press, 2020), 85.

37. Perry, *Prophets of the Hood*, 50.

38. Kevlexicon, "Still Strong." Cess is a British English word meaning tax or taxes.

39. Halifu Osumare, "Keeping It Real: Race, Class, and Youth Connections through Hip-Hop in the US and Brazil," *Humboldt Journal of Social Relations* 37 (2015): 6.

40. For more, see Kevlexicon, "Hip Hop Fighting Economic Inequality," accessed June 10, 2024, https://kevlexicon.com/.

41. Daphne Brooks, *Liner Notes for the Revolution: The Intellectual Life of Black Feminist Sound* (Cambridge, MA: Belknap Press of Harvard University Press, 2021), 30.

42. Nadine George-Graves, "Diasporic Spidering: Constructing Contemporary Black Identities," in *Black Performance Theory*, ed. Thomas F. DeFrantz and Anita Gonzalez (Durham, NC: Duke University Press, 2014), 33.

43. Biko Mutsaurwa, "The Afrikan Hiphop Caravan: Building a Revolutionary Counterculture," *Journal of Hip Hop Studies* 1, no. 2 (2014): 227.

44. To this day, Dzamara's whereabouts are unknown. For more, see Kim Chakanetsa, "Itai Dzamara: The Man Who Stood Up to Zimbabwe's Robert Mugabe and Vanished," BBC News, May 23, 2018, sec. Africa, https://www.bbc.com/news/world-africa-44209183. In 2016, a group of activists were sent to prison, convicted of organizing a rebellion against the Angolan government. The group had held a book club meeting, discussing political reform and nonviolent resistance. See Kayla Ruble, "Angola Sends a Rapper and 16 Activists to Prison for Plotting Rebellion," www.vice.com, March 28, 2016, https://www.vice.com/en /article/wja74m/angola-sends-a-rapper-and-16-activists-to-prison-for-plotting-rebellion.

45. Nomadik Studio, "'Amandla' Ft. Khusta, Mic Crenshaw, Ran-D, Judge and MC Bagol," YouTube, December 14, 2015, https://www.youtube.com/watch?v = usamqjWxtyk.

46. Nomadik Studio, "'Amandla.'"

47. Zeleza, "Dancing to the Beat," 228.

48. See Culture Hub Live, "YouTube," www.youtube.com, May 16, 2015, http://www .youtube.com.

49. Here, Bagol also cites Haile Selassie, who famously stated, "It is important that spiritual advancement must keep pace with material advancement."

50. Jean Muteba Rahier and Percy C. Hintzen, "Introduction: Theorizing the African Diaspora: Metaphor, Misrecognition, and Self-Recognition," in *Global Circuits of Blackness: Interrogating the African Diaspora*, ed. Jean Muteba Rahier, Percy C Hintzen, and Felipe Smith (Urbana: University of Illinois Press, 2010), xi.

51. Nomadik Studio, "'Amandla.'"

52. Evan Mwangi and Wanjiru Mbure, "Passion in a Mathree: Metropolitan Love in Nazizi Hirji's 'Kenyan Girl / Kenyan Boy,'" *Women & Language* 32, no. 2 (2009): 26.

53. Zeleza, "Diaspora Dialogues," 46.

54. George-Graves, "Diasporic Spidering," 37.

55. See John Fenn and Alex Perullo, "Language Ideologies, Choices, and Practices in Eastern African Hip Hop," in *Global Pop, Local Language*, ed. Harris M. Berger and Michael Thomas Carroll (Jackson: University Press of Mississippi, 2003), 19–52; Msia Kibona Clark, "Hip Hop as Social Commentary in Accra and Dar es Salaam," *African Studies Quarterly* 13, no. 3 (2012): 23–46.

56. The figure of the badman is the Black antihero, one who is positioned at the margins of society. Because the badman engages in risky economic activities, he often must use violence to defend himself. The bad nigga, in many ways, pushes the boundaries by eschewing most discourses of morality, even within U.S. Black culture. In U.S. hip hop, the drug dealer is a bad nigga, one who ignores community addiction and indeed profits from it. The bad nigga celebrates pernicious cishet masculinity by boasting about an endless willingness to kill those who threaten him, making the defiant and nihilistic way of living attractive and desirable. See Elaine B. Richardson, *Hiphop Literacies* (London: Routledge, 2007), 13–18.

57. Perry, *Prophets of the Hood*, 102–8.

58. In a discussion of postindependence army mutinies, Wunyabari O. Maloba cites the then-settler newspaper, *East Africa and Rhodesia*: "[The newspaper] speculated that the mutinies were the result of 'thousands of Mau Mau thugs' having been 'set free to engage in whatever nefarious activities they like. . .'"; Maloba, *Anatomy of Neo-colonialism*, 52.

Emily Baughan, in a discussion of rehabilitation campaigns during the Emergency, cites a 1955 article in the *Sunday Post*, where a worker in a children's home describes them as a "the plague of Nairobi, accomplished little thieves and posse of thugs, many of whom were tainted with the Mau Mau doctrine"; Emily Baughan, "Rehabilitating an Empire: Humanitarian Collusion with the Colonial State during the Kenyan Emergency, ca. 1954–1960," *Journal of British Studies* 59, no. 1 (2020): 57–79, at 65.

59. S. M. Shamsul Alam, *Rethinking the Mau Mau in Colonial Kenya* (New York: Springer, 2007), 187.

60. See Kamore Maina, "Four Suspected Thugs Shot Dead in Industrial Area," *The Star*, October 3, 2016, https://www.the-star.co.ke/news/2016–10–03-four-suspected-thugs-shot-dead-in-industrial-area/; Abdi Latif Dahir and Lily Kuo, "Kenyan Police Reportedly Killed Two Teenagers in Broad Daylight—and Much of the Public Approved," *Quartz*, April 4, 2017, https://qz.com/africa/948491/kenyan-police-killed-two-teenagers-in-broad-daylight-in-eastleigh-and-much-of-the-public-approved.

61. Judge, interview by RaShelle Peck, November 16, 2012.

62. Nafsi Huru, interview by RaShelle Peck, November 11, 2011.

63. During colonialism, the Kenyan state, rather than eliminating circumcision for boys, used it to produce a larger labor force. For instance, in precolonial contexts, many Kenyan communities circumcised boys in their late teens. However, because the colonial state wanted to increase the number of laboring men in the population, officials encouraged or coerced leaders into circumcising boys in their early teenage years, around twelve or thirteen, so that they would "be men" and could thus go off to work. The practice of teenage boys being ritualized at a younger age has remained a standard practice. For more, see Ocobock, *An Uncertain Age.*

Furthermore, during the presidencies of Jomo Kenyatta and Daniel Moi, politician Oginga Odinga ran campaigns to challenge both. Later, his son, Raila Odinga, would challenge Kenyatta's son, Uhuru. Both the Kenyattas and Mois are from communities that circumcise: the Gikuyu and Kalenjin, respectively. The Odingas are Luo and traditionally do not perform the practice. During the Odingas' challenges, conversations circulated in the public and media about whether a Luo man could lead a country given the fact that he is "not really a man and thus a child" due to his supposed uncircumcised status. For more, see Grace A. Musila, "Phallocracies and Gynocratic Transgressions Gender, State Power and Kenyan Public Life," *Africa Insight* 39, no. 1 (2009): 39–57.

64. Judge, interview by RaShelle Peck, November 16, 2012.

65. Mungiki emerged in the 1980s during conflicts over land in the Rift Valley. The organization is a secretive and illicit Kikuyu organization of many poor urban youth involved in racketeering and extortion in Nairobi. It holds monopolies over many parts of the *matatu* industry. Members partake in Mau Mau–style oathing and Kikuyu cultural traditions. During the 2007–8 postelection violence, claims were made that Uhuru had paid members to participate in violence. See Susan Kilonzo, "The Trajectories of Survival of the Mungiki Youth in Nairobi," *International Journal of Sociology* 43, no. 1 (2017): 27–42; Peter Mwangi Kagwanja, "Clash of Generations? Youth Identity, Violence and the Politics of Transition in Kenya, 1997–2002," in *Vanguard or Vandals Youth, Politics and Conflict in Africa*, ed. Jon Abbink (Leiden, Neth.: Brill, 2005), 81–109.

66. Msia Kibona Clark, *Hip-Hop in Africa: Prophets of the City and Dustyfoot Philosophers* (Athens: Ohio University Press, 2018), 148–182.

67. Jeffries, *Thug Life*, 100, emphasis in original.

68. #id33ke musiq, "Snarl Evaredi Ft Krunkid- Ukweli Official Video," YouTube, October 15, 2012, https://www.youtube.com/watch?v = EDrAH3BwXco.

69. Citizen. Colloquially, the phrase is "the common man" or "common person." This is a regularly used phrase.

70. Evaredi, interview by RaShelle Peck, November 22, 2012.

71. #id33ke musiq, "Snarl."

72. Miles White, *From Jim Crow to Jay-Z: Race, Rap, and the Performance of Masculinity* (Urbana: University of Illinois Press, 2011), 42.

73. See Msia Kibona Clark, "The Role of New and Social Media in Tanzanian Hip-Hop Production," *Cahiers d'études africaines* no. 216 (2014): 1115–36.

74. Brenda Dixon Gottschild, *Digging the Africanist Presence in American Performance: Dance and Other Contexts* (Westport, CT: Greenwood Press, 1996); Halifu Osumare, *The Africanist Aesthetic in Global Hip-Hop: Power Moves*, 1st ed. (New York: Palgrave Macmillan, 2007).

75. Richardson and Pough, "Hiphop Literacies."

76. Toni Blackman, "Introductory Statement/Background," *Journal of Popular Music Education* 2, no. 1/2 (2018): 173–80.

77. Binyavanga Wainaina, *One Day I Will Write about This Place: A Memoir* (Lagos: Farafina, 2013); Binyavanga Wainaina, *How to Write about Africa: Collected Works* (New York: One World, 2024).

78. After a high-profile conviction was vacated in 1997 for a murder he did not commit, Pratt worked for the remainder of his life with other political prisoners before moving out of the U.S. See Jack Olsen, *Last Man Standing: The Tragedy and Triumph of Geronimo Pratt* (New York: Anchor Books, 2000).

79. See Paul J. Magnarella, *Black Panther in Exile: The Pete O'Neal Story* (Gainesville: University Press of Florida, 2020).

80. S. Craig Watkins, "Black Youth and the Ironies of Capitalism," in *That's the Joint! The Hip-Hop Studies Reader*, ed. Murray Forman and Mark Anthony Neal (New York: Routledge, 2004), 568.

81. The Universal Negro Association's (UNIA) paper, *The Negro World*, was disseminated within Kenya. See Claudius Fergus, "From Prophecy to Policy: Marcus Garvey and the Evolution of Pan-African Citizenship," *Global South* 4, no. 2 (2010): 37.

82. Michael Wanguhu, ed., *Ni Wakati (It's Time!)*, dir. Russell Kenya (Kenya: Emerge Media Films, 2010), DVD.

83. It is also important to note that there are large populations of African Americans and other peoples of African descent who practice spiritualities and religions that are derived from Yoruba traditions.

84. See Melbourne S. Cummings and Abhik Roy, "Manifestations of Afrocentricity in Rap Music," *Howard Journal of Communication* 13, no. 1 (2002): 59–76; S. Craig Watkins, "A Nation of Millions: Hip Hop Culture and the Legacy of Black Nationalism,"*Communication Review* 4, no. 3 (2001): 373–98.

85. Paul Gilroy, *The Black Atlantic: Modernity and Double Consciousness* (Cambridge, MA: Harvard University Press, 1993), 87.

86. Wanguhu, *Ni Wakati*.

87. Wanguhu, *Ni Wakati*.

88. Wanguhu, *Ni Wakati*.

89. Perry, "Global Black Self-Fashionings," 658.

90. Wanguhu, *Ni Wakati*; Malcolm X, "Message to the Grassroots," in *American Identities: An Introductory Textbook*, ed. Lois P. Rudnick, Judith E. Smith, and Rachel Lee Rubin (Malden, MA: Blackwell, 2006), 121–22.

91. Zeleza, "Dancing to the Beat," 229.

92. Kim D. Butler, "Defining Diaspora, Refining a Discourse," *Diaspora: A Journal of Transnational Studies* 10, no. 2 (2001): 194.

4. THE SOUNDS OF IMPERFECT RESISTANCE

1. Caroline Mose, "Jua Cali-Justice: Navigating the 'Mainstream-Underground' Dichotomy in Kenyan Hip-Hop Culture," in *Native Tongues: The African Hip-Hop Reader*, ed. Paul Khalil Saucier (New York: African World Press, 2011), 69–104.

2. Mose, "Jua Cali-Justice," 71.

3. Frank West Mshamba later joined the group after its formation and began to make music both with the group and individually around 2015.

4. Henriques, *Sonic Bodies*, xvi.

5. Henriques, *Sonic Bodies*, 16.

6. To this end, Mbũgua wa Mũngai asserts, "Kenyan musicians are aware of the politics of (mis)representation and they are consciously deconstructing this discourse by placing themselves and other 'ordinary' persons (hawkers, shopkeepers, matatu drivers, and bar tenders amongst others) as central performers in their VCDs"; Mũngai, "'Made in River-wood,'" 62.

7. Mwangi, "The Incomplete Rebellion," 88. See also Mose, "Hip-Hop Halisi"; Koster, "The Hip Hop Revolution."

8. Mwangi, "The Incomplete Rebellion," 93.

9. Flamez Mshamba Mwenza, "Shupavu by Washamba Wenza Ft Judge Black Duo Prod. by Sniper G Ganji," YouTube, November 4, 2022, https://www.youtube.com/watch?v = R5m19-H0Hxk.

10. Smalls, "'Make the Music with Your Mouth.'"

11. Henriques, *Sonic Bodies*, 14.

12. Henriques, *Sonic Bodies*, xv.

13. Flamez Mshamba Mwenza, "Shupavu."

14. Mwangi, "The Incomplete Rebellion," 105.

15. Judge stated that the Sheng from "Shupavu" is from Ngara. For purposes of analysis, I had this song translated. Jaja Yogo, the translator I worked with, stated that the Sheng is specifically from Dandora. In the main text, I opted to defer to Judge's perspective.

16. Eric Kioko discusses how Sheng began in Kaloleni, an Eastlands community near the Central Business District; Kioko, "Regional Varieties."

17. See Hang Ren, Wei Guo, Zhenke Zhang, Leonard Musyoka Kisovi, and Priyanko Das, "Population Density and Spatial Patterns of Informal Settlements in Nairobi, Kenya," *Sustainability* 12, no. 18 (2020): 1–14.

18. Flamez Mshamba Mwenza, "Shupavu."

19. Flamez Mshamba Mwenza, "Shupavu."

20. UN-Habitat, *Kenya 2023 Country Brief: A Better Quality of Life for All in an Urbanizing World*, 2023, https://unhabitat.org/sites/default/files/2023/07/kenya_country_brief _final_en.pdf, 4.

21. See Kamuyu-Wa-Kang'ethe, "African Response to Christianity: A Case Study of the Agikuyu of Central Kenya," *Missiology* 16, no. 1 (1988): 23–44; Hassan Mwakimako, "Christian–Muslim Relations in Kenya: A Catalogue of Events and Meanings," *Islam–Christian Muslim Relations* 18, no. 2 (2007): 287–307; Yonatan N. Gez and Yvan Droz, "'It's All under Christianity': Religious Territories in Kenya," *Journal of Africana Religions* 7, no. 1 (2019): 37–61.

22. See Paul Gifford, "Some Recent Developments in African Christianity," *African Affairs* 93, no. 373 (1994): 513–34; Mary A. Porter, "Talking at the Margins: Kenyan Discourses on Homosexuality," in *Beyond the Lavender Lexicon: Authenticity, Imagination, and Appropriation in Lesbian and Gay Languages*, ed. William Leap (Amsterdam: Gordon and Breach, 1995), 133–53; Gregory Deacon, "'I Will Make You into a Great Nation, and I Will Bless You': Citizens, Traitors and Christianity in Kenya," in *Christian Citizens and the Moral Regeneration of the African State*, ed. Barbara Bompani and Caroline Valois (New York: Routledge, 2017), 149–62.

23. Kidula, "Polishing the Luster," 410–12.

24. Kidula, "Polishing the Luster," 410.

25. Kidula, "Polishing the Luster," 414.

26. Damaris Seleina Parsitau, "'Then Sings My Soul': Gospel Music as Popular Culture in the Spiritual Lives of Kenyan Pentecostal/Charismatic Christians," *Journal of Religion and Popular Culture* 14, no. 1 (2006): 7.

27. Mark Lamont, "Lip-Synch Gospel: Christian Music and the Ethnopoetics of Identity in Kenya," *Africa* 80, no. 3 (2010): 473.

28. Julius Gathogo, "Afro-Pentecostalism and the Kenyan Political Landscape," *Swedish Missiological Themes* 101, no. 2 (2013): 203–30.

29. See Julius Gathogo, "Evangelicals and Public Life in Kenya," in *Christian Responses to Terrorism: The Kenyan Experience*, vol. 10, ed. Gordon L. Heath and David Kirwa Tarus (Eugene, OR: Pickwick, 2017), 72–87.

30. Parsitau, "'Then Sings My Soul.'"

31. Parsitau, "'Then Sings My Soul.'"

32. Jean Kidula, "'There Is Power': Contemporizing Old Music Traditions for New Gospel Audiences in Kenya," *Yearbook for Traditional Music* 42 (2010): 62–80.

33. Kidula, "'There Is Power,'" 62.

34. Sue Timon, interview by RaShelle Peck, November 20, 2012.

35. *Kabisa* means absolutely, completely, or totally, and in this context the phrase translates to: "I wouldn't say that I *only* talk about the Bible."

36. Decence, interview by RaShelle Peck, December 10, 2012.

37. Flamez Mshamba Mwenza, "Ulimi Sue Timon & Flamez (Washamba Wenza) Official Video," YouTube, January 28, 2013, https://www.youtube.com/watch?v = zkwxRj BpoLs.

38. Mwenza, "Ulimi."

39. Wema TV, "Mustard Seed Faith | Testimony | the Conquerors Show," YouTube, June 20, 2021, https://www.youtube.com/watch?v = zayOjuoEnvg.

40. Anonymous, interview by RaShelle Peck, n.d.

41. Nduta Wa, "Juliani Planning a Kalamashaka Concert," *The Standard*, 2017, https://www.standardmedia.co.ke/entertainment/news/article/2001259287/juliani-planning-a-kalamashaka-concert.

42. Anonymous, interview by RaShelle Peck, n.d.

43. Wanguhu, *Ni Wakati*.

44. Wanguhu, *Ni Wakati*.

45. It should be noted that these ideologies of late capitalism aligned with similar ideals in precolonial Kenya. For example, John Lonsdale, in a larger discussion about the deep structures of morality in ethnic communities, discusses a "Kikuyu labor theory" wherein people learned through the family institution that obedience is a way of achieving self-respect and is attached to how hard one works; John Lonsdale, "The Moral Economy of Mau Mau: Wealth, Poverty and Civic Virtue in Kikuyu Political Thought," in *Unhappy Valley: Conflict in Kenya and Africa*, ed. Bruce Berman and John Lonsdale (London: James Currey, 1992), 315–504, at 333–37.

46. Demaine Jabez, interview by RaShelle Peck, December 10, 2011.

47. L-Ness, interview by RaShelle Peck, November 20, 2012.

48. See "Kenyans for Kenya (K4K) Initiative," PrepareCenter, accessed June 12, 2024, https://preparecenter.org/story/kenyans-for-kenya-k4k-initiative/.

49. Charis Enns and Brock Bersaglio, "Enclave Oil Development and the Rearticulation of Citizenship in Turkana, Kenya: Exploring 'Crude Citizenship,'" *Geoforum* 67 (2015): 78–88.

50. Enns and Bersaglio, "Enclave Oil Development," 83.

51. See Alexander Betts, Naohiko Omata, and Olivier Sterck, "Self-Reliance and Social Networks: Explaining Refugees' Reluctance to Relocate from Kakuma to Kalobeyei," *Journal of Refugee Studies* 33, no. 1 (2020): 62–85; Hanno Brankamp, "Camp Abolition: Ending Carceral Humanitarianism in Kenya (and Beyond)," *Antipode* 54, no. 1 (2022): 106–29.

52. See Maloba, *The Anatomy of Neo-colonialism*.

53. See Faith Mabera, "Kenya's Foreign Policy in Context (1963–2015)," *South African Journal of International Affairs* 23, no. 3 (2016): 365–84.

54. Judge, interview by RaShelle Peck, November 16, 2012.

55. Baby T, interview by RaShelle Peck, November 20, 2012.

56. Baby T, interview by RaShelle Peck, November 20, 2012.

57. Mose, "Jua Cali-Justice," 93.

58. Ogopa Deejays, "Jaguar—Matapeli (Official Ogopa Video)," YouTube, August 5, 2012, https://www.youtube.com/watch?v = H1wj8Sy6vc4.

59. There was a well-known maize scandal in 2009. See *Nation*, "Revealed: Sh150 Million Maize Scandal," July 3, 2020, https://nation.africa/kenya/news/1056–513142-u18wmp/index.html#google_vignette.

60. See Mokua Ombati, "Public Artworks: Creative Spaces for Civic and Political Behaviour in Kenya," *Australasian Review of African Studies* 36, no. 1 (2015): 29–50.

61. See Tracey Lomrantz Lester, "A Member of Kenyan Parliament Is Dismissed for Wearing Too Much Bling!," *Glamour*, March 4, 2011, https://www.glamour.com/story/a-member-of-kenyan-parliament.

62. The following articles detail the controversies surrounding Sonko: Basillioh Mutahi, "Kenya's Mike Sonko: The Rise and Fall of Nairobi's Ex-Governor," BBC News, March 28, 2021, http://www.bbc.com/news/world-africa-56269628; Joseph Wangui, "US Bans Entry of Former Nairobi Governor Mike Sonko, Family," *East African*, March 8, 2022, http://www.theeastafrican.co.ke/tea/news/east-africa/us-bans-entry-of-former-nairobi-governor-mike-sonko-family-3741356; *Al Jazeera*, "Nairobi Governor Mike Sonko Denies Corruption Charges in Court," December 9, 2019, http://www.aljazeera.com/news/2019/12/9/nairobi-governor-mike-sonko-denies-corruption-charges-in-court.

63. Ogopa Deejays, "Jaguar."

64. National Assembly of the Republic of Kenya, "Hon. Njagua, Charles Kanyi | the Kenyan Parliament Website," n.d., http://www.parliament.go.ke/node/3411.

65. See *Nairobi Gossip & News*, "Rabbit-King Kaka Launches a New Lucrative Business," accessed May 30, 2024, https://web.archive.org/web/20151001033238/http://www.nairobigossips.com/2015/09/rabbit-king-kaka-launches-new-lucrative.html?m = 1.

66. For more on the scandal, see *The Star*, "Inside Story of the NCPB Maize Scam," May 25, 2018), http://www.the-star.co.ke/news/2018–05–25-inside-story-of-the-ncpb-maize-scam/. For more on the raid on Waiguru's home, see Mercy Asamba, "Governor Anne Waiguru's Homes, Office Raided by EACC Detectives," *The Standard*, 2020, https://www.standardmedia.co.ke/central/article/2001383238/eacc-detectives-raid-governor-anne-waigurus-homes-office. For more on the controversial laptop project, see Tebby Otieno,

"KNUT Boss Reveals Kenya's School Laptop Project Was a Scam," Talk Africa, May 12, 2021, http://www.talkafrica.co.ke/knut-boss-reveals-kenyas-school-laptop-project-was-a-scam/. For more on Miguna Miguna, see Lynete Lusike Mukhongo, "Participatory Media Cultures: Virality, Humour, and Online Political Contestations in Kenya," *Africa Spectrum* 55, no. 2 (2020): 148–69.

67. King Kaka, "Wajinga Nyinyi (Official Video)," YouTube, December 14, 2019, https://www.youtube.com/watch?v = WIuMZmagvUk.

68. See Claire Munde, "Waiguru Drops King Kaka Suit Bid, Calls Him Confused Attention Seeker," *The Star*, December 20, 2019, https://www.the-star.co.ke/news/2019 -12-20-waiguru-drops-king-kaka-suit-bid-calls-him-confused-attention-seeker/.

69. See Vincent Kejitan, "DCI Denies Summoning King Kaka," *The Standard*, 2019, http://standardmedia.co.ke/ureport/article/2001353563/dci-denies-summoning-king-kaka.

70. See Mutonya, "The Beat Goes On"; Emily Akuno, "Controversial Music: A Postcolonial Reading of D. O. Misiani 'Bim En Bim' and Wainaina 'Nchi ya Kitu Kidogo,'" in *Researching Music Censorship*, ed. Helmi Järviluoma, Annemette Kirkegaard, and Jan Sverre Knudsen (Newcastle upon Tyne, UK: Cambridge Scholars, 2017), 160–84.

71. Watch254 TV, "Eric Wainaina Unites with WajingaNyinyi AKA King Kaka in a Powerful Collaboration! #Kenya," YouTube, December 17, 2019, https://www.youtube.com /watch?v=cSs4Y9RIJDo&t=172s.

72. *Nation*, "King Kaka, Juliani, Boniface Mwangi Sing Juliani's—'Utawala' Song," YouTube, December 17, 2019, https://www.youtube.com/watch?v = kqkUnVtnnh8.

73. Boombavideo, "Juliani—Utawala (Official Video)," YouTube, May 15, 2013, https://www.youtube.com/watch?v = 9HNl8YAnpoQ.

74. See Ntarangwi, *The Street Is My Pulpit*.

75. See Juliani Owino, "Music as a Weapon to Fight Inequality | Oxfam in Kenya," kenya.oxfam.org, January 16, 2017, http://kenya.oxfam.org/blog/music-weapon-fight-inequality.

76. Glissant, *Poetics of Relation*, 111.

77. See Kipkogei Kirwa, Caroline Kinuu Kimathi, and Ouno Victor Onyango, "Redressive Action in Political Discourse in the Face of Conflicting Views: A Case of the Building Bridges Initiative in Kenya," *International Journal of English Literature and Social Sciences* 7, no. 5 (2022): 1–11.

78. See Nick Mwangi, "Juliani Takes Issue with Jubilee Using His Song to Promote BBI," *Nairobi Wire*, November 3, 2020, http://nairobiwire.com/2020/11/juliani-takes-issue-with -jubilee-for-using-his-song-to-promote-bbi.html.

79. Imani Sanga, "The Practice and Politics of Hybrid Soundscapes in Muziki wa Injili in Dar es Salaam, Tanzania," *Journal of African Cultural Studies* 22, no. 2 (2010): 145–56.

80. Sanga, "The Practice and Politics," 146.

81. See Jesse Weaver Shipley, "Transnational Circulation and Digital Fatigue in Ghana's Azonto Dance Craze," *American Ethnologist* 40, no. 2 (2013): 362–81; Orlando Woods, "Clashing Cyphers, Contagious Content: The Digital Geopolitics of Grime," *Transactions of the Institute of British Geographers* 46, no. 2 (2021): 464–77.

82. Sheila Kimani, "#MCM: Simon Kimani Aka Bamboo—of Avoiding 'Compe' and Fighting Illuminati," *The Standard*, accessed June 28, 2024, https://www.standardmedia .co.ke/entertainment/celeb-profiles/article/2000176306/mcm-simon-kimani-aka-bamboo -of-avoiding-compe-and-fighting-illuminati.

83. See Ken, "Rapper Bamboo Endorses Uhuru for President," *Nairobi Wire*, January 15, 2013, http://nairobiwire.com/2013/01/rapper-bamboo-endorses-uhuru-for.html.

84. John Wanjohi, "Kenyan Singer Bamboo Claims He Was Bewitched after Returning to Kenya from the US," Mwakilishi.com, March 31, 2021, https://www.mwakilishi.com/article/diaspora-news/2021–03–31/kenyan-singer-bamboo-claims-he-was-bewitched-after-returning-from-the-us#google_vignette.

85. Phoenix Recordz, "2-5-Flow—Bamboo Ft Sugar—(Official Music Video)," YouTube, January 24, 2013, https://www.youtube.com/watch?v = KtSnXziBTMw.

86. Bradley, "Contextualizing Hip Hop Sonic Cool Pose," 59.

87. Mecca Jamilah Sullivan, "Fat Mutha: Hip Hop's Queer Corpulent Poetics," *Palimpsest* 2, no. 2 (2013): 200–213; Bettina L. Love, "'I See Trayvon Martin': What Teachers Can Learn from the Tragic Death of a Young Black Male," *Urban Review* 46, no. 2 (2014): 292–306.

88. Mose, "'Swag' and 'Cred,'" 112.

89. Ntarangwi, *The Street Is My Pulpit*, 99.

90. Anonymous, interview by RaShelle Peck, n.d. In a discussion about Kenyans rapping in U.S. Black accents, Mwenda Ntarangwi similarly discusses how Kenyans do not adopt Indian accents when in India; Ntarangwi, *East African Hip Hop*, 54.

91. Shirley Alusa-Brown, "Interview with Bamboo," n.d., www.jamati.com.

92. Bradley, "Contextualizing Hip Hop Sonic Cool Pose," 61.

93. Anonymous, interview by RaShelle Peck, n.d.

94. Anonymous, interview by RaShelle Peck, n.d.

CONCLUSION: HIP HOP FLOW AS KENYAN, AS BLACK

1. José Esteban Muñoz, *Disidentifications: Queers of Color and the Performance of Politics* (Minneapolis: University of Minnesota Press, 1999), 11.

2. Muñoz, *Disidentifications*, 5.

3. Judge, interview by RaShelle Peck, October 20, 2021; L-Ness, interview by RaShelle Peck, September 24, 2021.

4. Nafsi Huru, interview by RaShelle Peck, October 15, 2021.

5. Nafsi Huru, interview by RaShelle Peck, October 15, 2021.

6. Baby T, interview by RaShelle Peck, October 15, 2021.

7. Judge, interview by RaShelle Peck, October 20, 2021.

8. Nafsi Huru, interview by RaShelle Peck, October 15, 2021.

9. L-Ness, interview by RaShelle Peck, September 24, 2021.

10. Aimee Meredith Cox, *Shapeshifters: Black Girls and the Choreography of Citizenship* (Durham, NC: Duke University Press, 2015), 29.

11. Saucier and Woods, "Hip Hop Studies in Black."

12. Saucier and Woods, "Hip Hop Studies in Black," 278.

13. Dwight Conquergood, "Rethinking Ethnography: Towards a Critical Cultural Politics," *Communications Monographs* 58, no. 2 (1991): 180, 188.

14. Bruce J. Berman, "Ethnicity, Patronage and the African State: The Politics of Uncivil Nationalism," *African Affairs* 97, no. 388 (1998): 305–41.

15. See Jessica Auchter, "Forced Male Circumcision: Gender-Based Violence in Kenya," *International Affairs* 93, no. 6 (2017): 1339–56.

16. Grace Musila, "Violent Masculinities and the Phallocratic Aesthetics of Power in Kenya," in *The New Violent Cartography: Geo-analysis after the Aesthetic Turn*, ed. Samson Opondo and Michael Shapiro, 1st ed. (New York: Routledge, 2012), 151–70.

17. Tanya Saunders, "Towards a Transnational Hip-Hop Feminist Liberatory Praxis: A View from the Americas," *Social Identities* 22, no. 2 (2016): 188.

18. Here I work from the scholarship Christen A. Smith has done with the Cite Black Women campaign, which addresses the erasure Black women experience in academia. For more, see Christen A. Smith, Erica L. Williams, Imani A. Wadud, Whitney NL Pirtle, and Cite Black Women Collective, "Cite Black Women: A Critical Praxis (A Statement)," *Feminist Anthropology* 2, no. 1 (2021): 10–17.

19. Jeff Chang, *Total Chaos: The Art and Aesthetics of Hip-Hop* (New York: Basic Civitas Books, 2006), xiii.

Agano, November 11, 2011.
Amora, November 20, 2012.
Baby T, November 20, 2012, October 15, 2021.
Decence, December 10, 2012.
DJ Mos, December 8, 2011.
Esen, July 15, 2010.
Evaredi, November 22, 2012.
Funzo Kuu, November 11, 2011.
Jabez, Demaine, December 10, 2011.
Jagero, Mick, November 18, 2012.
Judge, November 16, 2012, October 20, 2021.
L-Ness, November 20, 2012, September 24, 2021.
Mtawali, September 13, 2012.
Nafsi Huru, November 11, 2011, October 15, 2021.
Ndugus, November 11, 2011.
Snooker, December 10, 2011.
Timon, Sue, November 20, 2012.
Washika, Adrian, September 15, 2012.

#id33ke musiq. "Snarl Evaredi Ft Krunkid—Ukweli Official Video." YouTube, October 15, 2012. https://www.youtube.com/watch?v=EDrAH3BwXco.

Achitsa, Beth. "Kenyan Artists Protest Foreign Music Dominance." *Music in Africa*, August 11, 2015. https://www.musicinafrica.net/magazine/kenyan-artists-protest-foreign-music-dominance.

Adar, Korwa G., and Isaac M. Munyae. "Human Rights Abuse in Kenya under Daniel arap Moi, 1978." *African Studies Quarterly* 5, no. 1 (2001): 1–14.

"African Author Ngugi and Wife Njeeri wa Thiong'o Brutally Attacked on Tour in Nairobi, Kenya." *Black Scholar* 34, no. 3 (2004): 78.

Agamben, Giorgio. *Homo Sacer: Sovereign Power and Bare Life*. Stanford, CA: Stanford University Press, 1998.

Agawu, Kofi. "Contesting Difference: A Critique of Ethnomusicology." In *The Cultural Study of Music: A Critical Introduction*, edited by Martin Clayton, Trevor Herbert, and Richard Middleton, 227–37. New York: Routledge, 2003.

Agesa, Ruth M. "Dynamics of Music and Political Mobilization in Post-colonial Kenya." *Journal of African Interdisciplinary Studies* 3, no. 10 (2019): 41–54.

Akuno, Emily. "Controversial Music: A Postcolonial Reading of D. O. Misiani 'Bim En Bim' and Wainaina 'Nchi ya Kitu Kidogo.'" In *Researching Music Censorship*, edited by Helmi Järviluoma, Annemette Kirkegaard, and Jan Sverre Knudsen, 160–84. Newcastle upon Tyne, UK: Cambridge Scholars, 2017.

Alam, S. M. Shamsul. *Rethinking the Mau Mau in Colonial Kenya*. New York: Springer, 2007.

Alim, H. Samy. "Global Ill-Literacies: Hip Hop Cultures, Youth Identities, and the Politics of Literacy." *Review of Research in Education* 35, no. 1 (2011): 120–46.

———. "Intro: Straight Outta Compton, Straight aus München: Global Linguistic Flows, Identities, and the Politics of Language in a Global Hip Hop Nation." In *Global Linguistic Flows: Hip Hop Cultures, Youth Identities, and the Politics of Language*, edited by H. Samy Alim, Awad Ibrahim, and Alastair Pennycook. New York: Routledge, 2009.

———. *Roc the Mic Right: The Language of Hip Hop Culture*. New York: Routledge, 2006.

Alim, H. Samy, Awad Ibrahim, and Alastair Pennycook, eds. *Global Linguistic Flows: Hip Hop Cultures, Youth Identities, and the Politics of Language*. New York: Routledge, 2009.

Al Jazeera. "Kenya Lifts Longstanding COVID Curfew as Infections Ease." October 20, 2021. https://www.aljazeera.com/news/2021/10/20/kenya-lifts-longstanding-covid-curfew-as-infections-ease.

———. "Nairobi Governor Mike Sonko Denies Corruption Charges in Court." December 9, 2019. http://www.aljazeera.com/news/2019/12/9/nairobi-governor-mike-sonko-denies-corruption-charges-in-court.

Althusser, Louis. *On the Reproduction of Capitalism: Ideology and Ideological State Apparatuses*. Reprint. London: Verso, 2014 [1970].

Alusa-Brown, Shirley. "Interview with Bamboo." N.d. www.jamati.com.

Amutabi, Maurice N. *The NGO Factor in Africa: The Case of Arrested Development in Kenya*. London: Routledge, 2013.

Anderson, David M. "Briefing: Kenya's Elections 2002: The Dawning of a New Era?" *African Affairs* 102, no. 407 (2003): 331–42.

Androutsopoulos, Jannis, and Arno Scholz. "Spaghetti Funk: Appropriations of Hip-Hop Culture and Rap Music in Europe." *Popular Music and Society* 26, no. 4 (2003): 463–79.

Anya, Sylvester Ndubuisi, Adrian Osuagwu, Emmanuel Onyeabor, Joycelin Chinwe Okubuiro, Matthew Nwankwo, Daniel Onyeonagu, and Ifeoma Pamela Enemo. "Credible Commitment or Sham Devotion to the International Criminal Court: Whither Nigeria, Kenya and Uganda?" *African Journal of Legal Studies* 15, no. 2 (April 13, 2023): 242–69.

Appert, Catherine M. "On Hybridity in African Popular Music: The Case of Senegalese Hip Hop." *Ethnomusicology* 60, no. 2 (2016): 279–99.

Asamba, Mercy. "Governor Anne Waiguru's Homes, Office Raided by EACC Detectives." *The Standard*, 2020. https://www.standardmedia.co.ke/central/article/2001383238/eacc-detectives-raid-governor-anne-waigurus-homes-office.

Atieno-Odhiambo, Elisha S. "The Formative Years: 1945–55." In *Decolonization and Independence in Kenya, 1940–93*, edited by Bethwell A. Ogot and William R. Ochieng', 25–47. London: James Currey, 1995.

———. "The Invention of Kenya." In *Decolonization and Independence in Kenya, 1940–93*, edited by Bethwell A. Ogot and William R. Ochieng', 1–4. London: James Currey, 1995.

———. "Kula Raha: Gendered Discourses and the Contours of Leisure in Nairobi, 1946–63." *AZANIA: Journal of the British Institute in Eastern Africa* 36, no. 1 (2001): 254–64.

Atieno-Odhiambo, Elisha S., and John Lonsdale, eds. *Mau Mau and Nationhood: Arms, Authority and Narration*. Columbus: Ohio State University Press, 2003.

Auchter, Jessica. "Forced Male Circumcision: Gender-Based Violence in Kenya." *International Affairs* 93, no. 6 (2017): 1339–56.

Auslander, Philip. *Liveness: Performance in a Mediatized Culture*. Oxford: Routledge, 2002.

Bâ, Sylvia Washington. *The Concept of Negritude in the Poetry of Leopold Sedar Senghor*. Princeton, NJ: Princeton University Press, 2015. Web.

Banks, Daniel. "Hip Hop as Pedagogy: Something from Something." *Theatre Topics* 25, no. 3 (2015): 243–59. Web.

Barkan, Joel D. "Will the Kenyan Settlement Hold?" *Current History* 107, no. 708 (2008): 147–53.

Barrett, Lindon. *Blackness and Value: Seeing Double*. Cambridge: Cambridge University Press, 1999.

Barz, Gregory F. "Meaning in Benga Music of Western Kenya." *British Journal of Ethnomusicology* 10, no. 1 (2001): 107–15. Web.

Basu, Dipannita, and Sidney J. Lemelle. *The Vinyl Ain't Final: Hip-Hop and the Globalisation of Black Popular Culture*. Ann Arbor, MI: Pluto Press, 2006.

Baughan, Emily. "Rehabilitating an Empire: Humanitarian Collusion with the Colonial State during the Kenyan Emergency, ca. 1954–1960." *Journal of British Studies* 59, no. 1 (2020): 57–79.

BBC News. 2018. "Head of Kenya Youth Agency Arrested in $78m Corruption Scandal." May 28, 2018, sec. Africa. https://www.bbc.com/news/world-africa-44280453.

Bender, Wolfgang. "Modern African Music: An Autonomous Music." In *Sounds of Change: Social and Political Features of Music in Africa*, edited by Stig-Magnus Thorsén, 87–106. Stockholm: Sida, 2004.

———. *Sweet Mother: Modern African Music*. Chicago: University of Chicago Press, 1991. Web.

Berman, Bruce J. "Ethnicity, Patronage and the African State: The Politics of Uncivil Nationalism." *African Affairs* 97, no. 388 (1998): 305–41.

Berman, Bruce J., Jill Cottrell, and Yash Ghai. "Patrons, Clients, and Constitutions: Ethnic Politics and Political Reform in Kenya." *Canadian Journal of African Studies* 43, no. 3 (2009): 462–506.

Berman Bruce J., and John M. Lonsdale. "Crises of Accumulation, Coercion and the Colonial State: The Development of the Labor Control System in Kenya, 1919–1929." *Canadian Journal of African Studies* 14, no. 1 (1980): 55–81.

———. *Unhappy Valley: Conflict in Kenya and Africa*. London: James Currey, 1992. Web.

Betts, Alexander, Naohiko Omata, and Olivier Sterck. "Self-Reliance and Social Networks: Explaining Refugees' Reluctance to Relocate from Kakuma to Kalobeyei." *Journal of Refugee Studies* 33, no. 1 (2020): 62–85.

Blackman, Toni. "Introductory Statement/Background." *Journal of Popular Music Education* 2, no. 1/2 (2018): 173–80.

Boombavideo. "Juliani—Utawala (Official Video)." YouTube, May 15, 2013. https://www.youtube.com/watch?v=9HNl8YAnpoQ.

Bradley, Regina. "Becoming Outkasted: Archiving Contemporary Black Southernness in a Digital Age." In *Digital Sound Studies*, edited by Mary Caton Lingold, Darren Mueller, and Whitney Anne Trettien, 120–29. Durham, NC: Duke University Press, 2018.

———. "Contextualizing Hip Hop Sonic Cool Pose in Late Twentieth- and Twenty-First-Century Rap Music." *Current Musicology* 93 (2012): 55–70.

Brankamp, Hanno. "Camp Abolition: Ending Carceral Humanitarianism in Kenya (and Beyond)." *Antipode* 54, no. 1 (2022): 106–29.

Britton, Celia. *Introduction to a Poetics of Diversity: by Édouard Glissant*. Liverpool: Liverpool University Press, 2020.

Brooks, Daphne A. "Afro-sonic Feminist Praxis: Nina Simone and Adrienne Kennedy in High Fidelity." In *Black Performance Theory*, edited by Thomas F. DeFrantz and Anita Gonzalez, 204–22. Durham. NC: Duke University Press, 2014.

———. *Liner Notes for the Revolution: The Intellectual Life of Black Feminist Sound*. Cambridge, MA: Belknap Press of Harvard University Press, 2021.

Brown, Jayna. "Buzz and Rumble." *Social Text* 28, no. 1 (2010): 125–46. Web.

Brown, Stephen. "Authoritarian Leaders and Multiparty Elections in Africa: How Foreign Donors Help to Keep Kenya's Daniel arap Moi in Power." *Third World Quarterly* 22, no. 5 (2001): 725–39.

Brownhill, Leigh S., and Terisa Turner. "Subsistence Trade and World Trade: Gendered Class Struggle in Kenya, 1999–2002." *Canadian Woman Studies / Les cahiers de la femme* 4 and 1, vol. 21 and 22 (2002): 169–77.

Butler, Kim D. "Defining Diaspora, Refining a Discourse." *Diaspora: A Journal of Transnational Studies* 10, no. 2 (2001): 189–219.

Carrier, Neil, and Celia Nyamweru. "Reinventing Africa's National Heroes: The Case of Mekatilili, a Kenyan Popular Heroine." *African Affairs* 115, no. 461 (2016): 599–620.

Chakanetsa, Kim. 2018. "Itai Dzamara: The Man Who Stood Up to Zimbabwe's Robert Mugabe and Vanished." BBC News, May 23, 2018, sec. Africa. https://www.bbc.com/news/world-africa-44209183.

Chang, Jeff. *Total Chaos: The Art and Aesthetics of Hip-Hop.* New York: Basiccivitas Books, 2006.

Charry, Eric S., ed. *Hip Hop Africa: New African Music in a Globalizing World.* Bloomington: Indiana University Press, 2012.

Chude-Sokei, Louis. *The Sound of Culture: Diaspora and Black Technopoetics.* Middleton, CT: Wesleyan University Press, 2015.

Clark, Msia Kibona. "Feminisms in African Hip Hop." *Meridians: Feminism, Race, Transnationalism* 17, no. 2 (2018): 383–400. Web.

———. "Hip Hop as Social Commentary in Accra and Dar es Salaam." *African Studies Quarterly* 13, no. 3 (2012): 23–46.

———. *Hip-Hop in Africa: Prophets of the City and Dustyfoot Philosophers.* Athens: Ohio University Press, 2018.

———. "The Role of New and Social Media in Tanzanian Hip-Hop Production." *Cahiers d'études africaines* 216 (2014): 1115–36.

Clark, Msia Kibona, and Mickie Mwanzia Koster. *Hip Hop and Social Change in Africa: Ni Wakati.* Lanham, MD: Lexington Books, 2014. Web.

Clark, Msia Kibona, Quentin Williams, and Akosua Adomako Ampofo. *Hip-Hop in Africa: Prophets of the City and Dustyfoot Philosophers.* Athens: Ohio University Press, 2018. Web.

Cobb, William Jelani. *To the Break of Dawn: A Freestyle on the Hip Hop Aesthetic.* New York: New York University Press, 2007.

Colbert, Soyica Diggs. *Black Movements: Performance and Cultural Politics.* New Brunswick, NJ: Rutgers University Press, 2017. Web.

Collins, Patricia Hill. *From Black Power to Hip Hop: Racism, Nationalism, and Feminism.* Philadelphia: Temple University Press, 2006.

Conquergood, Dwight. "Rethinking Ethnography: Towards a Critical Cultural Politics." *Communications Monographs* 58, no. 2 (1991): 179–94.

Cooper, Brittney C., Susana M. Morris, and Robin M. Boylorn. *The Crunk Feminist Collection.* New York: Feminist Press at CUNY, 2017.

Cox, Aimee Meredith. *Shapeshifters: Black Girls and the Choreography of Citizenship.* Durham, NC: Duke University Press, 2015.

Culture Hub Live. "YouTube." www.youtube.com, May 16, 2015. http://www.youtube.com.

Cummings, Melbourne S., and Abhik Roy. "Manifestations of Afrocentricity in Rap Music." *Howard Journal of Communication* 13, no. 1 (2002): 59–76.

Dahir, Abdi Latif, and Lily Kuo. 2017. "Kenyan Police Reportedly Killed Two Teenagers in Broad Daylight—and Much of the Public Approved." *Quartz*, April 4, 2017. https://qz.com/africa/948491/kenyan-police-killed-two-teenagers-in-broad-daylight-in-eastleigh-and-much-of-the-public-approved.

Daily Nation. "World Bank Cancels Funding for Kazi Kwa Vijana over Graft." July 3, 2020. https://nation.africa/kenya/news/world-bank-cancels-funding-for-kazi-kwa-vijana-over-graft—787724.

DandoraMusic. "Looking Up Rmx X 254 Female Rappers (Official Music Video)." YouTube, November 6, 2014. https://www.youtube.com/watch?v=w6PoSkSuDqU&t=2s.

Deacon, Gregory. "'I Will Make You into a Great Nation, and I Will Bless You': Citizens, Traitors and Christianity in Kenya." In *Christian Citizens and the Moral Regeneration of the African State*, edited by Barbara Bompani and Caroline Valois, 149–62. New York: Routledge, 2017.

DeFrantz, Thomas. "The Black Beat Made Visible: Hip Hop Dance and Body Power." In *Of the Presence of the Body: Essays on Dance and Performance Theory*, edited by André Lepecki, 64–81. Middletown, CT: Wesleyan University Press, 2004.

Dingley, Zebulon. "The Transfiguration of Lukas Pkech: Dini ya Msambwa and the 'Kolloa Affray.'" *Journal of Religion and Violence* 8, no. 1 (2020): 5–34.

Durham, Aisha. "Behind Beats and Rhymes: Working Class from a Hampton Roads Hip Hop Homeplace." *Policy Futures in Education* 7, no. 2 (2009): 217–29.

———. "Using [Living Hip Hop] Feminism: Redefining an Answer (to) Rap." In *Home Girls, Make Some Noise!: Hip Hop Feminism Anthology*, edited by Gwendolyn D. Pough, Elaine Richardson, Aisha Durham, and Rachel Raimist, 304–12. Mira Loma, CA: Parker, 2007.

Eagleson, Ian. "Between Uptown and River Road: The Making and Undoing of Kenya's 1960s' 'Zilizopendwa.'" *World of Music* 3, no. 1 (2014): 25–45. http://www.jstor.org/stable/24318231.

Eisenberg, Andrew J. "Hip-Hop and Cultural Citizenship on Kenya's 'Swahili Coast.'" *Africa* 82, no. 4 (2012): 556–78.

———. "M-Commerce and the (Re)making of the Music Industry in Kenya: Preliminary Notes and Findings." Report presented to the Association for Social Anthropology, April 5, 2012.

Enns, Charis, and Brock Bersaglio. "Enclave Oil Development and the Rearticulation of Citizenship in Turkana, Kenya: Exploring 'Crude Citizenship.'" *Geoforum* 67 (2015): 78–88.

Eure, Joseph D., and James G. Spady. *Nation Conscious Rap.* New York: PC International Press, 1991.

Fenn, John, and Alex Perullo. "Language Ideologies, Choices, and Practices in Eastern African Hip Hop." In *Global Pop, Local Language*, edited by Harris M. Berger and Michael Thomas Carroll, 19–52. Jackson: University Press of Mississippi, 2003.

Fergus, Claudius. "From Prophecy to Policy: Marcus Garvey and the Evolution of Pan-African Citizenship." *Global South* 4, no. 2 (2010): 29–48.

Ferrari, Aurélia. "Hip-Hop in Nairobi: Recognition of an International Movement and the Main Means of Expression for the Urban Youth in Poor Residential Areas." In *Songs and Politics in Eastern Africa*, edited by Kimani Njogu and Hervé Maupeu, 107–28. Dar es Salaam: Mkuti na Nyota, 2007.

Flamez Mshamba Mwenza. "Shupavu by Washamba Wenza Ft Judge Black Duo Prod. by Sniper G Ganji." YouTube, November 4, 2022. https://www.youtube.com/watch?v=R5m19-HoHxk.

———. "Ulimi Sue Timon & Flamez (Washamba Wenza) Video Trailer." YouTube, January 11, 2013. https://www.youtube.com/watch?v=ShuCJ2992y0.

———. "Ulimi Sue Timon & Flamez (Washamba Wenza) Official Video." YouTube, January 28, 2013. https://www.youtube.com/watch?v=zkwxRjBpoLs.

Frederiksen, Bodil Folke. "Popular Culture, Gender Relations and the Democratization of Everyday Life in Kenya." *Journal of Southern African Studies* 26, no. 2 (2000): 209–22.

Gathogo, Julius. "Afro-Pentecostalism and the Kenyan Political Landscape." *Swedish Missiological Themes* 101, no. 2 (2013): 203–230.

———. "Evangelicals and Public Life in Kenya." In *Christian Responses to Terrorism: The Kenyan Experience, Vol. 10*, edited by Gordon L. Heath and David Kirwa Tarus, 72–87. Eugene, OR: Pickwick, 2017.

Gaunt, Kyra D. *The Games Black Girls Play Learning the Ropes from Double-Dutch to Hip-Hop*. New York: New York University Press, 2006. Web.

Gecaga, Margaret Gathoni. "Religious Movements and Democratisation in Kenya: Between the Sacred and the Profane." In *Kenya: The Struggle for Democracy*, edited by Godwin R. Murunga and Shadrack W. Nasong'o, 58–89. London: Zed Books, 2007.

Gecau, Kimani. "Popular Song and Social Change in Kenya." *Media, Culture & Society* 17, no. 4 (1995): 557–75.

George-Graves, Nadine. "Diasporic Spidering: Constructing Contemporary Black Identities." In *Black Performance Theory*, edited by Thomas F. DeFrantz and Anita Gonzalez, 33–44. Durham, NC: Duke University Press, 2014.

Gez, Yonatan N., and Yvan Droz. "'It's All under Christianity': Religious Territories in Kenya." *Journal of Africana Religions* 7, no. 1 (2019): 37–61.

Gifford, Paul. "Some Recent Developments in African Christianity." *African Affairs* 93, no. 373 (1994): 513–34.

Gilroy, Paul. *The Black Atlantic: Modernity and Double Consciousness*. Cambridge, MA: Harvard University Press, 1993.

Githinji, Peter. "Ambivalent Attitudes: Perception of Sheng and Its Speakers." *Nordic Journal of African Studies* 17, no. 2 (2008): 113–36.

Githiora, Chege. "Sheng: Peer Language, Swahili Dialect or Emerging Creole?" *Journal of African Cultural Studies* 15, no. 2 (2002): 159–81.

———. "Sheng: The Expanding Domains of an Urban Youth Vernacular." *Journal of African Cultural Studies* 30, no. 2 (2018): 105–20.

Glissant, Édouard. *Poetic Intention*. Callicoon, NY: Nightboat Books, 2018.

———. *Poetics of Relation*. Ann Arbor: University of Michigan Press, 1997.

GoDown Arts Centre—Home of Performing & Visual Arts. "Home." Accessed June 4, 2024. https://thegodown.org/.

Gottschild, Brenda Dixon. *Digging the Africanist Presence in American Performance: Dance and Other Contexts*. Westport, CT: Greenwood Press, 1996.

Government of Kenya. *National Policy on Culture and Heritage.* Nairobi: Government Printers, 2009.

Gowon-Adelabu, Nenpomingyi Sarah, Susan Mwangi Owino, and Washington Ndiiri. "The Dynamics of Political Corruption and Neo-patrimonialism in Kenya." *Dynamics* 8, no. 14 (2018): 160–69.

Graham, Ronnie. *The World of African Music.* London: Pluto Press, 1992. Web.

Hall, Stuart. "The Problem of Ideology-Marxism without Guarantees." *Journal of Communication Inquiry* 10, no. 2 (1986): 28–44.

Halliday, Craig. "Animating Political Protests through Artivism in 21st Century Nairobi, Kenya." *Law, Social Justice & Global Development* 24, no. 24 (2019): 100–114.

Harrison, Anthony Kwame. *Hip Hop Underground: The Integrity and Ethics of Racial Identification.* Philadelphia: Temple University Press, 2009. Web.

Hassan, Mai. "A State of Change: District Creation in Kenya after the Beginning of Multiparty Elections." *Political Research Quarterly* 69, no. 3 (2016): 510–21.

Hazzard-Donald, Katrina. "Dance in Hip-Hop Culture." In *That's the Joint! The Hip-Hop Studies Reader*, edited by Murray Forman and Mark Anthony Neal, 505–16. New York: Routledge, 2012.

———. "What Hip Hop Dance Says." In *Droppin' Science: Critical Essays on Rap Music and Hip Hop Culture*, edited by William Eric Perkins, 220–35. Philadelphia: Temple University Press, 1996.

Head, Emma. 2009. "The Ethics and Implications of Paying Participants in Qualitative Research." *International Journal of Social Research Methodology* 12, no. 4: 335–44.

Henriques, Julian. *Sonic Bodies: Reggae Sound Systems, Performance Techniques, and Ways of Knowing.* New York: Continuum, 2011.

Honan, Edith. 2014. "Outrage in Kenya: Attacks on Women in Mini-Skirts Spark Street Protest." *The Star*, November 19. https://www.thestar.com.my/lifestyle/people/2014/11/19/outrage-in-kenya-attacks-on-women-in-miniskirts-spark-street-protest.

Ibrahim, Awad. "Remixing Culture, Language, and the Politics of Boundaries in Education: Toward Critical Hip-Hop Ill-Literacies." In *Handbook of Cultural Studies and Education*, edited by Peter Pericles Trifonas and Susan Jagger, 224–35. New York: Routledge, 2018.

Jabbaar-Gyambrah, Tara. "Gender Politics of Hip-Hop and Hip-Life Music in New York and Ghana." *Afro-Americans in New York Life and History* 39, no. 1 (2015): 7–31.

Jeffries, Michael P. *Thug Life: Race, Gender, and the Meaning of Hip-Hop.* Chicago: University of Chicago Press, 2011. Web.

Johnson, Imani Kai. "From Blues Women to B-Girls: Performing Badass Femininity." *Women & Performance: A Journal of Feminist Theory* 24, no. 1 (2014): 15–28. Web.

Joseph, Figaro. "Domestic Actors and Liberalization: A Case Study of Internal and External Pressures in Moi's Kenya." *Contemporary Politics* 19, no. 3 (2013): 321–38.

Joseph, Richard A. "Class, State, and Prebendal Politics in Nigeria." *Journal of Commonwealth & Comparative Politics* 21, no. 3 (1983): 21–38.

Journo, Aurelie Marion. "Hip-Hop Literature: A Case Study from the New Kenyan Literary Scene." *Postcolonial Text* 5, no. 3 (2009): 1–22.

Judy, R.A.T. "On the Question of Nigga Authenticity." In *That's the Joint!: The Hip-Hop Studies Reader*, edited by Murray Forman and Mark A. Neal. New York: Routledge, 2012.

Kagwanja, Peter Mwangi. "Clash of Generations? Youth Identity, Violence and the Politics of Transition in Kenya, 1997–2002." In *Vanguard or Vandals Youth, Politics and Conflict in Africa*, edited by Jon Abbink, 81–109. Leiden, Neth.: Brill, 2005.

Kagwanja, Peter. "Courting Genocide: Populism, Ethno-nationalism and the Informalisation of Violence in Kenya's 2008 Post-election Crisis." *Journal of Contemporary African Studies* 27, no. 3 (2009): 365–87.

Kaka, King. "King Kaka- Wajinga Nyinyi (Official Video)." YouTube, December 14, 2019. https://www.youtube.com/watch?v=WIuMZmagvUk.

Kamau, Macharia. "Copyright Body Destroys Pirated CDs Estimated at Sh10m." *The Standard*, 2012. https://www.standardmedia.co.ke/article/2000052183/copyright-body -destroys-pirated-cds-estimated-at-sh10m.

Kamuyu-Wa-Kang'ethe. "African Response to Christianity: A Case Study of the Agikuyu of Central Kenya." *Missiology* 16, no. 1 (1988): 23–44.

Karanja, Lucy. "'Homeless' at Home: Linguistic, Cultural, and Identity Hybridity and Third Space Positioning of Kenyan Urban Youth." *Comparative and International Education* 39, no. 2 (2010): 1–19.

Kasarani Youth Congress. "Mobilization without Emancipation: The Case of Kazi Kwa Vijana in Kasarani Constituency." Nairobi, 2009.

Kejitan, Vincent. "DCI Denies Summoning King Kaka." *The Standard*, 2019. www.standard media.co.ke/ureport/article/2001353563/dci-denies-summoning-king-kaka.

Kelley, Robin D. G. *Race Rebels: Culture, Politics, and the Black Working Class.* New York: Free Press, 1994.

Ken. "Rapper Bamboo Endorses Uhuru for President," *Nairobi Wire*, January 15, 2013. http:// nairobiwire.com/2013/01/rapper-bamboo-endorses-uhuru-for.html.

Kevlexicon. "Hip Hop Fighting Economic Inequality." https://kevlexicon.com/.

———. "Still Strong—Musa Aka Nafsi Huru and Kevlexicon." YouTube, January 22, 2012. https://www.youtube.com/watch?v=aMQSVPP8g4c.

———. "Still Strong [Official Video]—Kevlexicon, Nafsi Huru & NJE—Ufuoni/Audio Kusini." YouTube, April 3, 2012. https://www.youtube.com/watch?v=eXcaXLldKQo.

Keyes, Cheryl L. "At the Crossroads: Rap Music and Its African Nexus." *Ethnomusicology* 40, no. 2 (1996): 223–48.

———. "Empowering Self, Making Choices, Creating Spaces: Black Female Identity via Rap Music Performance." *Journal of American Folklore* 113, no. 449 (2000): 255–69.

———. *Rap Music and Street Consciousness.* Urbana: University of Illinois Press, 2002. Web.

———. "Verbal Art Performance in Rap Music: The Conversation of the 80s." *Folklore Forum* 17, no. 2 (1984): 143–52.

Kidula, Jean. "The Local and Global in Kenyan Rap and Hip Hop Culture." In *Hip Hop Africa: New African Music in a Globalizing World*, edited by Eric Charry, 171–86. Bloomington: Indiana University Press, 2012.

———. "Polishing the Luster of the Stars: Music Professionalism Made Workable in Kenya." *Ethnomusicology* 44, no. 3 (2000): 408–28. Web.

———. "'There Is Power': Contemporizing Old Music Traditions for New Gospel Audiences in Kenya." *Yearbook for Traditional Music* 42 (2010): 62–80.

Kilonzo, Susan. "The Trajectories of Survival of the Mungiki Youth in Nairobi." *International Journal of Sociology* 43, no. 1 (2017): 27–42.

Kimani, Sheila. "#MCM: Simon Kimani Aka Bamboo—of Avoiding 'Compe' and Fighting Illuminati." *The Standard*. Accessed June 28, 2024. https://www.standardmedia.co.ke /entertainment/celeb-profiles/article/2000176306/mcm-simon-kimani-aka-bamboo -of-avoiding-compe-and-fighting-illuminati.

Kinyanjui, Mary Njeri. "Situating Fireside Knowledge in Development Feminist Academy." *Journal of Language, Technology & Entrepreneurship in Africa* 10, no. 2 (2019): 1–14.

Kinyatti, Maina Wa, ed. *Thunder from the Mountains: Mau Mau Patriotic Songs.* Trenton, NJ: Africa World Press, 1990.

Kioko, Eric. "Regional Varieties and 'Ethnic' Registers of Sheng." In *Youth Language Practices in Africa and Beyond*, edited by Nico Nassenstein and Andrea Hollington, 119–48. University of Cologne, Ger.: De Gruyter Mouton, 2015.

Kirwa, Kipkogei, Caroline Kinuu Kimathi, and Ouno Victor Onyango. "Redressive Action in Political Discourse in the Face of Conflicting Views: A Case of the Building Bridges Initiative in Kenya." *International Journal of English Literature and Social Sciences* 7, no. 5 (2022): 1–11.

Klugman, Jeni. "Kenya: Economic Decline and Ethnic Politics." In *War, Hunger, and Displacement: The Origins of Humanitarian Emergencies*, vol. 2, *Case Studies*, edited by E. Wayne Nafziger, Frances Stewart, and Raimo Väyrynen, 295–331. New York: Oxford University Press, 2000.

Koster, Mickie Mwanzia. "The Hip Hop Revolution in Kenya: UkooFlani Mau Mau, Youth Politics and Memory, 1990–2012." *Journal of Pan African Studies* 6, no. 3 (2013): 82–105.

Kubik, Gerhard. "Neo-traditional Popular Music in East Africa since 1945." *Popular Music* 1 (1981): 83–104. Web.

Lamont, Mark. "Lip-Synch Gospel: Christian Music and the Ethnopoetics of Identity in Kenya." *Africa* 80, no. 3 (2010): 473–96.

Lane, Jeremy F. *Jazz and Machine-Age Imperialism: Music, "Race," and Intellectuals in France, 1918–1945.* Ann Arbor: University of Michigan Press, 2013.

Lester, Tracey Lomrantz. "A Member of Kenyan Parliament Is Dismissed for Wearing Too Much Bling!" *Glamour*, March 4, 2011. https://www.glamour.com/story/a-member-of-kenyan-parliament.

Ligaga, Dina. "Mapping Emerging Constructions of Good Time Girls in Kenyan Popular Media." *Journal of African Cultural Studies* 26, no. 3 (2014): 249–61.

Lloyd, Tom. "Liminal 'Criminals': Re-thinking Historiographies of, and through, the 'Thuggee' Phenomenon." *History Compass* 5, no. 2 (2007): 362–74.

Lonsdale, John. "The Moral Economy of Mau Mau: Wealth, Poverty and Civic Virtue in Kikuyu Political Thought." In *Unhappy Valley: Conflict in Kenya and Africa*, edited by Bruce Berman and John Lonsdale, 315–504. London: James Currey, 1992.

Loureiro-Rodríguez, Verónica. "'If We Only Speak Our Language by the Fireside, It Won't Survive': The Cultural and Linguistic Indigenization of Hip Hop in Galicia." *Popular Music and Society* 36, no. 5 (2013): 659–76.

Love, Bettina L. "'I See Trayvon Martin': What Teachers Can Learn from the Tragic Death of a Young Black Male." *Urban Review* 46, no. 2 (2014): 292–306.

Low, John. "A History of Kenyan Guitar Music: 1945—1980." *African Music* 6, no. 2 (1982): 17. Web.

Lukalo, Fibian Kavulani. *Extended Handshake or Wrestling Match? Youth and Urban Culture Celebrating Politics in Kenya.* Uppsala: Nordic Africa Institute, 2006.

Mabera, Faith. "Kenya's Foreign Policy in Context (1963–2015)." *South African Journal of International Affairs* 23, no. 3 (2016): 365–84.

Macharia, Keguro. "Love." *Critical Ethnic Studies* 1, no. 1 (2015): 68–75.

———. "Unhoming Kenyan Women." *Gukira*, October 3, 2014. https://gukira.wordpress .com/2014/10/03/unhoming-kenyan-women/.

Magnarella, Paul J. *Black Panther in Exile: The Pete O'Neal Story*. Gainesville: University Press of Florida, 2020.

Magubane, Zine. "Ni Wapi Tunakwenda: Hip Hop Culture and the Children of Arusha." In *The Vinyl Ain't Final: Hip Hop and the Globalization of Black Popular Culture*, edited by Dipannita Basu and Sidney J. Lemelle, 230–54. London: Pluto, 2006.

Mahone, Sloan. "The Psychology of Rebellion: Colonial Medical Responses to Dissent in British East Africa." *Journal of African History* 47, no. 2 (2006): 241–58.

Maina, Kamore. "Four Suspected Thugs Shot Dead in Industrial Area." *The Star*, October 3, 2016. https://www.the-star.co.ke/news/2016–10–03-four-suspected-thugs-shot-dead-in -industrial-area/.

Malcolm X. "Message to the Grassroots." In *American Identities: An Introductory Textbook*, edited by Lois P. Rudnick, Judith E. Smith, and Rachel Lee Rubin, 119–25. Malden, MA: Blackwell, 2006.

Malm, Krister. "The Music Industry." In *Ethnomusicology: An Introduction*, 349–64. London: Macmillan, 1992.

Malm, Krister, and Roger Wallis. *Media Policy and Music Activity*. London: Routledge, 1992.

Maloba, Wunyabari O. *The Anatomy of Neo-colonialism in Kenya: British Imperialism and Kenyatta, 1963–1978*. Cham, Switz.: Springer Science and Business Media, Palgrave Macmillan, 2017.

Marsh, Charity, and Sheila Petty. "Globalization, Identity, and Youth Resistance: Kenya's Hip Hop Parliament." *MUSICultures* 38, no. 1 (2011): 132–43.

Martin, Stephen H. "Brass Bands and the Beni Phenomenon in Urban East Africa." *African Music: Journal of the International Library of African Music* 7, no. 1 (1991): 72–81.

———. "Popular Music in Urban East Africa: From Historical Perspective to a Contemporary Hero." *Black Music Research Journal* (1991): 39–53.

Mbae, Peaceloise. "Fraudsters Stole Sh791 Million from National Youth Service, Says Devolution Cabinet Secretary Anne Waiguru." *The Standard*, n.d. https://www.standard media.co.ke/article/2000176045/fraudsters-stole-sh791-million-from-national-youth -service-says-devolution-cabinet-secretary-anne-waiguru.

Mbembé, Achille. *On the Postcolony*. Berkeley: University of California Press, 2001. Web.

Mgbako, Chi. *To Live Freely in This World: Sex Worker Activism in Africa*. New York: New York University Press, 2016.

Milu, Esther. "'Hatucheki Na Watu': Kenyan Hip-Hop Artists' Theories of Multilingualism, Identity and Decoloniality." PhD diss., Michigan State University, 2016.

———. "Translingualism, Kenyan Hip-Hop and Emergent Ethnicities: Implications for Language Theory and Pedagogy." *International Multilingual Research Journal* 12, no. 2 (2018): 96–108.

Mindoti, Kaskon W., and Hellen Agak. "Political Influence on Music Performance in Kenya between 1963–2002." *Bulletin of the Council for Research in Music Education*, no. 161/162 (2004): 155–64. Web.

Ministry of Sports, Culture, and Heritage. *The National Policy on Culture and Heritage*. Edited by Amina Chawahir Mohamed Jibril, 2023. https://www.tourism.go.ke/wp -content/uploads/2023/05/NATIONAL-POLICY-ON-CULTURE-AND-HERITAGE .pdf.

Mitchell, Tony, ed. *Global Noise: Rap and Hip-Hop outside the USA*. Middleton, CT: Wesleyan University Press, 2001.

Morgan, Joan. *When Chickenheads Come Home to Roost: A Hip-Hop Feminist Breaks It Down*. New York: Simon and Schuster, 2017.

Morgan, Marcyliena. *The Real Hiphop: Battling for Knowledge, Power, and Respect in the LA Underground*. Durham, NC: Duke University Press, 2009.

Morrison, Matthew D. "The Sound(s) of Subjection: Constructing American Popular Music and Racial Identity through Blacksound." *Women & Performance: A Journal of Feminist Theory* 27, no. 1 (2017): 13–24.

Mose, Caroline. "Hip Hop Halisi: Continuities of Heroism on the African Political Landscape." In *Hip Hop and Social Change in Africa: Ni Wakati*, edited by Msia Kibona Clark and Mickie Mwanzia Koster, 3–26. New York: Lexington Books, 2014.

———. "Jua Cali-Justice: Navigating the 'Mainstream-Underground' Dichotomy in Kenyan Hip-Hop Culture." In *Native Tongues: The African Hip-Hop Reader*, edited by Paul Khalil Saucier, 69–104. New York: African World Press, 2011.

———. "'Swag' and 'Cred': Representing Hip-Hop in the African City." *Journal of Pan African Studies* 6, no. 3 (2013): 106–32.

Mueller, Susanne D. "Kenya and the International Criminal Court (ICC): Politics, the Election and the Law." *Journal of Eastern African Studies* 8, no. 1 (2014): 25–42.

Muendo, Steven Kisuli. "Revealed: Kenyan Singer Sugar's Baby Secrets." *Pulse Magazine*, n.d.

Muendo, Steven. "How 'Budget Song' Landed Baba Otonglo Singer in Trouble." *The Standard*, 2023. https://www.standardmedia.co.ke/entertainment/news/article/2001475215/how-budget-song-landed-baba-otonglo-singer-in-trouble.

Mūgo, Mĩcere Githae. "The Woman Artist in Africa Today: A Critical Commentary." Africa Development / *Afrique et Développement* 19, no. 1 (1994): 49–69.

Muhonja, Besi Brillian. "Gender, Archiving, and Recognition: Naming and Erasing in Nairobi's Cityscape." In *Kenya after 50: Reconfiguring Education, Gender, and Policy*, edited by Michael Mwenda Kithinji, Mickie Mwanzia Koster, and Jerono P. Rotich, 171–96. New York: Palgrave Macmillan, 2016.

Mūhoro, P. Mwangi. "The Poetics of Gĩkũyũ Mwomboko: Narrative as a Technique in HIV-AIDS Awareness Campaign in Rural Kenya." In *Songs and Politics in Eastern Africa*, edited by Kimani Njogu and Hervé Maupeu. Dar es Salaam: Mkuti na Nyota, 2007.

Mukhongo, Lynete Lusike. "Participatory Media Cultures: Virality, Humour, and Online Political Contestations in Kenya." *Africa Spectrum* 55, no. 2 (2020): 148–69.

Muller, Carol. "South Africa and American Jazz: Towards a Polyphonic Historiography." *History Compass* 5, no. 4 (2007): 1062–77.

Munde, Claire. "Waiguru Drops King Kaka Suit Bid, Calls Him Confused Attention Seeker." *The Star*, December 20, 2019. https://www.the-star.co.ke/news/2019–12–20-waiguru-drops-king-kaka-suit-bid-calls-him-confused-attention-seeker/.

Mūngai, Mbũgua wa. "'Is Marwa!' It's Ours': Popular Music and Identity Politics in Kenyan Youth Culture." In *Cultural Production and Change in Kenya: Building Bridges*, edited by K. Njogu and G. Oluoch-Olunya, 47–62. Nairobi: Twaweza Communications, 2007.

———. "'Made in Riverwood': (Dis)locating Identities and Power through Kenyan Pop Music." *Journal of African Cultural Studies* 20, no. 1 (2008): 57–70.

Mũngai, Mbũgua wa, and David A. Samper. "'No Mercy, No Remorse': Personal Experience Narratives about Public Passenger Transportation in Nairobi, Kenya." *Africa Today* 52, no. 3 (2006): 51–81.

Muñoz, José Esteban. *Disidentifications: Queers of Color and the Performance of Politics.* Minneapolis: University of Minnesota Press, 1999.

Muñoz, Luis. "Nu Nairobi: Inside Nairobi's Music Scene." *Fact Magazine*, April 9, 2018. https://www.factmag.com/2018/04/09/nu-nairobi-inside-nairobis-music-scene.

Murunga, Godwin. "Governance and the Politics of Structural Adjustment in Kenya." In *Kenya: The Struggle for Democracy*, edited by Godwin Murunga and Shadrack Nasong'o, 263–300. Dakar: Codesria, 2007.

———, eds. *Kenya: The Struggle for Democracy.* New York: Zed Books, 2008.

———. *Spontaneous or Premeditated?: Post-election Violence in Kenya.* Discussion paper, 1–58. Uppsala: Nordic Africa Institute, 2011.

Murunga, Godwin R., and Shadrack W. Nasong'o. "Bent on Self-Destruction: The Kibaki Regime in Kenya." *Journal of Contemporary African Studies* 24, no. 1 (2006): 1–28.

———. "Prospects for Democracy in Kenya." In *Kenya: The Struggle for Democracy*, edited by Godwin R. Murunga and Shadrack W. Nasong'o, 3–16. New York: Zed Books, 2008.

Musambi, Evelyne. "Kenyan Artistes, MCSK Lock Horns over Royalties." *Daily Nation* [Nairobi, Kenya], October 22, 2014. Gale in Context: Global Issues. https://link.gale.com/apps/doc/A387039575/GIC?u=cuny_mancc&sid=bookmark-GIC&xid=21b7fc55.

Music in Africa. "Music in Africa," n.d. https://www.musicinafrica.net/.

Musila, Grace A. "Phallocracies and Gynocratic Transgressions: Gender, State Power and Kenyan Public Life." *Africa Insight* 39, no. 1 (2009): 39–57.

———. "Violent Masculinities and the Phallocratic Aesthetics of Power in Kenya." In *The New Violent Cartography: Geo-analysis after the Aesthetic Turn*, edited by Samson Opondo and Michael Shapiro, 151–70, 1st ed. New York: Routledge, 2012.

Mutahi, Basillioh. "Kenya's Mike Sonko: The Rise and Fall of Nairobi's Ex-Governor." BBC News, March 28, 2021, www.bbc.com/news/world-africa-56269628.

Mutahi, Patrick, and Mutuma Ruteere. "Violence, Security and the Policing of Kenya's 2017 Elections." *Journal of Eastern African Studies* 13, no. 2 (2019): 253–71.

Mutongi, Kenda. *Matatu: A History of Popular Transportation in Nairobi.* Chicago: University of Chicago Press, 2017.

Mũtonya, Maina wa. "The Beat Goes On: Performing Postcolonial Disillusionment in Kenya." *Humania del Sur* 5, no. 8 (2010): 47–66.

———. 2004. "Praise and Protest: Music and Contesting Patriotism in Postcolonial Kenya." *Social Dynamics* 30, no. 2 (2004): 20–35.

Mũtonya, Maina wa, and Catherine Bosire. *The Politics of Everyday Life in Gĩkũyũ Popular Music of Kenya (1990–2000).* Nairobi: Twaweza Communications, 2013.

Mutsaurwa, Biko. "The Afrikan Hiphop Caravan: Building a Revolutionary Counterculture." *Journal of Hip Hop Studies* 1, no. 2 (2014): 226–31.

Mwakimako, Hassan. "Christian–Muslim Relations in Kenya: A Catalogue of Events and Meanings." *Islam–Christian Muslim Relations* 18, no. 2 (2007): 287–307.

Mwangi, Evan. "Masculinity and Nationalism in East African Hip-Hop Music." *Tydskrif vir Letterkunde* 41, no. 2 (2004): 5–20.

———. "The Incomplete Rebellion: Mau Mau Movement in Twenty-First-Century Kenyan Popular Culture." *Africa Today* 57, no. 2 (2010): 86–113.

Mwangi, Evan, and Wanjiru Mbure. "Passion in a Mathree: Metropolitan Love in Nazizi Hirji's 'Kenyan Girl / Kenyan Boy.'" *Women & Language* 32, no. 2 (2009): 25–31.

Mwangi, Nick. "Juliani Takes Issue with Jubilee Using His Song to Promote BBI." *Nairobi Wire*, November 3, 2020. nairobiwire.com/2020/11/juliani-takes-issue-with-jubilee-for -using-his-song-to-promote-bbi.html.

Mwangi, Peter Muhoro. "The Poetics of Gĩkũyũ Mwomboko: Narrative as a Technique in HIV-AIDS Awareness Campaign in Rural Kenya." In *Songs and Politics in Eastern Africa*, edited by Kimani Njogu and Hervé Maupeu, 73–105. Dar es Salaam: Mkuki na Nyota, 2007.

———. "Silencing Musical Expression in Colonial and Post-Colonial Kenya." In *Popular Music Censorship in Africa*, edited by Michael Drewett and Martin Cloonan, 157–69. Burlington, VT: Ashgate, 2006.

Mwangola, Mshaï S. "Njia Panda: Kenyan Theatre in Search of Identity." In *Getting Heard: [Re]claiming Performance Space in Kenya*, edited by Kimani Njogu, 1–24. Nairobi: Twaweza Communications, 2008.

Mwaura, Bantu. "Kenyan Youth and the Entropic Destruction of a Hopeful Social Order." In *Cultural Production and Social Change in Kenya: Building Bridges*, edited by Kimani Njogu, 63–74. Nairobi: Twaweza Communications, 2007.

MzukaFlani. "MIC—Black Duo." YouTube, January 31, 2009. https://www.youtube.com /watch?v=1LbmBvQVU3s&t=4s.

Nairobi Gossip & News. "Rabbit-King Kaka Launches a New Lucrative Business." 2015. https://web.archive.org/web/20151001033238/http://www.nairobigossips.com/2015/09 /rabbit-king-kaka-launches-new-lucrative.html?m=1.

Nash, Jennifer C. "Practicing Love: Black Feminism, Love-Politics, and Post-Intersectionality." *Meridians* 11, no. 2 (2013): 1–24.

Nation. "King Kaka, Juliani, Boniface Mwangi Sing Juliani's—'Utawala' Song." YouTube, December 17, 2019. https://www.youtube.com/watch?v=kqkUnVtnnh8.

———. "Malaika: Who Was the Real Composer?" June 21, 2020. https://nation.africa/kenya /life-and-style/weekend/malaika-who-was-the-real-composer—567794.

———. "Revealed: Sh150 Million Maize Scandal," July 3, 2020. https://nation.africa/kenya /news/1056–513142-u18wmp/index.html#google_vignette.

National Assembly of the Republic of Kenya. "Hon. Njagua, Charles Kanyi | The Kenyan Parliament Website." N.d. http://www.parliament.go.ke/node/3411.

Ndanyi, Samson Kaunga. "Film Censorship and Identity in Kenya." *Ufahamu: A Journal of African Studies* 42, no. 2 (2021): 23–41.

Ndavula, John, and Jackline U. Lidubwi. "Can Vernacular Radio Be Conflict Sensitive? An Analysis of Vernacular Radio Programming in Western Kenya." In *Indigenous Language for Social Change Communication in the Global South*, edited by Abiodun Salawu, Tshepang Bright Molale, Enrique Uribe-Jongbloed, and Mohammad Sahid Ullah, 229–42. New York: Rowman & Littlefield, 2023.

Ndii, David. "Crony Capitalism and State Capture: The Kenyatta Family Story." *The Elephant: African Analysis, Opinion and Investigation*, July 7, 2018. https://www.theelephant .info/opinion/2018/07/07/crony-capitalism-and-state-capture-the-kenyatta-family -story/.

Neal, Mark Anthony. *Soul Babies: Black Popular Culture and the Post-Soul Aesthetic*. New York: Routledge, 2002. Web.

Njogu, Kimani, ed. *Culture, Performance and Identity. Paths of Communication in Kenya.* Nairobi: Twaweza Communications, 2008.

Nomadik Studio. "'Amandla' Ft. Khusta, Mic Crenshaw, Ran-D, Judge and MC Bagol." YouTube, December 14, 2015. https://www.youtube.com/watch?v=usamqjWxtyk.

Ntarangwi, Mwenda. *East African Hip Hop: Youth Culture and Globalization.* Urbana: University of Illinois Press, 2009. Web.

———. "Hip-Hop, Westernization and Gender in East Africa." In *Songs and Politics in Eastern Africa*, edited by Kimani Njogu and Hervé Maupeu, 273–302. Dar es Salaam: Mkuki na Nyota, 2007.

———. *The Street Is My Pulpit: Hip Hop and Christianity in Kenya.* Urbana: University of Illinois Press, 2016.

Nyairo, Joyce. "Kenyan Gospel Soundtracks: Crossing Boundaries, Mapping Audiences." *Journal of African Cultural Studies* 20, no. 1 (2008): 71–83.

Nyairo, Joyce, and James Ogude. "Popular Music, Popular Politics: Unbwogable and the Idioms of Freedom in Kenyan Popular Music." *African Affairs* 104, no. 415 (2005): 225–49.

———. "Specificities: Popular Music and the Negotiation of Contemporary Kenyan Identity: The Example of Nairobi City Ensemble." *Social Identities* 9, no. 3 (2003): 383–400.

Nyong'o, Tavia. "Afro-philo-sonic Fictions: Black Sound Studies after the Millennium." *Small Axe* 18, no. 2 (2014): 173–79.

Ocobock, Paul. *An Uncertain Age: The Politics of Manhood in Kenya.* Athens: Ohio University Press, 2017.

Odhiambo, Tom. "Specificities: Troubled Love and Marriage as Work in Kenyan Popular Fiction." *Social Identities* 9, no. 3 (2003): 423–36.

Ogopa Deejays. "Jaguar—Matapeli (Official Ogopa Video)." YouTube, August 5, 2012. https://www.youtube.com/watch?v=H1wj8Sy6vc4.

Ogot, Bethwell. "Construction of a National Culture." In *Decolonization and Independence in Kenya, 1940–93*, edited by Bethwell A. Ogot and William R. Ochieng', 214–38. London: James Currey, 1995.

———. "The Decisive Years: 1956–63." In *Decolonization and Independence in Kenya, 1940–93*, edited by Bethwell A. Ogot and William R. Ochieng', 48–79. London: James Currey, 1995.

Ogot, Bethwell, and William Robert Ochieng'. *Decolonization and Independence in Kenya: 1940–93.* London: James Currey, 1995.

Ogude, James. "The Invention of Traditional Music in the City: Exploring History and Meaning in Urban Music in Contemporary Kenya." *Research in African Literatures* 43, no. 4 (2012): 147–65.

Okande, Austine, and Mkala Mwangesha. "Artistes Royalties 'to Shoot Up Soon.'" *The Standard*, October 15, 2012.

Okumu, Caleb C. "Reclaiming Kenya's Popular Music: A Solution to a Dilemma." In *Emerging Solutions for Musical Arts Education in Africa*, edited by Anri Herbst, 228–34. Cape Town: African Minds, 2005.

Olsen, Jack. *Last Man Standing: The Tragedy and Triumph of Geronimo Pratt.* New York: Anchor Books, 2000.

Ombati, Cyrus. "Four Thugs Shot Dead in Nairobi, a Pistol with 18 Bullets Recovered." *The Standard*, n.d. https://www.standardmedia.co.ke/article/2000183450/standard-digital.

Ombati, Mokua. "Public Artworks: Creative Spaces for Civic and Political Behaviour in Kenya." *Australasian Review of African Studies* 36, no. 1 (2015): 29–50.

Ombuor, Joe. "Musician Declared to the World That Malaika Was His Original Composition." *The Standard*, 2022. https://www.standardmedia.co.ke/counties/article/2001437254/musician-declared-to-the-world-that-malaika-was-his-original-composition.

Omondi, Washington. *Report of the Presidential National Music Commission*. Nairobi: Government Printers, 1984.

Opondo, Patricia A. "Cultural Policies in Kenya." *Arts Education Policy Review* 101, no. 5 (2000): 18–24.

Osamba, Joshia. "The Dynamics of Ethnopolitical Conflict and Violence in the Rift Valley Province of Kenya." *Nationalism and Ethnic Politics* 7, no. 4 (2001): 87–112.

Osumare, Halifu. *The Africanist Aesthetic in Global Hip-Hop: Power Moves*. 1st ed. New York: Palgrave Macmillan, 2007. Web.

———. "Global Breakdancing and the Intercultural Body." *Dance Research Journal* 34, no. 2 (2002): 30–45.

———. "Keeping It Real: Race, Class, and Youth Connections through Hip-Hop in the US and Brazil." *Humboldt Journal of Social Relations* 37 (2015): 6–18.

———. "Motherland Hip-Hop: Connective Marginality and African American Youth Culture in Senegal and Kenya." In *Rhythms of the Afro-Atlantic World: Rituals and Remembrances*, edited by Ifeoma C. K. Nwankwo and Mamadou Diouf, 161–77. Ann Arbor: University of Michigan Press, 2010.

Otieno, Tebby. "KNUT Boss Reveals Kenya's School Laptop Project Was a Scam." *Talk Africa*, May 12, 2021. www.talkafrica.co.ke/knut-boss-reveals-kenyas-school-laptop-project-was-a-scam/.

Owino, Juliani. "Music as a Weapon to Fight Inequality | Oxfam in Kenya." kenya.oxfam.org, January 16, 2017. http://kenya.oxfam.org/blog/music-weapon-fight-inequality.

Owuor, Samuel O., and Teresa Mbatia. "Post-Independence Development of Nairobi City, Kenya." Paper presented at Workshop on African Capital Cities, Dakar, September 22–23, 2008.

Pabón-Colón, Jessica Nydia. *Graffiti Grrlz: Performing Feminism in the Hip Hop Diaspora*. New York: New York University Press, 2018. Web.

Pardue, Derek. *Ideologies of Marginality in Brazilian Hip Hop*. New York: Palgrave Macmillan, 2008.

Park, Jeong Kyung, James Nyachae Michira, and Seo Young Yun. "African Hip Hop as a Rhizomic Art Form Articulating Urban Youth Identity and Resistance with Reference to Kenyan Genge and Ghanaian Hiplife." *Journal of the Musical Arts in Africa* 16, no. 1/2 (2019): 99–118.

Parsitau, Damaris Seleina. "'Then Sings My Soul': Gospel Music as Popular Culture in the Spiritual Lives of Kenyan Pentecostal/Charismatic Christians." *Journal of Religion and Popular Culture* 14, no. 1 (2006): 1–11.

Peck, RaShelle R. "Love, Struggle, and Compromises: The Political Seriousness of Nairobi Underground Hip Hop." *African Studies Review* 61, no. 2 (2018): 111–33.

Pennycook, Alastair, and Tony Mitchell. "Hip Hop as Dusty Foot Philosophy: Engaging Locality." In *Global Linguistic Flows: Hip Hop Cultures, Youth Identities, and the Politics of Language*, edited by H. Samy Alim, Awad Ibrahim, and Alastair Pennycook, 25–42. New York: Routledge, 2008.

Peoples, Whitney A. "'Under Construction': Identifying Foundations of Hip-Hop Feminism and Exploring Bridges between Black Second-Wave and Hip-Hop Feminisms." *Meridians* 8, no. 1 (2008): 19–52.

Perkins, William Eric, ed. *Droppin' Science: Critical Essays on Rap Music and Hip Hop Culture*, vol. 79. Philadelphia: Temple University Press, 1996.

Perry, Marc D. "Global Black Self-Fashionings: Hip Hop as Diasporic Space." *Identities: Global Studies in Culture and Power* 15, no. 6 (2008): 635–64.

Perry, Imani. *Prophets of the Hood: Politics and Poetics in Hip Hop*. Durham, NC: Duke University Press, 2004.

Perullo, Alex. "Rumba in the City of Peace: Migration and the Cultural Commodity of Congolese Music in Dar es Salaam, 1968–1985." *Ethnomusicology* 52, no. 2 (2008): 296–323.

Perullo, Alex, and Andrew Eisenberg. "Musical Property Rights Regimes in Tanzania and Kenya after TRIPS." In *The SAGE Handbook of Intellectual Property*, edited by Matthew David and Debora Halbert, 148–64. Los Angeles: SAGE, 2014.

Perullo, Alex, and John Fenn. "Language Ideologies, Choices, and Practices in Eastern African Hip Hop." In *Global Pop, Local Language*, edited by Harris M. Berger and Michael Thomas Carroll, 19–52. Jackson: University Press of Mississippi, 2003.

Phoenix Recordz. "2-5-Flow—Bamboo Ft Sugar—(Official Music Video)." YouTube, January 24, 2013. https://www.youtube.com/watch?v=KtSnXziBTMw.

Porter, Mary A. "Talking at the Margins: Kenyan Discourses on Homosexuality." In *Beyond the Lavender Lexicon: Authenticity, Imagination, and Appropriation in Lesbian and Gay Languages*, edited by William Leap, 133–53. Amsterdam: Gordon and Breach, 1995.

Pough, Gwendolyn D. *Check It while I Wreck It: Black Womanhood, Hip Hop Culture, and the Public Sphere*. Boston: Northeastern University Press, 2004. Web.

PrepareCenter. "Kenyans for Kenya (K4K) Initiative." Accessed June 12, 2024. https://preparecenter.org/story/kenyans-for-kenya-k4k-initiative/.

Rahier, Jean Muteba, and Percy C. Hintzen, "Introduction. Theorizing the African Diaspora: Metaphor, Misrecognition, and Self-Recognition." In *Global Circuits of Blackness: Interrogating the African Diaspora*, edited by Jean Muteba Rahier, Percy C Hintzen, and Felipe Smith, ix–xxvi. Urbana: University of Illinois Press, 2010.

Ren, Hang, Wei Guo, Zhenke Zhang, Leonard Musyoka Kisovi, and Priyanko Das. "Population Density and Spatial Patterns of Informal Settlements in Nairobi, Kenya." *Sustainability* 12, no. 18 (2020): 1–14.

Richardson, Elaine B. "Global Linguistic Flows: Hip Hop Cultures, Youth Identities, and the Politics of Language, edited by H. Samy Alim, Awad Ibrahim and Alastair Pennycook." *Journal of Sociolinguistics* 14, no. 2 (2010): 266–72.

———. *Hiphop Literacies*. London: Routledge, 2007.

Richardson, Elaine, and Gwendolyn Pough. "Hiphop Literacies and the Globalization of Black Popular Culture." *Social Identities* 22, no. 2 (2016): 129–32.

Rosberg, Carl Gustav, and John Nottingham. *The Myth of "Mau Mau": Nationalism in Kenya*. New York: Praeger, 1966.

Rose, Tricia. *Black Noise: Rap Music and Black Culture in Contemporary America*. Hanover, NH: University Press of New England, 1994.

Rosenberg, Aaron Louis. "Zairo-Congolese Musicians and the Sound of Assimilation in East Africa." In *Music and Messaging in the African Political Arena*, edited by Uche T. Onyebadi, 201–20. Hershey, PA: IGI Global, 2019.

Rubin, Joel. "Hip Hop Videos and Black Identity in Virtual Space." *Journal of Hip Hop Studies* 3, no. 1 (2016): 74–85.

Ruble, Kayla. "Angola Sends a Rapper and 16 Activists to Prison for Plotting Rebellion." www.vice.com, March 28, 2016. https://www.vice.com/en/article/wja74m/angola-sends -a-rapper-and-16-activists-to-prison-for-plotting-rebellion.

Samper, David A. "'Africa Is Still Our Mama': Kenyan Rappers, Youth Identity, and the Revitalization of Traditional Values." *African Identities* 2, no. 1 (2004): 37–51.

Sanga, Imani. "The Practice and Politics of Hybrid Soundscapes in Muziki wa Injili in Dar es Salaam, Tanzania." *Journal of African Cultural Studies* 22, no. 2 (2010): 145–56.

Sanya, Brenda Nyandiko, and Anne Namatsi Lutomia. "Feminism Unfinished: Towards Gender Justice and Women's Rights in Kenya." In *Kenya after 50: Reconfiguring Education, Gender, and Policy*, edited by Michael Mwenda Kithinji, Mickie Mwanzia Koster, and Jerono P. Rotich, 227–52. London: Palgrave Macmillan, 2016.

Sarakasi Dome—Sarakasi Trust. "Sarakasi Dome—Sarakasi Trust." October 21, 2023. https://sarakasi.org/sarakasidome/.

Saucier, P. Khalil, and Tryon P. Woods. "Hip Hop Studies in Black." *Journal of Popular Music Studies* 26, no. 2/3 (2014): 268–94.

Saunders, Tanya L. *Cuban Underground Hip Hop: Black Thoughts, Black Revolution, Black Modernity*. Austin: University of Texas Press, 2015. Web.

———. "Towards a Transnational Hip-Hop Feminist Liberatory Praxis: A View from the Americas." *Social Identities* 22, no. 2 (2016): 178–94.

Scott, James C. *Domination and the Arts of Resistance: Hidden Transcripts*. New Haven, CT: Yale University Press, 1990. Web.

Sex Worker Film and Arts Festival Movies. "Mwili Wangu, Cha[g]uo Langu—My Body, My Choice | Sex Worker Fest Movies." Accessed June 8, 2024. http://www.sexworkerfest .com/videos/video_type/mwili-wangu-chauo-langu-my-body-my-choice-part-1/.

Shaw, Carolyn Martin. *Colonial Inscriptions: Race, Sex and Class in Kenya*. Minneapolis: University of Minnesota Press, 1995.

Shilaho, Westen K. *Political Power and Tribalism in Kenya*. Cham, Switz.: Springer International, 2018.

Shipley, Jesse Weaver. "Aesthetic of the Entrepreneur: Afro-Cosmopolitan Rap and Moral Circulation in Accra, Ghana." *Anthropological Quarterly* (2009): 631–68.

———. "Transnational Circulation and Digital Fatigue in Ghana's Azonto Dance Craze." *American Ethnologist* 40, no. 2 (2013): 362–81.

Shitemi, Naomi L. "Orality: Aesthetic and Expressive Literary Genre Exemplified by Kenyan Hip Hop Discourse." *Muziki* 7, no. 1 (2010): 1–30.

Slocum, Karla. "Negotiating Identity and Black Feminist Politics in Caribbean Research." In *Black Feminist Anthropology: Theory, Politics, Praxis, and Poetics*, edited by Irma McClaurin, 126–48. New Brunswick, NJ: Rutgers University Press, 2001.

Smalls, Shanté Paradigm. "'Make the Music with Your Mouth': Sonic Subjectivity and Postmodern Identity Formations in Beatboxing." *Lateral* 3 (2014): 1–15.

Smith, Christen A., Erica L. Williams, Imani A. Wadud, Whitney NL Pirtle, and Cite Black Women Collective. "Cite Black Women: A Critical Praxis (A Statement)." *Feminist Anthropology* 2, no. 1 (2021): 10–17.

Spady, James G. "Mapping and Re-Membering Hip Hop History, Hiphopography and African Diasporic History." *Western Journal of Black Studies* 37, no. 2 (2013): 126–57.

Spronk, Rachel. "Sex, Sexuality and Negotiating Africanness in Nairobi." *Africa* 79, no. 4 (2009): 500–519.

Southern, Eileen. "*Thunder from the Mountains*, edited by Maina Wa Kinyatti (Book Review)." Cambria Heights, NY: Foundation for Research in the Afro-American Creative Arts, 1982. Web.

Stapleton, Chris, and Chris May. *African Rock: The Pop Music of a Continent*. New York: Dutton, 1990.

Strumpf, Mitchel. "Early Studies of the Music of East Africa." In *Ethnomusicology in East Africa: Perspectives from Uganda and Beyond*, edited by Sylvia Nannyonga-Tamusuza and Thomas Solomon, 33–48. Kampala: Fountain, 2012.

Sullivan, Mecca Jamilah. "Fat Mutha: Hip Hop's Queer Corpulent Poetics." *Palimpsest* 2, no. 2 (2013): 200–213.

Terkourafi, Marina, ed. *The Languages of Global Hip Hop*. London: Continuum International, 2010.

The Star. "Inside Story of the NCPB Maize Scam." May 25, 2018. http://www.the-star.co.ke /news/2018-05-25-inside-story-of-the-ncpb-maize-scam/.

Thiong'o, Ngũgĩ wa. *Decolonising the Mind: The Politics of Language in African Literature*. Nairobi: East African, 1992.

———. *Globalectics: Theory and the Politics of Knowing*. New York: Columbia University Press, 2014.

———. "On the Abolition of the English Department." *Présence Africaine* 1 (2018): 103–109.

———. *Penpoints, Gunpoints, and Dreams: Towards a Critical Theory of the Arts and the State in Africa*. Oxford: Oxford University Press, 1998.

———. "The Politics of National Theatre: The Example of Kenya." *TDR/The Drama Review* 62, no. 2 (2018): 16–21.

Thompson, Robert F. "An Aesthetic of the Cool." *African Arts* 7, no. 1 (1973): 40–43.

———. "An Aesthetic of Cool: West African Dance." In *Signifyin(g), Sanctifyin' & Slam Dunking: A Reader in African American Expressive Culture*, edited by Gena Caponi-Tabery, 72–86. Amherst: University of Massachusetts Press, 1999.

Tully, Melissa, and Brian Ekdale. "Sites of Playful Engagement: Twitter Hashtags as Spaces of Leisure and Development in Kenya." *Information Technologies & International Development* 10, no. 3 (2014): 67–82.

Turner, Victor. "Body, Brain, and Culture." *Cross Currents* 36, no. 2 (1986): 156–78.

UN-Habitat. *Kenya 2023 Country Brief: A Better Quality of Life for All in an Urbanizing World*. July 2023. https://unhabitat.org/sites/default/files/2023/07/kenya_country_brief _final_en.pdf.

Vernon, Paul. "Feast of the East." www.bolingo.org, 1997. http://www.bolingo.org/audio /texts/fr145eastafrica.html.

Wa, Nduta. "Juliani Planning a Kalamashaka Concert." *The Standard*, 2017. https://www .standardmedia.co.ke/entertainment/news/article/2001259287/juliani-planning-a-kala mashaka-concert.

Wainaina, Binyavanga. *How to Write about Africa: Collected Works*. New York: One World, 2024.

———. *One Day I Will Write about This Place: A Memoir*. Lagos: Farafina, 2013.

Wallis, Roger, and Krister Malm. *Big Sounds from Small Peoples: The Music Industry in Small Countries*. New York: Pendragon Press, 1984. Web.

Wambui, John M. "A Cosmopolitan Ghetto: The Shifting Image of Kibera Slum from 'Flying Toilets' to a Centre for Metropolitan Innovation." *The Thinker* 85, no. 3 (2020): 19–35.

Wanguhu, Michael, ed. *Ni Wakati (It's Time!)*. Directed by Russell Kenya. DVD. Kenya: Emerge Media Films, 2010.

Wangui, Joseph. "US Bans Entry of Former Nairobi Governor Mike Sonko, Family." *East African*, March 8, 2022. www.theeastafrican.co.ke/tea/news/east-africa/us-bans-entry -of-former-nairobi-governor-mike-sonko-family-3741356.

Wanjala, Henry, and Charles Kebaya. "Popular Music and Identity Formation among Kenyan Youth." *Muziki* 13, no. 2 (2016): 20–35.

Wanjohi, John. "Kenyan Singer Bamboo Claims He Was Bewitched after Returning to Kenya from the US." Mwakilishi.com, March 31, 2021. https://www.mwakilishi.com /article/diaspora-news/2021–03–31/kenyan-singer-bamboo-claims-he-was-bewitched -after-returning-from-the-us#google_vignette.

Wanyama, Mellitus Nyongesa. "Policy and Implementation: A Case of Music Copyright Laws in Kenya." *Muziki* 4, no. 1 (2007): 27–41.

Wasike, Chris. "Jua Cali, Genge Rap Music and the Anxieties of Living in the Glocalized City of Nairobi." *Muziki* 8, no. 1 (2011): 18–33.

Watch254 TV. "Eric Wainaina Unites with WajingaNyinyi AKA King Kaka in a Powerful Collaboration! #Kenya." YouTube, December 17, 2019. https://www.youtube.com/watch ?v=cSs4Y9RIJD0&t=172s.

Watkins, S. Craig. "Black Youth and the Ironies of Capitalism." In *That's the Joint! The Hip-Hop Studies Reader*, edited by Murray Forman and Mark Anthony Neal, 557–78. New York: Routledge, 2004.

———. *Hip Hop Matters: Politics, Pop Culture, and the Struggle for the Soul of a Movement*. Boston: Beacon Press, 2005.

———. "A Nation of Millions: Hip Hop Culture and the Legacy of Black Nationalism." *Communication Review* 4, no. 3 (2001): 373–98.

Weheliye, Alexander G. *Phonographies: Grooves in Sonic Afro-Modernity*. Durham, NC: Duke University Press, 2005.

Wema TV. "Mustard Seed Faith | Testimony | The Conquerors Show." 2021. https://www .youtube.com/watch?v=zayOjuoEnvg.

White, Miles. *From Jim Crow to Jay-Z: Race, Rap, and the Performance of Masculinity*. Urbana: University of Illinois Press, 2011.

Williams, Quentin. "Youth Multilingualism in South Africa's Hip-Hop Culture: A Metapragmatic Analysis." *Sociolinguistic Studies* 10, no. 1/2 (2016): 109–33.

Wipper, Audrey. *Riot and Rebellion among African Women: Three Examples of Women's Political Clout*. East Lansing: Office of WID, Michigan State University, 1986. Web.

Wolf, Thomas P. "Immunity or Accountability? Daniel Toroitich arap Moi: Kenya's First Retired President." In *Legacies of Power: Leadership Change and Former Presidents in African Politics*, edited by Roger Southall and Henning Melber, 197–232. Cape Town: Human Sciences Research Council, Democracy and Governance Research Programme, 2006.

Woods, Orlando. "Clashing Cyphers, Contagious Content: The Digital Geopolitics of Grime." *Transactions of the Institute of British Geographers* 46, no. 2 (2021): 464–77.

Zeleza, Paul Tiyambe. "Dancing to the Beat of the Diaspora: Musical Exchanges between Africa and Its Diasporas." *African and Black Diaspora: An International Journal* 3, no. 2 (2010): 211–36.

———. "Diaspora Dialogues: Engagements Between Africa and Its Diasporas." In *The New African Diaspora*, edited by Isidore Okpewho and Nkiru Nzegwu, 31–58. Bloomington: Indiana University Press, 2009.

NOTE: Page numbers followed by *fig.* refer to figures. Those followed by *n* refer to notes, with note number.